MCA
Modern Desktop Administrator

Study Guide
Exam MD-101

MCA
Modern Desktop
Administrator
Study Guide
Exam MD-101

William Panek

SYBEX®
A Wiley Brand

This book is dedicated to the three ladies of my life: Crystal, Alexandria, and Paige.

Acknowledgments

I would like to thank my wife and best friend, Crystal. She is always the light at the end of my tunnel. I want to thank my two daughters, Alexandria and Paige, for all of their love and support during the writing of all my books. The three of them are my support system and I couldn't do any of this without them.

I want to thank my family, and especially my brothers, Rick, Gary, and Rob. They have always been there for me. I want to thank my father, Richard, who helped me become the man I am today, and my mother, Maggie, for all of her love and support.

I would like to thank all of my friends and co-workers at StormWind Studios (www.stormwindstudios.com). Thanks to all of you for everything that you do. I would not have been able to complete this book without all of your help and support.

I want to thank everyone on my Sybex team, especially my development editor, Kim Wimpsett who helped me make this the best book possible, and Jon Buhagiar, who is the technical editor of this book and an outstanding resource on this book. It's always good to have the very best technical guy backing you up. I want to thank Katie Wisor, who was my production editor, and Judy Flynn for being the copyeditor.

Special thanks to my acquisitions editor, Kenyon Brown, who was the lead for the entire book. Finally, I want to thank everyone else behind the scenes that helped make this book possible. It's truly an amazing thing to have so many people work on my books to help make them the very best. I can't thank you all enough for your hard work.

About the Author

William Panek holds the following certifications: MCP, MCP+I, MCSA, MCSA+ Security and Messaging, MCSE-NT (3.51 and 4.0), MCSE (2000, 2003, 2012/2012 R2), MCSE+Security and Messaging, MCDBA, MCT, MCTS, MCITP, CCNA, CCDA, and CHFI. Will is also a four-time and current Microsoft MVP winner.

After many successful years in the computer industry, Will decided that he could better use his talents and his personality as an instructor. He began teaching for schools such as Boston University and the University of Maryland, just to name a few. He has done consulting and training for some of the biggest government and corporate companies in the world, including the United States Secret Service, Cisco, United States Air Force, and United States Army.

In 2015, Will became a Sr. Microsoft Instructor for StormWind Studios (www.stormwindstudios.com). He currently lives in New Hampshire with his wife and two daughters. Will was also a Representative in the New Hampshire House of Representatives from 2010 to 2012. In his spare time, he likes to do blacksmithing, shooting (trap and skeet), snowmobiling, playing racquetball, and riding his Harley. Will is also a commercially rated helicopter pilot.

Contents at a Glance

Contents

Table of Exercises

Introduction

This book was written from over 25 years of IT experience. I have taken that experience and translated it into a Windows 10 book that will help you not only prepare for the Microsoft 365 Certified: Modern Desktop Administrator Associate exams but also to develop a clear understanding of how to install and configure Windows 10 while avoiding all the possible configuration pitfalls.

Many Microsoft books just explain the Windows operating system, but with *this book*, I will go a step further, providing many in-depth, step-by-step procedures to support my explanations of how the operating system performs at its best.

Microsoft Windows 10 is the newest version of Microsoft's client operating system software. Microsoft has taken the best of Windows 7 and Windows 8 and combined them into the latest creation, Windows 10.

Windows 10 eliminates many of the problems that plagued the previous versions of Windows clients and it includes a much faster boot time and shutdown. It is also easier to install and configure, and it barely stops to ask the user any questions during installation. In this book, I will show you what features are installed during the automated installation and where you can make changes if you need to be more in charge of your operating system and its features.

This book takes you through all the ins and outs of Windows 10, including installation, configuration, online Microsoft subscriptions, auditing, backups, and so much more.

Windows 10 has improved on Microsoft's desktop environment, made networking easier, working with Microsoft Azure, enhanced search ability, improved performance—and that's only scratching the surface.

When all is said and done, this is a technical book for IT professionals who want to take Windows 10 to the next step and get certified. With this book, you will not only learn Windows 10 and hopefully pass the exams, you will also become a Windows 10 expert.

The Microsoft Certification Program

Since the inception of its certification program, Microsoft has certified more than two million people. As the computer network industry continues to increase in both size and complexity, this number is sure to grow—and the need for proven ability will also increase. Certifications can help companies verify the skills of prospective employees and contractors.

The Microsoft certification tracks for Windows include just some of the following certifications:

Microsoft 365 Certified: Modern Desktop Administrator Associate: Windows 10   The Microsoft 365 Certified: Modern Desktop Administrator Associate is now the highest-level certification you can achieve with Microsoft in relation to Windows 10. It requires passing exams MD-100 and MD-101. This book assists in your preparation for exam MD-101.

Microsoft Certified Technology Associate (MTA)   This is Microsoft's newest certification program. This certification targets those new to the IT field and tests candidates on the core competencies necessary to become an IT professional.

How Do You Become Certified on Windows 10?

Attaining Microsoft certification has always been a challenge. In the past, students have been able to acquire detailed exam information—even most of the exam questions—from online "brain dumps" and third-party "cram" books or software products. For the new generation of exams, this is simply not the case.

Microsoft has taken strong steps to protect the security and integrity of its new certification tracks. Now prospective candidates must complete a course of study that develops detailed knowledge about a wide range of topics. It supplies them with the true skills needed, derived from working with the technology being tested.

The new generations of Microsoft certification programs are heavily weighted toward hands-on skills and experience. It is recommended that candidates have troubleshooting skills acquired through hands-on experience and working knowledge.

Fortunately, if you are willing to dedicate the time and effort to learn Windows 10, you can prepare yourself well for the exam by using the proper tools. By working through this book, you can successfully meet the requirements to pass the Windows 10 exams.

Microsoft 365 Certified: Modern Desktop Administrator Associate Exam Requirements

Candidates for MCSA certification on Windows 10 must pass two Windows 10 MCSA tests:

- MD-100: Windows 10
- MD-101: Managing Modern Desktops

Microsoft provides exam objectives to give you a general overview of possible areas of coverage on the Microsoft exams. Keep in mind, however, that exam objectives are subject to change at any time without prior notice and at Microsoft's sole discretion. Please visit the Microsoft Learning website (www.microsoft.com/learning) for the most current listing of exam objectives.

For a more detailed description of the Microsoft certification programs, including a list of all the exams, visit the Microsoft Learning website at www.microsoft.com/learning.

Types of Exam Questions

In an effort to both refine the testing process and protect the quality of its certifications, Microsoft has focused its latest certification exams on real experience and hands-on proficiency. There is a greater emphasis on your past working environments and responsibilities and less emphasis on how well you can memorize. In fact, Microsoft says that certification candidates should have hands-on experience before attempting to pass any certification exams.

 Microsoft will accomplish its goal of protecting the exams' integrity by regularly adding and removing exam questions, limiting the number of questions that any individual sees in a beta exam, limiting the number of questions delivered to an individual by using adaptive testing, and adding new exam elements.

Exam questions may be in a variety of formats: Depending on which exam you take, you'll see multiple-choice questions as well as select-and-place and prioritize-a-list questions. Simulations and case study–based formats are included as well. Let's take a look at the types of exam questions, so you'll be prepared for all of the possibilities.

Multiple-Choice Questions

Multiple-choice questions come in two main forms. One is a straightforward question followed by several possible answers of which one or more is correct. The other type of multiple-choice question is more complex and based on a specific scenario. The scenario may focus on several areas or objectives.

Select-and-Place Questions

Select-and-place exam questions involve graphical elements that you must manipulate to successfully answer the question. For example, you might see a diagram of a computer network. A typical diagram will show computers and other components next to boxes that contain the text "Place here." The labels for the boxes represent various computer roles on a network, such as a print server and a file server. Based on information given for each computer, you are asked to select each label and place it in the correct box. You need to place *all* of the labels correctly. No credit is given for the question if you correctly label only some of the boxes.

In another select-and-place problem, you might be asked to put a series of steps in order by dragging items from boxes on the left to boxes on the right and placing them in the correct order. One other type requires that you drag an item from the left and place it under an item in a column on the right.

 For more information on the various exam question types, go to www.microsoft.com/learning/mcpexams/policies/innovations.asp.

Simulations

Simulations are the kinds of questions that most closely represent actual situations and test the skills you use while working with Microsoft software interfaces. These exam questions include a mock interface on which you are asked to perform certain actions according to a given scenario. The simulated interfaces look nearly identical to what you see in the actual product.

Because of the number of possible errors that can be made on simulations, be sure to consider the following recommendations from Microsoft:

- Do not change any simulation settings that don't pertain to the solution directly.

- When related information has not been provided, assume that the default settings are used.

- Make sure that your entries are spelled correctly.

- Close all the simulation application windows after completing the set of tasks in the simulation.

The best way to prepare for simulation questions is to spend time working with the graphical interface of the product on which you will be tested.

Case Study–Based Questions

Case study–based questions first appeared in the MCSD program. These questions present a scenario with a range of requirements. Based on the information provided, you answer a series of multiple-choice and select-and-place questions. The interface for case study–based questions has a number of tabs, each of which contains information about the scenario. At present, this type of question appears only in most of the Design exams.

Tips for Taking the Windows 10 Exams

Here are some general tips for achieving success on your certification exam:

- Arrive early at the exam center so that you can relax and review your study materials. During this final review, you can look over tables and lists of exam-related information.

- Read the questions carefully. Do not be tempted to jump to an early conclusion. Make sure that you know *exactly* what the question is asking.

- Answer all questions. If you are unsure about a question, mark it for review and come back to it at a later time.

- On simulations, do not change settings that are not directly related to the question. Also, assume default settings if the question does not specify or imply which settings are used.

- For questions that you're not sure about, use a process of elimination to get rid of the obviously incorrect answers first. This improves your odds of selecting the correct answer when you need to make an educated guess.

Exam Registration

At the time this book was released, Microsoft exams are given using more than 1,000 Authorized VUE Testing Centers around the world. For the location of a testing center near you, go to VUE's website at www.vue.com. If you are outside the United States and Canada, contact your local VUE registration center.

Find out the number of the exam you want to take, and then register with the VUE registration center nearest to you. At this point, you will be asked for advance payment for the exam. The exams are $165 each and you must take them within one year of payment. You can schedule exams up to six weeks in advance or as late as one working day prior to the date of the exam. You can cancel or reschedule your exam if you contact the center at least two working days prior to the exam. Same-day registration is available in some locations, subject to space availability. Where same-day registration is available, you must register a minimum of two hours before test time.

When you schedule the exam, you will be provided with instructions regarding appointment and cancellation procedures, ID requirements, and information about the testing center location. In addition, you will receive a registration and payment confirmation letter from VUE.

Microsoft requires certification candidates to accept the terms of a nondisclosure agreement before taking certification exams.

Who Should Read This Book?

This book is intended for individuals who want to earn their Microsoft 365 Certified: Modern Desktop Administrator Associate: Windows 10 certification.

This book will not only help anyone who is looking to pass the Microsoft exams, it will also help anyone who wants to learn the real ins and outs of the Windows 10 operating system.

What's Inside?

Here is a glance at what's in each chapter:

Chapter 1: Installing and Updating Windows 10   In the first chapter, I explain the requirements and steps to install and configure Windows 10. I will also show you the different versions of Windows 10. This chapter also shows you how to configure automated installation of Windows 10.

Chapter 2: Managing Authentication   This chapter shows you how to configure user authorization and authentication. Understanding how users authenticate onto your network and Azure is one of the most important tasks that administrators must perform. I will also teach you how to manage user profiles.

Chapter 3: Managing Devices   I show you how to implement conditional access and compliance policies for devices. I will show you how to configure device profiles and also how to plan and implement co-management between your on-site network with your Azure based network.

Chapter 4: Planning and Managing Microsoft Intune   This chapter takes you through the different ways to manage Intune device enrollment and inventory. I will also show you how to deploy and update your applications. Finally, I will talk about implanting Mobile Application Management.

Chapter 5: Managing Security   This chapter teaches you how to configure and manage Windows Defender. I will show you how to use Windows Defender Credential Guard, Windows Defender Exploit Guard, Windows Defender Advanced Threat Protection, Windows Defender Application Guard, and Windows Defender Antivirus.

Chapter 6: Configuring Auditing   This chapter will show you how to monitor your different devices. I will also talk about how to monitor the health of your devices using Windows Analytics and cloud-based tools.

What's Included with the Book

There are many helpful items intended to prepare you for the Microsoft 365 Certified: Modern Desktop Administrator Associate certification included in this book:

Assessment Test   There is an Assessment Test at the conclusion of the introduction that can be used to quickly evaluate where you are with Windows 10. This test should be taken prior to beginning your work in this book and should help you identify areas in which you are either strong or weak. Note that these questions are purposely more simple than the types of questions you may see on the exams.

Opening List of Objectives   Each chapter includes a list of the exam objectives that are covered in that chapter.

Helpful Exercises   Throughout the book, I have included step-by-step exercises of some of the more important tasks you should be able to perform. Some of these exercises have corresponding videos that can be downloaded from the book's website. Also, later in this introduction you'll find a recommended home lab setup that will be helpful in completing these tasks.

Video Resources   After each chapter summary, if the chapter includes exercises with corresponding videos, a list or description of the exercises with video resources will be provided. The videos can be accessed at www.wiley.com/go/Sybextestprep.

Exam Essentials   The end of each chapter also includes a listing of exam essentials. These are essentially repeats of the objectives, but remember that any objective on the exam blueprint could show up on the exam.

Chapter Review Questions   Each chapter includes review questions. These are used to assess your understanding of the chapter and are taken directly from the chapter. These questions are based on of the exam objectives and are similar in difficulty to items you might actually receive on the MCSA: Windows 10 exams.

NOTE   The Sybex Interactive Online Test Bank, flashcards, videos, and glossary can be accessed at www.wiley.com/go/Sybextestprep.

Interactive Online Learning Environment and Test Bank

The interactive online learning environment that accompanies the MCA Modern Desktop Administrator Study Guide, Exam MD-101 study guide provides a test bank with study tools to help you prepare for the certification exams and increase your chances of passing the exam the very first time! The test bank includes the following elements:

Sample Tests   All of the questions in this book are provided, including the assessment test, which you'll find at the end of this introduction, and the chapter tests that include the review questions at the end of each chapter. In addition, there are two practice exams. Use these questions to test your knowledge of the study guide material. The online test bank runs on multiple devices.

Electronic Flashcards   The flashcards are included for quick reference and are great tools for learning quick facts. You can even consider these as additional simple practice questions, which is essentially what they are.

Videos   Some of the exercises include corresponding videos. These videos show you how the author does the exercises. There is also a video that shows you how to set up virtualization so that you can complete the exercises within a virtualized environment. I also have videos to help you on the Microsoft exams at www.youtube.com/c/williampanek.

PDF of Glossary of Terms   There is a glossary included that covers the key terms used in this book.

Recommended Home Lab Setup

To get the most out of this book, you will want to make sure that you complete the exercises throughout the chapters. To complete the exercises, you will need one of two setups. First, you can set up a machine with Windows 10 and complete the labs using a regular Windows 10 machine.

The second way to set up Windows 10 is by using virtualization. I set up Windows 10 as a virtual hard disk (VHD) and I did all the labs this way. The advantages of using virtualization are that you can always just wipe out the system and start over without losing a real server. Plus, you can set up multiple virtual servers and create a full lab environment on one machine.

I created a video for this book showing you how to set up a virtual machine and how to install Windows 10 onto that virtual machine. This video can be seen at www.youtube .com/c/williampanek.

How to Contact Sybex or the Author

Sybex strives to keep you supplied with the latest tools and information you need for your work. Please check the website at www.wiley.com/go/Sybextestprep, where I'll post additional content and updates that supplement this book should the need arise.

You can contact Will Panek by going to his website at www.willpanek.com. Will Panek also has videos and test prep information located at www.youtube.com/c/williampanek. Will also has a Windows 10 Facebook page and a Twitter account @AuthorWillPanek.

Objective Mapping

Table I.1 contains an objective map to show you at-a-glance where you can find each objective covered.

TABLE I.1   MD-101 Objective Map

Objective	Chapter
Deploy and update operating systems (35-40%)	
Plan and implement Windows 10 by using dynamic deployment	**Chapter 1**
■ evaluate and select an appropriate deployment options ■ pilot deployment ■ manage and troubleshoot provisioning packages	Chapter 1
Plan and implement Windows 10 by using Windows Autopilot	**Chapter 1**
■ evaluate and select an appropriate deployment options ■ pilot deployment ■ create, validate, and assign deployment profile ■ extract device HW information to CSV file ■ import device HW information to cloud service ■ troubleshoot deployment	Chapter 1

Objective	Chapter
Upgrade devices to Windows 10	**Chapter 1**
▪ identify upgrade and downgrade paths ▪ manage in-place upgrades ▪ configure a Windows analytics environment ▪ perform Upgrade Readiness assessment ▪ migrate user profiles	Chapter 1
Manage updates	**Chapter 1**
▪ configure Windows 10 delivery optimization ▪ configure Windows Update for Business ▪ deploy Windows updates ▪ implement feature updates ▪ monitor Windows 10 updates	Chapter 1
Manage device authentication	**Chapter 2**
▪ manage authentication policies ▪ manage sign-on options ▪ perform Azure AD join	Chapter 2
Manage policies and profiles (25-30%)	
Plan and implement co-management	**Chapter 3**
▪ implement co-management precedence ▪ migrate group policy to MDM policies ▪ recommend a co-management strategy	Chapter 3
Implement conditional access and compliance policies for devices	**Chapter 3**
▪ implement conditional access policies ▪ manage conditional access policies ▪ plan conditional access policies ▪ implement device compliance policies ▪ manage device compliance policies ▪ plan device compliance policies	Chapter 3

TABLE I.1   MD-101 Objective Map *(continued)*

Objective	Chapter
Configure device profiles	**Chapter 3**
▪ implement device profiles ▪ manage device profiles ▪ plan device profiles	Chapter 3
Manage user profiles	**Chapter 2**
▪ configure user profiles ▪ configure Enterprise State Roaming in Azure AD ▪ configure sync settings ▪ implement Folder Redirection, including OneDrive	Chapter 2
Manage and protect devices (20-25%)	
Manage Windows Defender	**Chapter 5**
▪ implement and manage Windows Defender Application Guard ▪ implement and manage Windows Defender Credential Guard ▪ implement and manage Windows Defender Exploit Guard ▪ implement Microsoft Defender Advanced Threat Protection ▪ integrate Windows Defender Application Control ▪ manage Windows Defender Antivirus	Chapter 5
Manage Intune device enrollment and inventory	**Chapter 4**
▪ configure enrollment settings ▪ configure Intune automatic enrollment ▪ enable device enrollment ▪ enroll non-Windows devices ▪ enroll Windows devices ▪ generate custom device inventory reports' Review device inventory	Chapter 4
Monitor devices	**Chapter 6**
▪ monitor device health (e.g., log analytics, Windows Analytics, or other cloud-based tools, etc.) ▪ monitor device security	Chapter 6

Objective	Chapter
Manage apps and data (10-15%)	
Deploy and update applications	**Chapter 4**
<ul><li>assign apps to groups</li><li>deploy apps by using Intune</li><li>deploy apps by using Microsoft Store for Business</li><li>deploy O365 ProPlus</li><li>enable sideloading of apps into images</li><li>gather Office readiness data</li><li>configure and implement kiosk (assigned access) or public devices</li></ul>	Chapter 4
Implement Mobile Application Management (MAM)	**Chapter 4**
<ul><li>implement MAM policies</li><li>manage MAM policies</li><li>plan MAM</li><li>configure Windows Information Protection</li><li>implement Azure Information Protection templates</li><li>securing data by using Intune</li></ul>	Chapter 4

Assessment Test

1. You need to automatically register all the existing computers to the Azure AD network and also enroll all of the computers in Intune. What should you use?

    A. Use a DNS Autodiscover address record.

    B. Use a Windows Autopilot deployment profile.

    C. Use an Autodiscover service connection point (SCP).

    D. Set up a Group Policy Object (GPO).

2. You have a Windows 10 Windows Image (WIM) that is mounted. You need to view the list of third-party drivers installed on the WIM. What should you do?

    A. Run DISM and specify the /get-drivers parameter.

    B. Run Driverquery.exe and use the /si parameter.

    C. From Device Manager, view all hidden drivers.

    D. From Windows Explorer, open the mount folder.

3. You have a computer that runs Windows 10 Pro. The computer is joined to Azure Active Directory (Azure AD) and enrolled in Microsoft Intune. You need to upgrade the computer to Windows 10 Enterprise for another user. What should you configure in Intune?

    A. Windows Autopilot device profile

    B. A device enrollment policy

    C. A device cleanup rule

    D. A device compliance policy

4. You decide to install Windows Deployment Services (WDS). You are using a Windows Server 2019 domain and have verified that your network meets the requirements for using WDS. What command-line utility can you use to configure the WDS server?

    A. dism.exe

    B. wdsutil.exe

    C. setup.exe

    D. The WDS icon in Control Panel

5. You have installed a clean installation of Windows 10 on your computer. You want to create an image of the new installation to use as a basis for remote installs. What Windows 10 utility should you use to accomplish this?

    A. WDS

    B. Windows SIM

    C. DISM

    D. Sysprep

6. You are the administrator in charge of a computer that runs both Windows 7 and Windows 10. Windows 10 is installed on a different partition from Windows 7. You have to make sure that the computer always starts Windows 7 by default. What action should you perform?

A. Run bcdedit.exe and the /default parameter.

B. Run bcdedit.exe and the /bootcd parameter.

C. Create a boot.ini file in the root of the Windows 10 partition.

D. Create a boot.ini file in the root of the Windows 7 partition.

7. An administrator wants to look at an Azure Active Directory application policy for your user's applications. What PowerShell command would you use to accomplish this task?

A. Add-AzureADPolicy

B. Add-AzureADApplicationPolicy

C. Create-AzurePolicy

D. Install-AzureADPolicy

8. Your boss has asked you about Azure security and making sure that user logins are secure. What feature can you explain to your boss to ease their concerns?

A. Azure AD User Security

B. Azure AD Identity Protection

C. Azure AD Security add-on

D. Azure Identity Protection

9. An administrator wants to change an Azure Active Directory policy for one of their users. What PowerShell command would you use to accomplish this task?

A. New-AzureADPolicy

B. Edit-AzureADPolicy

C. New-AzurePolicy

D. Set-AzureADPolicy

10. An administrator wants to view their Azure AD directory settings for the company's Azure AD subscription. What PowerShell command would you use to accomplish this task?

A. View-AzureADDirectorySetting

B. Get-AzureADDirectorySetting

C. Add-AzureADDirectorySetting

D. Set-AzureADDirectorySetting

11. You need to upgrade 100 Windows 10 Pro computers to Windows 10 Enterprise. What should you configure in Intune?

A. A device enrollment policy

B. A device cleanup rule

C. A device compliance policy

D. A device configuration profile

12. An administrator needs to create a device configuration profile in Microsoft Intune. You need to implement an ADMX-backed policy. Which profile type should you use?

    A. Identity protection

    B. Custom

    C. Device restrictions

    D. System restrictions

13. You need to set up a Windows 10 system in a break room where all employees can use it. Which device configuration profile type should you use?

    A. Kiosk

    B. Endpoint protection

    C. Identity protection

    D. Device restrictions

14. You have compressed a 4 MB file into 2 MB. You are copying the file to another computer that has a FAT32 partition. How can you ensure that the file will remain compressed?

    A. When you copy the file, use the xcopy.exe command with the /comp switch.

    B. When you copy the file, use the Windows Explorer utility and specify the option Keep Existing Attributes.

    C. On the destination folder, make sure that you set the option Compress Contents To Save Disk Space in the folder's properties.

    D. You can't maintain disk compression on a non-NTFS partition.

15. An administrator suspects that a problem in Windows 10 is related to the files being spread over the disk. What utility can be used to store the files contiguously on the disk?

    A. Disk Defragmenter

    B. Disk Manager

    C. Disk Administrator

    D. Disk Cleanup

16. When your users get added to Intune and get licensed, how many devices can each user use by default?

    A. 14

    B. 15

    C. 16

    D. 17

17. How do you allow your tablets to connect to your cell phones for Internet access?

    A. Configure the broadband connection as a metered network.

    B. Turn on cellular tethering.

    C. Enable tablet tethering.

    D. Enable tablet metering in the tablets settings.

18. An administrator needs to secure some of the Microsoft operating system's loopholes that hackers use. What type of updates would you need to install to help solve this problem?

    A. Security Updates

    B. Definition Updates

    C. Critical Updates

    D. Software Updates

19. You want to enable self-service password reset on the sign-in screen. Which settings should you configure from the Microsoft Intune blade?

    A. Device configuration

    B. Device compliance

    C. Device enrollment

    D. Conditional access

20. What do you need to do to be sure that all iOS devices can be managed by the Intune Administrators?

    A. Add an Employee Portal app from the Apple App Store.

    B. Create a device enrollment manager account.

    C. Configure an Intune Service Connector for Exchange.

    D. Import an Apple Push Notification service (APNs) certificate.

21. Your work computer network is protected by a firewall. You have configured your Windows 10 computer to use HTTPS. What port should you open on the firewall?

    A. 25

    B. 110

    C. 443

    D. 995

22. Your home computer network is protected by a firewall. You have configured your Windows 10 home computer to use Windows Mail. After you configure your email accounts, you discover that you are unable to send email messages from Windows Mail. Your email provider uses POP3 and SMTP. What port should you open on the firewall?

    A. 25

    B. 110

    C. 443

    D. 995

23. Your company is using Microsoft Azure Active Directory and all computers are enrolled in Microsoft Intune with EMS. The administrator needs to make sure that only approved applications are allowed to run on all of these computers. What should you implement to ensure this?

    A. Windows Defender Credential Guard

    B. Windows Defender Exploit Guard

    C. Windows Defender Application Control

    D. Windows Defender Antivirus

24. What two ports use FTP?

    A. Ports 12 and 15

    B. Ports 20 and 21

    C. Ports 80 and 443

    D. Ports 80 and 110

25. You have a Windows 10 machine that has a virus that was caused by a malicious font. You need to stop this type of threat from affecting your corporate computers in the future. What should you use?

    A. Windows Defender Exploit Guard

    B. Windows Defender Application Guard

    C. Windows Defender Credential Guard

    D. Windows Defender System Guard

26. What port does DNS use?

    A. Port 20

    B. Ports 25

    C. Ports 53

    D. Ports 80

27. The IT manager wants CPU utilization, disk utilization, and memory utilization all included in the data collected. How should you accomplish this?

    A. Create a User Defined Data Collector set.

    B. Create a custom performance set.

    C. Create a Trace event.

    D. Create a session Data Collector set.

28. You need to use a Microsoft Azure monitoring tool to monitor devices and change settings. Which of the following tools can you use?

    A. Performance Monitor

    B. Microsoft Azure IoT Central Application

    C. Azure Performance Center

    D. Intune Performance Center

29. You need to stop an application from running in Task Manager. Which tab would you use to stop an application from running?

   A. Performance

   B. Users

   C. Options

   D. Details

30. You have a computer named Portable1. You need to view the events collected from Portable1. Which query would an administrator run in Log Analytics?

   A. Eventview | where SourceSystem = = "Portable1"

   B. Eventview | where Computer = = "Portable1"

   C. Event | where SourceSystem = = "Portable1"

   D. Event | where Computer = = "Portable1"

Answers to Assessment Test

1. B. Windows Autopilot profiles allow an administrator to choose how the Windows 10 system will be set up and configured on Azure AD and Intune. See Chapter 1 for more information.

2. A. The DISM utility with the /get-drivers switch allows you to find out which drivers are installed on the WIM. See Chapter 1 for more information.

3. A. Windows Autopilot profiles allow an administrator to choose how the Windows 10 system will be set up and configured on Azure AD and Intune. See Chapter 1 for more information.

4. B. wdsutil.exe is a command-line utility that can be used to configure the WDS server. Several other configuration options need to be specified on the WDS server, and you can set them using wdsutil.exe. See Chapter 1 for more information.

5. C. You can use the DISM utility to create an image of a Windows 10 installation. After the image has been created, you can prepare the image with a utility such as the System Preparation Tool (Sysprep). The image can then be used for remote installations of Windows 10. See Chapter 1 for more information.

6. A. The Boot Configuration Data (BCD) store contains boot information parameters that were previously found in boot.ini in older versions of Windows. To edit the boot options in the BCD store, use the bcdedit utility, which can be launched only from a command prompt. See Chapter 1 for more information.

7. B. Administrators can use the Add-AzureADApplicationPolicy command to add an application policy. See Chapter 2 for more information.

8. B. Azure AD Identity Protection allows an Azure administrator to use the same type of protection that Microsoft uses to protect and secure users' identities. See Chapter 2 for more information.

9. D. Administrators can use the Set-AzureADPolicy command to update an Azure AD policy. See Chapter 2 for more information.

10. B. Administrators can use the Get-AzureADDirectorySetting command to view their directory settings. See Chapter 2 for more information.

11. D. You can upgrade your devices by using a device configuration profile. The option that you want to configure is Edition Upgrade. Edition Upgrade allows you to upgrade Windows 10 (and later) devices to a newer version of Windows. See Chapter 3 for more information.

12. B. One of the options you have in device configuration profiles is the ability to set up custom profiles. Custom profile settings allow an Intune administrator to configure options that are not automatically included with Intune. See Chapter 3 for more information.

13. A. Kiosk systems are normally designed in a location where many people can use the same device and that device will only run limited applications. See Chapter 3 for more information.

14. D. Windows 10 data compression is supported only on NTFS partitions. If you move the file to a FAT32 partition, then it will be stored as uncompressed. See Chapter 3 for more information.

15. A. The Disk Defragmenter utility is used to rearrange files so that they are stored contiguously on the disk. This optimizes access to those files. You can also defragment disks through the command-line utility Defrag. See Chapter 3 for more information.

16. B. By default, licensed users can add up to 15 devices to their accounts. Device Administrators have the ability to add devices to Intune, but users do have the ability to enroll 15 devices on their own. See Chapter 4 for more information.

17. B. Tethering means that users can connect one device to another for Internet services. See Chapter 4 for more information.

18. A. Security updates are updates that need to be applied to fix a security issue. These security issues are used by hackers to either hack into a device or software. See Chapter 4 for more information.

19. A. You will want to configure device configuration settings. To do this, sign in to the Azure portal and click Intune. Create a new device configuration profile by going to Device Configuration ➤ Profiles ➤ Create Profile. See Chapter 4 for more information.

20. D. An Apple Push Notification service (APNs) certificate must be imported from Apple so that the company can manage iOS devices. See Chapter 4 for more information.

21. C. Port 443 should be opened on the firewall. Simple Mail Transfer Protocol (SMTP) is used for outbound mail and uses port 25. Post Office Protocol (POP3), which is used for receiving inbound mail, uses port 110. See Chapter 5 for more information.

22. A. Port 25 should be opened on the firewall. Simple Mail Transfer Protocol (SMTP) is used for outbound mail and uses port 25. Post Office Protocol (POP3), which is used for receiving inbound mail, uses port 110. See Chapter 5 for more information.

23. C. Administrators can use Windows Defender Application Control to ensure that only applications that you explicitly allow can run on the Windows 10 computers. See Chapter 5 for more information.

24. B. File Transfer Protocol (FTP) servers use port 20 and port 21. See Chapter 5 for more information.

25. A. Windows Defender Exploit Guard helps protect your system from common malware hacks that use executable files and scripts to attack applications like Microsoft Office. See Chapter 5 for more information.

26. C. Domain Name System (DNS) servers use Port 53. See Chapter 5 for more information.

27. A. Data Collector Sets are used to collect data into a log so that the data can be reviewed. You can view the log files with Performance Monitor. See Chapter 6 for more information.

28. B. Use Microsoft Azure Internet of Things (IoT) Central Application to monitor devices and change settings. Azure IoT Central Applications are hosted by Microsoft, which reduces the administration overhead of managing applications. See Chapter 6 for more information.

29. D. All of the applications that are running on the Windows 10 machine will show up under the Details tab. Right-click the application and end the process. See Chapter 6 for more information.

30. D. Administrator can view the events collected from a specific computer in Azure is to run a query in the Logs Analytics. See Chapter 6 for more information.

Chapter

1

Installing and Updating Windows 10

MICROSOFT EXAM OBJECTIVES COVERED IN THIS CHAPTER:

✓ **Plan and implement Windows 10 by using dynamic deployment**

- Evaluate and select an appropriate deployment options; pilot deployment; manage and troubleshoot provisioning packages.

✓ **Plan and implement Windows 10 by using Windows Autopilot**

- Evaluate and select an appropriate deployment options; pilot deployment; create, validate, and assign deployment profile; extract device HW information to CSV file; import device HW information to cloud service; troubleshoot deployment.

✓ **Upgrade devices to Windows 10**

- Identify upgrade and downgrade paths; manage in-place upgrades; configure a Windows analytics environment; perform Upgrade Readiness assessment; migrate user profiles.

✓ **Manage updates**

- Configure Windows 10 delivery optimization; configure Windows Update for Business; deploy Windows updates; implement feature updates; monitor Windows 10 updates.

This book is for exam MD-101, and this is the second of two Windows 10 exams (MD-100 and MD-101) for the Microsoft 365 Certified: Modern Desktop Administrator Associate. If you are using both of the Sybex books for the Microsoft 365 Certified: Modern Desktop Administrator Associate, you will notice that some of the topics in Chapter 1 are the same in both books. The reason for this is that no matter what test you take, installing Windows 10 is the same. Where the two books start to differ is with automated installations. Many of these automated installations will require an Azure subscription along with Intune.

But as with the start of any journey, we must take our first steps. The first steps for this exam is with learning about the Windows 10 installation process. It is important that you understand the different versions of Windows 10 and which one is right for you and your organization.

Understanding the Basics

Microsoft Windows 10 is the latest version of Microsoft's client operating system software and according to Microsoft, it's the last. Microsoft has announced that Windows 10 will be the last client operating system and they will just continue to do edition updates. Windows 10 combines the best of Windows 7 and Windows 8 and it also makes it much easier to work within the cloud.

Microsoft has released many different editions of the Windows 10 operating system. The following list is just a few of the more popular editions:

- Windows 10 Home
- Windows 10 Pro
- Windows 10 Pro for Workstation
- Windows 10 Enterprise
- Windows 10 Enterprise E3
- Windows 10 Enterprise E5
- Windows 10 Education

Microsoft also offers some of these operating systems as slimmed down versions called "Windows 10 IoT Core." This edition is one of the above Windows 10 versions that don't require a monitor or system. For example, suppose you are building a toy robot and you want to load Windows 10 into his core computer. You can use the IoT versions to run the robot's functionality.

Windows 10 has been improved in many of the weak areas that plagued Windows 8. Windows 10 has a much faster boot time and shutdown compared to Windows 8. It also brings back the Start button that we are all so familiar with from previous editions.

The Windows 10 operating system functions are also faster than their previous counterparts. The processes for opening, moving, extracting, compressing, and installing files and folders are more efficient than they were in previous versions of Microsoft's client operating systems.

Let's take a look at some of the features of each Windows 10 edition (this is just an overview of some of the benefits to using Windows 10). Table 1.1 and Table 1.2 show each edition and what some of the features are for those editions.

 The information in Table 1.1 and Table 1.2 was taken directly from Microsoft's website and documentation.

TABLE 1.1 Windows 10 Security and Protection

Description	Home	Pro	Pro for Workstation	E3	E5
Integrity enforcement of operating system boot up process	■	■	■	■	■
Integrity enforcement of sensitive operating system components	■	■	■	■	■
Advanced vulnerability and zero-day exploit mitigations	■	■	■	■	■
Reputation based network protection for Microsoft Edge, Internet Explorer, and Chrome	■	■	■	■	■
Host based firewall	■	■	■	■	■
Ransomware mitigations	■	■	■	■	■
Pre-execution emulation executables and scripts	■	■	■	■	■
Runtime behavior monitoring	■	■	■	■	■
In memory anomaly and behavior monitoring	■	■	■	■	■

TABLE 1.1   Windows 10 Security and Protection *(continued)*

Description	Home	Pro	Pro for Workstation	E3	E5
Machine learning and AI based protection from viruses and malware threats	▪	▪	▪	▪	▪
Cloud protection for fastest responses to new/unknown web-based threats	▪	▪	▪	▪	▪
Protection from fileless based attacks	▪	▪	▪	▪	▪
Industry standards based multifactor authentication	▪	▪	▪	▪	▪
Support for biometrics (Facial and Fingerprints)	▪	▪	▪	▪	▪
Support for Microsoft Authenticator	▪	▪	▪	▪	▪
Support for Microsoft compatible security devices	▪	▪	▪	▪	▪
Automatic encryption on capable devices	▪	▪	▪	▪	▪
Advanced encryption configuration options		▪	▪	▪	▪
Removable storage protection		▪	▪	▪	▪
Supports for Active Directory and Azure Active Directory		▪	▪	▪	▪
Hardware based isolation for Microsoft Edge		▪	▪	▪	▪
Application control powered by the Intelligent Security Graph		▪	▪	▪	▪
Device Control (e.g.: USB)		▪	▪	▪	▪
Personal and business data separation		▪	▪	▪	▪
Application access control		▪	▪	▪	▪

Description	Home	Pro	Pro for Workstation	E3	E5
Copy and paste protection		▪	▪	▪	▪
Removable storage protection		▪	▪	▪	▪
Integration with Microsoft Information Protection		▪	▪	▪	▪
Network protection for web-based threats				▪	▪
Enterprise management of hardware-based isolation for Microsoft Edge				▪	▪
Hardware isolation of single sign-in tokens				▪	▪
Direct Access & Always On VPN device Tunnel				▪	▪
Centralized configuration mgmt, analytics, reporting, and security operations					▪
Centralized management, analytics, reporting, and operations					▪
Customizable network protection for web-based threats					▪
Host intrusion prevention rules					▪
Device-based conditional access					▪
Tamper protection of operating system					▪
Advanced monitoring, analytics, and reporting for attack surface					▪
Advanced machine learning and AI based protection for apex level viruses and malware threats					▪
Advanced cloud protection that includes deep inspection and detonation					▪

TABLE 1.1   Windows 10 Security and Protection *(continued)*

Description	Home	Pro	Pro for Workstation	E3	E5
Emergency outbreak protection from the Intelligent Security Graph					▪
ISO 27001 compliance					▪
Geolocation and sovereignty of sample data					▪
Sample data retention policy					▪
Monitoring, analytics- and reporting for Next Generation Protection capabilities					▪

TABLE 1.2   Windows 10 Updates

Description	Home	Pro	Pro for Workstation	E3	E5
In-place upgrades	▪	▪	▪	▪	▪
Express updates	▪	▪	▪	▪	▪
Delivery optimization	▪	▪	▪	▪	▪
Windows Analytics Upgrade Readiness		▪	▪	▪	▪
Windows Analytics Update Compliance		▪	▪	▪	▪
Windows Update for Business		▪	▪	▪	▪
Windows Analytics Device Health				▪	▪
30 months of support for September targeted releases				▪	▪
Windows 10 LTSC Access				▪	▪

Windows 10 Features

Now that you have seen which editions contain which features, let's take a look at some of the Windows 10 features in greater detail. This section describes only a few of these features, but all features will be explained throughout this book.

Cortana Integration   Windows 10 comes with Cortana integration. Cortana is your very own personal assistant. You can type in or ask Cortana a question and Cortana will seek out the best possible answer based on your question.

Secure Boot   Windows 10 provides the ability for securely booting the operating system. Secure boot validates all drivers and operating system components before they are loaded against the signature database. If you are going to implement the Secure Boot feature of Windows 10, then make sure the system firmware is set up as Unified Extensible Firmware Interface (UEFI) and not BIOS. You also need to make sure the disks are converted from Master Boot Record (MBR) disks to a GUID Partition Table (GPT) disk.

Virtual Smart Cards   Windows 10 has started offering a new way to do two-factor authentication with virtual smart cards. Virtual smart cards help an IT department that doesn't want to invest in extra hardware and smart cards. Virtual smart cards use Trusted Platform Module (TPM) devices that allow for the same capabilities as physical smart cards with the physical hardware.

Miracast   Windows 10 allows you to project your Windows 10 laptop or mobile device to a projector or television. Miracast allows you to connect to an external device through the use of your mobile wireless display (WiDi) adapter.

Hyper-V   Windows 10 (except Home version) comes with Hyper-V built into the operating system. Hyper-V is Microsoft's version of a Virtual Server.

Enterprise Data Protection   Windows 10 Enterprise Data Protection (EDP) helps protect corporate data in a world that is increasingly becoming a Bring Your Own Device (BYOD) environment. Since many organizations are allowing employees to connect their own devices to their network, the possibility of corporate data being compromised because of noncorporate programs running on these personnel devices is increasing. For example, many third-party apps may put corporate data at risk by accidentally disclosing corporate information through the application.

Enterprise Data Protection helps protect information by separating corporate applications and corporate data from being disclosed by personal devices and personal applications.

Device Guard   Because employees can use multiple types of Windows 10 devices (Surface Pros, Windows Phones, and Windows 10 computer systems), Device Guard is a feature that helps guarantee that only trusted applications will run on any of these devices.

Device Guard uses both hardware and software security features to lock down a device so it can run only trusted and approved applications. This also helps protect against hackers running malicious software on these devices.

Microsoft Passport / Windows Hello   Microsoft has introduced two security features for Windows 10 called Windows Hello and Microsoft Passport. Windows Hello is a biometrics system integrated into Windows 10 and it is a piece of the user's authentication experience. Microsoft Passport allows users to use a two-factor authentication system that combines a PIN or biometrics with an encrypted key from a user's device to provide two-factor authentication.

Start Menu   Windows 10 has brought back the Start Menu that users are familiar with. The Windows 10 Start Menu combines the best of both Windows 7 and Windows 8. So the Start Menu gives you a menu that we were familiar with in Windows 7 as well as the Live Tiles that users liked in Windows 8.

Microsoft Edge and Internet Explorer 11   Windows 10 has introduced a new way to surf the Internet with Microsoft Edge. But Windows 10 also still comes with Internet Explorer 11 in the event that you need to run ActiveX controls or run backward-compatible web services or sites.

Microsoft Edge allows users to start using many new Microsoft features, including Web Note (allows you to annotate, highlight, and call things out directly on web pages), Reading View (allows you to print and save as a PDF for easy reading), and Cortana (personal assistant).

Domain Join and Group Policy   Depending on the version of Windows 10 that you are using, administrators have the ability to join Windows 10 clients to either a corporate version of Active Directory or a cloud-based version of Azure Active Directory.

Microsoft Store for Business   Microsoft Store has included many applications that allow users to get better functionality and productivity out of their Windows 10 devices. One advantage for corporations is that they can create their own applications and load them into the Microsoft Store for users to download (called *sideloading*).

Mobile Device Management   Mobile Device Management (MDM) allows administrators to set up Windows 10 policies that can integrate many corporate scenarios, including the ability to control users' access to the Windows Store and the ability to use the corporate VPN. MDM also allows administrators to manage multiple users who have accounts set up on Microsoft Azure Active Directory (Azure AD). Windows 10 MDM support is based on the Open Mobile Alliance (OMA) Device Management (DM) protocol 1.2.1 specification.

Understanding the Windows 10 Architecture

Windows 10 has limited the number of files that load at system startup to help with the core performance of the operating system. Microsoft has also removed many of the fluff items that Windows Vista used, allowing for better performance.

Microsoft offers both a 32-bit version and a 64-bit version of Windows 10. The terms *32-bit* and *64-bit* refer to the CPU, or processor. The number represents how the data is processed. It is processed either as 2^{32} or 2^{64}. The larger the number, the larger the amount of data that can be processed at any one time.

To get an idea of how 32-bit and 64-bit processors operate, think of a large highway with 32 lanes. Vehicles can travel on those 32 lanes only, so when traffic gets backed up, the result is delays. Now think of how many more vehicles can travel on a 64-lane highway. The problem here is that a 32-lane highway can't handle the number of vehicles a 64-lane highway can. You need to have the infrastructure to allow for that volume of vehicles. The same is true for computers. Your computer has to be configured to allow you to run a 64-bit processor.

So what does all of this mean to the common user or administrator? It's all about random access memory, or RAM. A 32-bit operating system can handle up to 4 GB of RAM, and a 64-bit processor can handle up to 16 exabytes (EB) of RAM. None of this is new. Although 64-bit processors are just starting to get accepted with Windows systems, other operating systems, such as Apple, have been using 64-bit processors for many years.

When you're installing or upgrading Windows 10, the version of Windows 10 must match the CPU version. For example, if your system is a 32-bit system, you must use a 32-bit OS. If your system is a 64-bit system, you can install either the 32-bit or 64-bit version of Windows 10.

Computer processors are typically rated by speed. The speed of the processor, or central processing unit (CPU), is rated by the number of clock cycles that can be performed in 1 second. This measurement is typically expressed in gigahertz (GHz). One GHz is one billion cycles per second. Keep in mind that processor architecture must also be taken into account when considering processor speed. A processor with a more efficient pipeline will be faster than a processor with a less-efficient pipeline at the same CPU speed.

Preparing to Install Windows 10

Installing Windows 10 can be relatively simple because of the installation wizard. The installation wizard will walk you through the entire installation of the operating system.

The most difficult part of installing Windows 10 is preparing and planning for the installation. One thing I often say to IT pros is, "An hour of planning will save you days of work." Planning a Windows 10 rollout is one of the hardest and most important tasks that you will perform when installing Windows 10.

There are many decisions that should be made before you install Windows 10. The first decision is which edition of Windows 10 you want to install. As mentioned previously, Microsoft has six different editions of the Windows 10 operating system. This allows an administrator to custom-fit a user's hardware and job function to the appropriate version of Windows 10. Many times, Microsoft releases multiple editions of the operating system contained within the same Windows 10 media disk. You can choose to unlock the one you want based on the product key you have. Let's take a closer look at the different versions of Windows 10.

> In this book, I will not talk much about Windows 10 Education. Windows 10 Education is the counterpart to Windows 10 Enterprise, but it is a volume-licensed version of Windows 10 that is specifically priced for educational institutions. Educational institutions receive the same Enterprise functionality, but they pay much less than a corporation.

Windows 10 Pro

Windows 10 Pro is designed for small-business owners. Microsoft designed Windows 10 Pro for users to get more done and safeguard their data. Pro offers the following features:

- Broad application and device compatibility with unlimited concurrent applications.
- A safe, reliable, and supported operating system.
- Microsoft Passport/Windows Hello.
- Domain Join.
- Improved Taskbar and Jump Lists.
- Enterprise Mode Internet Explorer (EMIE).
- Advanced networking support (ad hoc wireless networks and Internet connection sharing).
- View Available Networks (VAN). Windows 10 by default has the ability, when you use a wireless network adapter, to choose the wireless network that you want to connect to by using the wireless network adapter properties.
- Mobility Center.
- Action Center, which makes it easier to resolve many IT issues yourself.
- Easy networking and sharing across all your PCs and devices.
- Group Policy Management.
- Windows Update and Windows Update for Business.
- Multitouch.
- Improved handwriting recognition.
- Domain Join, which enables simple and secure server networking.
- BitLocker, which protects data on removable devices.
- Device Encryption.
- Encrypting File System, which protects data.

- Client Hyper-V.
- Location Aware Printing, which helps find the right printer when moving between the office and home.
- Start Menu that includes Live Tiles.

Windows 10 Enterprise

Windows 10 Enterprise is the version designed for midsize and large organizations. This operating system has the most features and security options of all Windows 10 versions. Here are some of the features:

- Broad application and device compatibility with unlimited concurrent applications.
- A safe, reliable, and supported operating system.
- Microsoft Passport/Windows Hello.
- Enterprise Mode Internet Explorer (EMIE).
- Group Policy Management.
- Windows Update and Windows Update for Business.
- Advanced networking support (ad hoc wireless networks and Internet connection sharing).
- View Available Networks (VAN). Windows 10 by default has the ability, when you use a wireless network adapter, to choose the wireless network that you want to connect to by using the wireless network adapter properties.
- Mobility Center.
- Easy networking and sharing across all your PCs and devices.
- Multitouch.
- Start Menu that includes Live Tiles.
- Improved handwriting recognition.
- Domain Join, which enables simple and secure server networking.
- Device Encryption.
- Encrypting File System, which protects data.
- Location Aware Printing, which helps find the right printer when you are moving between the office and home.
- Client Hyper-V.
- Credential Guard.
- Device Guard.
- BitLocker, which protects data on removable devices.
- DirectAccess, which links users to corporate resources from the road without a virtual private network (VPN).

- BranchCache, which makes it faster to open files and web pages from a branch office.
- AppLocker, which restricts unauthorized software and also enables greater security hardware requirements

Windows 10 Enterprise E3 and E5

Microsoft has released a new cloud-based way to deploy Windows 10 Enterprise with the introduction of Windows 10 Enterprise E3 and E5. Windows 10 Enterprise E3 and E5 are subscription-based versions of Windows 10 for organizations that like to work with Microsoft Office 365.

When Microsoft released Windows 10 version 1703, it included a Windows 10 Enterprise E3 and E5 benefit for Microsoft customers with either Enterprise Agreements (EA) or Microsoft Products & Services Agreements (MPSA).

One of the advantages of using the subscription-based service for Windows 10 E3 and E5 is that the Windows 10 license can be purchased per user or per device. If the licenses are per user, the users can then choose to download the corporate version of Windows 10 E3 or E5 onto either their work systems or personal systems (depending on corporate policies).

As you saw in Table 1.1 and Table 1.2, by purchasing the Windows 10 E3 and E5 subscriptions, you get many additional features, including enterprise-level security and control. Some of the E3 and E5 components are available if you would like to purchase them separately.

New Install or Upgrade?

Once you've determined that your hardware meets the minimum requirements, you need to decide whether you want to do an upgrade or a clean install. An upgrade allows you to retain your existing operating system's applications, settings, and files.

The bad news is that if you are moving from Windows Vista, Windows XP, or earlier versions of Windows to Windows 10, you must perform a clean install. You can perform an upgrade to Windows 10 if the following conditions are true:

- You are running Windows 7 or Windows 8.
- You want to keep your existing applications and preferences.
- You want to preserve any local users and groups you've created.

You must perform a clean install of Windows 10 if any of the following conditions are true:

- There is no operating system currently installed.
- You have an operating system installed that does not support an in-place upgrade to Windows 10 (such as DOS, Windows 9x, Windows NT, Windows Me, Windows 2000 Pro, Windows Vista, or Windows XP).
- You want to start from scratch, without keeping any existing preferences.
- You want to be able to dual-boot between Windows 10 and your previous operating system.

Table 1.3 shows each operating system that can be upgraded and the edition of Windows 10 to which it should be upgraded.

TABLE 1.3 Windows 7 and Windows 8 upgrade options

From Current Edition	Windows 10 Edition
Windows 7 Pro	Windows 10 Pro
Windows 7 Ultimate	Windows 10 Pro
Windows 7 Enterprise	Windows 10 Enterprise
Windows 8.1 Home	Windows 10 Home
Windows 8.1 Pro	Windows 10 Pro
Windows 8.1 Enterprise	Windows 10 Enterprise
Windows 8.1 Pro for Students	Windows 10 Pro

Upgrade Considerations

Almost all Windows 7 and Windows 8 applications should run with the Windows 10 operating system. However, possible exceptions to this statement include the following:

- Applications that use file-system filters, such as antivirus software, may not be compatible.
- Custom power-management tools may not be supported.

Before upgrading to Windows 10, be sure to stop any antivirus scanners, network services, or other client software. These software packages may see the Windows 10 install as a virus and cause installation issues.

If you are performing an upgrade installation to the same partition as an existing version of Windows, the contents of the existing Users (or Documents and Settings), Program Files, and Windows directories will be placed in a directory named Windows.old, and the old operating system will no longer be available.

Another issue that you may need to look at is the user's profile. Depending if your company uses roaming profiles, these profiles will be stored on a local server. Starting with Windows 7, Microsoft started using roaming profile version numbers to identify what operating system is using what profile. The following list shows some of the different operating systems and what roaming profile version numbers go with the operating system:

- Windows XP and Windows Server 2003 \\<servername>\<fileshare>\<username>
- Windows Vista and Windows Server 2008 \\<servername>\<fileshare>\<username>.V2

- Windows 7 and Windows Server 2008 R2 \\<servername>\<fileshare>\<username>.V2
- Windows 8 and Windows Server 2012 (after updates) \\<servername>\<fileshare>\<username>.V3
- Windows 8.1 and Windows Server 2012 R2 (after updates) \\<servername>\<fileshare>\<username>.V4
- Windows 10 (before version 1607) \\<servername>\<fileshare>\<username>.V5
- Windows 10 (after version 1607) \\<servername>\<fileshare>\<username>.V6

Hardware Compatibility Issues

You need to ensure that you have Windows 10 device drivers for your hardware. If you have a video driver without a Windows 10–compatible driver, the Windows 10 upgrade will install the Standard VGA driver, which will display the video with an 800×600 resolution. Once you get the Windows 10 driver for your video, you can install it and adjust video properties accordingly.

Application Compatibility Issues

Not all applications that were written for earlier versions of Windows will work with Windows 10. After the upgrade, if you have application problems, you can address the problems in any of the following ways:

- If the application is compatible with Windows 10, reinstall the application after the upgrade is complete.
- If the application uses dynamic-link libraries (DLLs) and there are migration DLLs for the application, apply the migration DLLs.
- Use the Microsoft Application Compatibility Toolkit (ACT) to determine the compatibility of your current applications with Windows 10. ACT will determine which applications are installed, identify any applications that may be affected by Windows updates, and identify any potential compatibility problems with User Account Control and Internet Explorer. Reports can be exported for detailed analysis.
- If applications were written for earlier versions of Windows but are incompatible with Windows 10, use the Windows 10 Program Compatibility Wizard. From the Control Panel, click the Programs icon, and then click the Run Programs From Previous Versions link to start the Program Compatibility Wizard. If the application is not compatible with Windows 10, upgrade your application to a Windows 10–compliant version.

An Upgrade Checklist

Once you have made the decision to upgrade, you should develop a plan of attack. The following upgrade checklist (valid for upgrading from Windows 7 or Windows 8/8.1) will help you plan and implement a successful upgrade strategy:

- Verify that your computer meets the minimum hardware requirements for Windows 10.
- Make sure you have the Windows 10 drivers for the hardware. You can verify this with the hardware manufacturer.

- To audit the current configuration and status of your computer, run the Get Windows 10 App tool from the Microsoft website, which also includes documentation on using the utility. It will generate a report of any known hardware or software compatibility issues based on your configuration. You should resolve any reported issues before you upgrade to Windows 10.

- Make sure your BIOS is current. Windows 10 requires that your computer has the most current BIOS. If it does not, it may not be able to use advanced power-management features or device-configuration features. In addition, your computer may cease to function during or after the upgrade. Use caution when performing BIOS updates because installing the incorrect BIOS can cause your computer to fail to boot.

- If you are going to implement the Secure Boot feature of Windows 10, then make sure the system firmware is set up as Unified Extensible Firmware Interface (UEFI) and not BIOS. You also need to make sure the disks are converted from Master Boot Record (MBR) disks to a GUID Partition Table (GPT) disk.

- Take an inventory of your current configuration. This inventory should include documentation of your current network configuration, the applications that are installed, the hardware items and their configuration, the services that are running, and any profile and policy settings.

- Back up your data and configuration files. Before you make any major changes to your computer's configuration, you should back up your data and configuration files and then verify that you can successfully restore your backup. Chances are, if you have a valid backup, you won't have any problems. Likewise, if you don't have a valid backup, you will likely have problems.

- Delete any unnecessary files or applications, and clean up any program groups or program items you don't use. Theoretically, you want to delete all the junk on your computer before you upgrade. Think of this as the spring-cleaning step.

- Verify that there are no existing problems with your hard drive prior to the upgrade. Perform a disk scan, a current virus scan, and defragmentation. These too are spring-cleaning chores. This step just prepares your hard drive for the upgrade.

- Perform the upgrade. In this step, you upgrade from the Windows 7 or Windows 8/8.1 operating system to Windows 10.

- Verify your configuration. After Windows 10 has been installed, use the inventory to compare and test each element that was inventoried prior to the upgrade to verify that the upgrade was successful.

Handling an Upgrade Failure

Before you upgrade, you should have a contingency plan in place. Your plan should assume the worst-case scenario. For example, what happens if you upgrade and the computer doesn't work anymore? It is possible that, after checking your upgrade list and verifying that everything should work, your attempt at the actual upgrade may not work. If this happens, you may want to return your computer to the original, working configuration.

Indeed, I have made these plans, created my backups (two, just in case), verified them, and then had a failed upgrade anyway—only to discover that I had no clue where to find the original operating system CD. A day later, with the missing CD located, I was able to get up and running again. My problem was an older BIOS, and the manufacturer of my computer did not have an updated BIOS.

Disk Partitioning

Disk partitioning is the act of taking the physical hard drive and creating logical partitions. A logical drive is how space is allocated to the drive's primary and logical partitions. For example, if you have a 500 GB hard drive, you might partition it into three logical drives:

- C: drive, which might be 200 GB
- D: drive, which might be 150 GB
- E: drive, which might be 150 GB

The following list details some of the major considerations for disk partitioning:

Partition Size   One important consideration in your disk-partitioning scheme is determining the partition size. You need to consider the amount of space taken up by your operating system, the applications that will be installed, and the amount of stored data. It is also important to consider the amount of space required in the future.

Microsoft recommends that you allocate at least 16 GB of disk space for Windows 10. This allows room for the operating system files and for future growth in terms of upgrades and installation files that are placed with the operating system files.

The System and Boot Partitions   When you install Windows 10, files will be stored in two locations: the system partition and the boot partition. The system partition and the boot partition can be the same partition.

The system partition contains the files needed to boot the Windows 10 operating system. The system partition can be set as either a Master Boot Record (MBR) disk or a GUID Partition Table (GPT) disk. It is often the first physical hard drive in the computer and normally contains the necessary files to boot the computer. The files stored on the system partition do not take any significant disk space. The active partition is the system partition that is used to start your computer. The C: drive is usually the active partition.

The boot partition contains the Windows 10 operating system files. By default, the Windows operating system files are located in a folder named Windows.

Disk Partition Configuration Utilities   If you are partitioning your disk prior to installation, you can use several utilities, such as the DiskPart utility, or a third-party utility, such as Paragon Partition Magic. You can also configure the disks during the installation of the Windows 10 operating system.

You might want to create only the first partition where Windows 10 will be installed. You can then use the Disk Management utility in Windows 10 to create any other partitions you need.

Language and Locale

Language and locale settings determine the language the computer will use. Windows 10 supports many languages for the operating system interface and utilities.

Locale settings are for configuring the format for items such as numbers, currencies, times, and dates. For example, English for the United States specifies a short date as mm/dd/yyyy (month/day/year), while English for South Africa specifies a short date as yyyy/mm/dd (year/month/day).

It is very important to only choose the locales that this machine will need to use. The reason for this is that for every locale you choose, your system will get updates for all chosen locales that you set up.

Installing Windows 10

The first step to installing Windows 10 is to know what type of media you need to install the Windows 10 operating system. Windows 10 gives you multiple ways to do an install.

You can install Windows 10 either from the bootable DVD or through a network installation using files that have been copied to a network share point or USB device. You can also install Windows 10 by using a virtual hard drive (vhd). You can also launch the setup.exe file from within the Windows 10 operating system to upgrade your operating system.

To start the installation, you simply restart your computer and boot to the DVD. The installation process will begin automatically. You will walk through the steps of performing a clean install of Windows 10 from the DVD in Exercise 1.1.

If you are installing Windows 10 from the network, you need a distribution server and a computer with a network connection. A distribution server is a server that has the Windows 10 distribution files copied to a shared folder. The following steps are used to install Windows 10 over the network:

1. Boot the target computer.
2. Attach to the distribution server and access the share that has the files copied to it.
3. Launch setup.exe.
4. Complete the Windows 10 installation using either the clean install method or the upgrade method. These methods are discussed in detail in the following sections.

Performing a Clean Install of Windows 10

On any installation of Windows 10, there are three stages.

Collecting Information During the collection phase of the installation, Windows 10 gathers the information necessary to complete the installation. This is where Windows 10 gathers your local time, location, keyboard, license agreement, installation type, and installation disk partition information.

Installing Windows This section of the installation is where your Windows 10 files are copied to the hard disk and the installation is completed. This phase takes the longest because the files are installed.

Setting Up Windows In this phase, you set up a username, computer name, and password; enter the product key; configure the security settings; and review the date and time. Once this is finished, your installation will be complete.

As explained earlier, you can run the installation from the optical media, from a USB, or over a network. The only difference in the installation procedure is your starting point: from your optical drive or USB or a network share. The steps in Exercise 1.1 and Exercise 1.2 assume you are using the Windows 10 DVD to install Windows 10.

When you boot to the Windows 10 installation media, the Setup program will automatically start the Windows 10 installation. In Exercise 1.1, you will perform a clean install of Windows 10. This exercise assumes that you have access to Windows 10 Enterprise; other editions may vary slightly. You can also download an evaluation version of Windows 10 from the Microsoft website.

Also, I may list steps that you may not see or I may not list steps that you see—this is because my version of Windows may be different. For example, I am installing an MSDN Windows 10 Enterprise edition. At this time, I am not required to enter a license number during install. A normal version bought from a vendor may ask for the license during the actual install.

 I am loading Windows 10 Enterprise into a Hyper-V virtual machine. Again, this may make your installation a little different than the steps listed in Exercise 1.1. Plus, depending on your version and license model, not all screens may appear.

EXERCISE 1.1

Performing a Clean Install of Windows 10

1. Insert the Windows 10 DVD or .iso image in the machine or virtual machine with no operating system and start the computer.

2. If you are directed to "Hit any key" to start the DVD, press Enter.

3. The first screen will ask you to enter your language, time and currency format, and keyboard or input method (see Figure 1.1). After filling in these fields, click Next.

FIGURE 1.1 Windows Setup screen

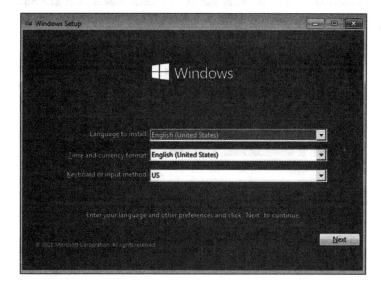

4. On the next screen, click the Install Now button (see Figure 1.2).

FIGURE 1.2 Windows install screen

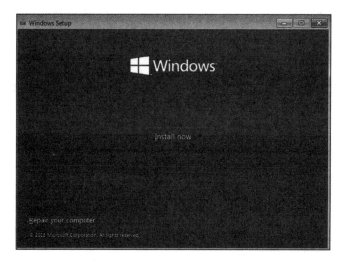

5. Depending on your installation media, the next screen will ask you which version of Windows 10 you want to install. I am choosing Windows 10 Enterprise (see Figure 1.3).

FIGURE 1.3 Windows version screen

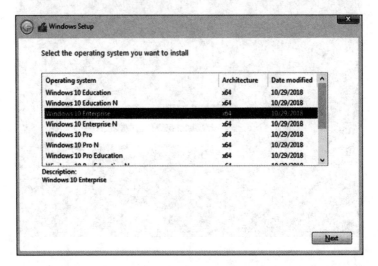

6. A message appears to tell you that the setup is starting. The licensing screen will be first. Read the license agreement and then check the I Accept The License Terms check box. Click Next.

7. When asked which type of installation you want, click Custom (Advanced) as shown in Figure 1.4.

FIGURE 1.4 Type of install screen

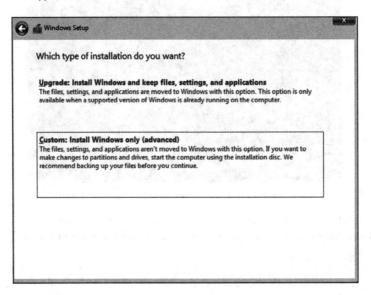

8.   The next screen asks you to identify the disk to which you would like to install Windows 10. Choose an unformatted free space or a partition (partition will be erased) with at least 32 GB available. You can also click the Drive Options (Advanced) link to create and format your own partition as shown in Figure 1.5. Click the New link and click Apply to create the new partition for Windows 10. A message will appear stating that Windows 10 will set some partitions for system files. Just click the OK button. After you choose your partition, click Next.

FIGURE 1.5   Windows disk setup screen

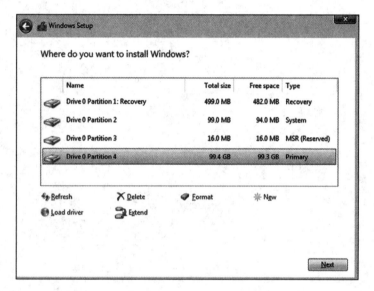

9.   When your partition is set, the installation will start (as shown in Figure 1.6). You will see the progress of the installation during the entire process. When the installation is complete, the machine will reboot.

FIGURE 1.6   Windows installation status screen

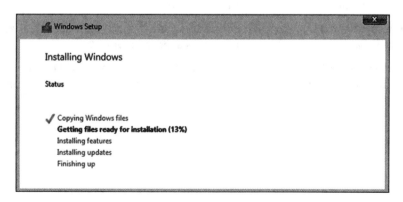

10. After the restart, a screen appears that asks you to choose your region. Select your region (see Figure 1.7), and then click the Next button.

FIGURE 1.7   Choose your region screen

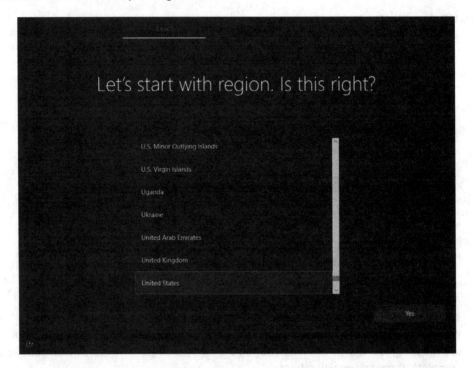

11. The next screen will ask you about your keyboard layout. Choose your keyboard layout (see Figure 1.8) and then click the Yes button.

12. The next screen will ask you if you have a second keyboard. If you do, click the Add Layout button. If not, click the Skip button (as seen in Figure 1.9).

13. At the sign in with Microsoft screen, choose the Domain Join Instead link. It will ask you who is going to use this PC. Enter your username and click the Next button.

FIGURE 1.8　Choosing your keyboard layout

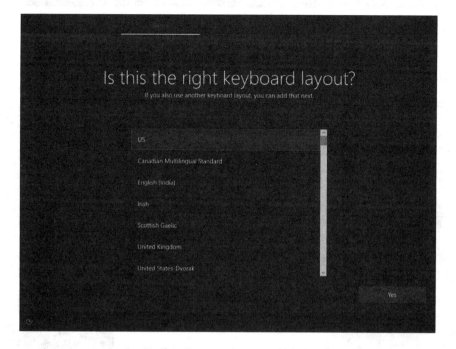

FIGURE 1.9　Adding a second keyboard

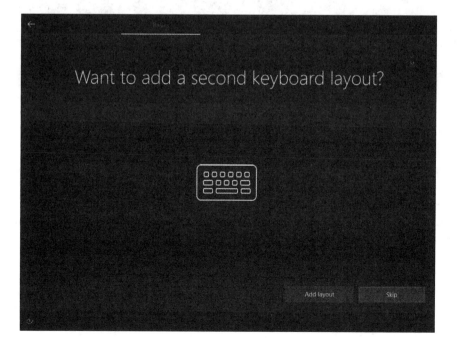

14. Next it's going to ask you to enter a super memorable password (as shown in Figure 1.10). Type in your password and click the Next button.

FIGURE 1.10   Windows 10 screen

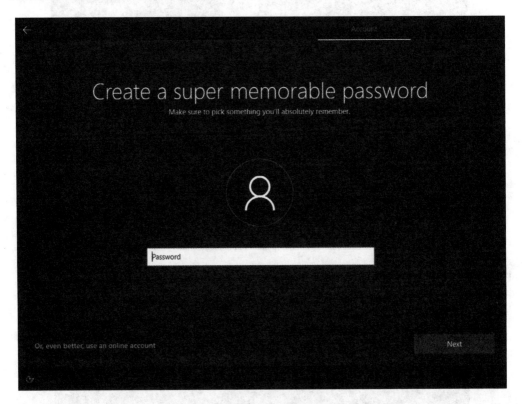

15. You will be asked to reenter your password. Enter your password again and click the Next button.

16. Depending on your version, you may be asked to create three security questions. If your edition asks this, put in your security questions and click the Next button for each security question. After the third question, click the Next button to move on.

17. The next screen will ask if you want to make Cortana your personal assistant. You can choose either Accept or Decline. I am going to choose Decline.

18. The next screen will ask if you want Microsoft to save your activity history. If you accept this, you will send Microsoft information about all activities that you are doing. This allows you to continue to finish these activities from any other device. Since this is a corporate machine, I will choose not to send Microsoft my activity history by choosing the No button (see Figure 1.11).

FIGURE 1.11   Windows activity screen

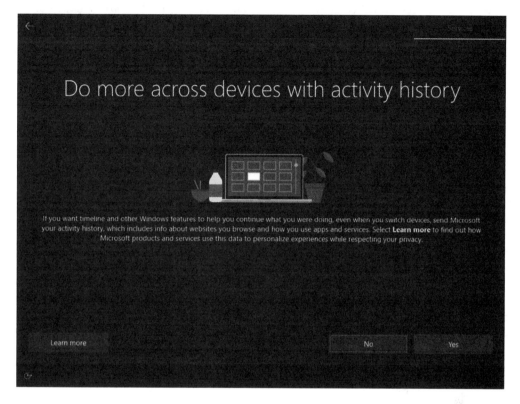

19. The next screen will be the privacy settings screen. Enable or disable any of the privacy settings that you want disabled (all will be enabled by default). Once you're complete, click the Accept button.

20. A different screen will appear letting you know that the system is being set up. This may take a few minutes. Be sure not to turn off the machine during this process. Once this is all completed, the system may ask you to log in. Put in your password and click the right arrow next to the password box. Your installation is now complete.

Before we talk about the Windows 10 upgrade procedure, I want to quickly explain something that you saw during the Windows 10 install. In step 13, I had you choose "Domain Join Instead" instead of using a Microsoft account. We will explore both of the choices in greater detail, but I wanted to quickly explain why we chose one over the other.

Microsoft offers two main networks: workgroup-based or domain-based. *Workgroups* (also referred to also as peer-to-peer networks) is when you just connect your computers together directly to each other. A perfect example for most of us is what you do in your home network. Most home users connect their machines together without the use of a main server.

Corporations normally do things a bit differently than that. *Domains* are networks that are controlled by servers called domain controllers. Domain controllers are Windows servers that have a copy of a database called Active Directory (AD). Recently Microsoft took domain-based networks a step further by allowing companies to set up a cloud-based version of an Active Directory domain (Azure AD). This means that companies no longer need to maintain and manage their own domain controllers.

Most companies that decide to start moving to an Azure based network will also have an onsite domain. This is a hybrid network that includes both on-site and cloud-based networks. This book will focus heavily on that type of hybrid set up.

Performing an Upgrade to Windows 10

This section describes how to perform an upgrade to Windows 10 from Windows 8.1. Similar to a clean install, you can run the installation from the installation DVD, from a USB drive, or over a network. The only difference in the installation procedure is your starting point: from your optical or USB drive or from a network share. For the steps in this section, it is assumed that you are using the Windows 10 DVD to install the Windows 10 operating system.

Upgrading a Windows 7 or Windows 8/8.1 system to Windows 10 will save you a lot of time and trouble. Because we are upgrading the system, all of the user's data and applications will remain installed and most likely still work the exact same way. Sometimes when we upgrade a system, we run into problems with applications. But many times that is caused by a driver or a needed software update that will most likely solve the issue.

The three main steps in the Windows 10 upgrade process are very similar to the ones for a clean install. The three steps of upgrading to Windows 10 are as follows:

1. Collecting information
2. Installing Windows
3. Setting up Windows

In Exercise 1.2, you will go through the process of installing Windows 10 by upgrading Windows 8.1. I have a Windows 8.1 Enterprise system that I will update to Windows 10 Enterprise.

EXERCISE 1.2

Upgrading Windows 8.1 to Windows 10

1. Insert the Windows 10 DVD. (We are upgrading Windows 8.1 Enterprise to Windows 10 Enterprise.)

2. If Autorun does not start, navigate to the DVD drive and click setup.exe. Once the setup starts (via either setup.exe or Autorun), click Run Setup.exe as shown in Figure 1.12.

FIGURE 1.12   DVD setup screen

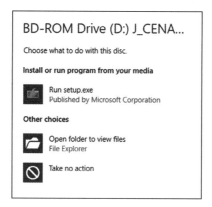

3. If a pop-up box appears for User Account Control, click the Yes button (see Figure 1.13).

FIGURE 1.13   User Account Control screen

You should then see a message appear stating that Windows is preparing the system, as shown in Figure 1.14.

FIGURE 1.14   Preparing screen

4. You may be prompted to Get Important Updates. You can choose to either download the updates or not do them at this time. Make a choice and click the Next button. (During my installation, I decided to download the updates.)

5. The Microsoft Windows 10 license terms appear. Read the terms and then click Accept. (The installation will not allow you to continue until you click Accept.)

6. At the Ready To Install screen (shown in Figure 1.15), you can change what files and/ or apps you want to keep by clicking the Change What To Keep link. Once you're ready, click the Install button.

FIGURE 1.15   Ready To Install screen

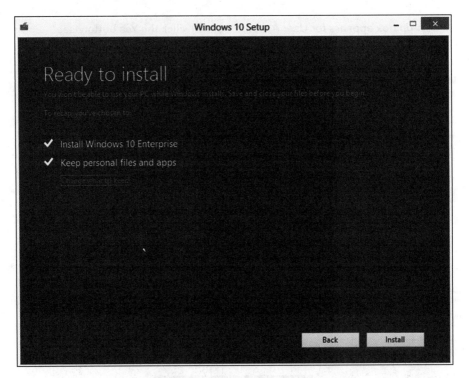

7. Windows 10 will begin to install (as shown in Figure 1.16). Your computer may restart multiple times. This is normal. As the upgrade status screen states, "Sit back and relax."

8. After the upgrade has completed, a welcome screen will be displayed, similar to the one shown in Figure 1.17. Click Next.

FIGURE 1.16   Installing status screen

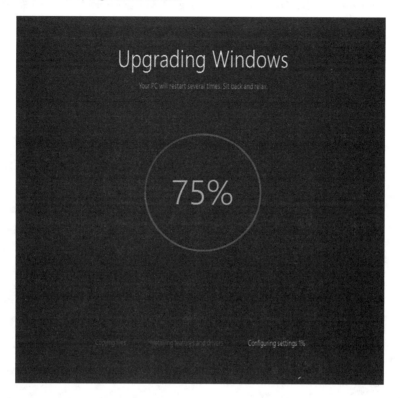

FIGURE 1.17   Welcome screen

9. At the Get Going Fast screen, click the Use Express Settings button.

10. At the New Apps screen, just click Next.

And that's it—Windows 10 is installed (see Figure 1.18). Congrats.

FIGURE 1.18 Windows 10 screen

Now that we have installed the Windows 10 operating system, let's take a look at how to change your system's locales. Earlier I explained that the locale settings help you with the system's language format, settings, and region specific details.

In Exercise 1.3, I will show you how to change your current locale. This helps when you take your Windows 10 laptop, tablet, or phone to another part of the world.

EXERCISE 1.3

Configuring Locales

1. Click the Start button and choose Settings.

2. Once in the Settings screen, choose Time And Language.

3. This should place you on the Date & Time screen. Make sure your time zone is set correctly. If it's not, pull down the time zone options and choose your time zone.

4. Scroll down and make sure the date and time formats are set the way you want. If they are not, click the Change Date And Time Formats link. Change the formats to the way you want them set.

5. Click the Region And Language link on the left-hand side.

6. Make sure the country or region is set properly. If you want to add a second language to this Windows 10 system, click the Add A Language link. Choose the language you want.

7. Once completed, close the Settings screen.

Troubleshooting Installation Problems

The Windows 10 installation process is designed to be as simple as possible. The chances for installation errors are greatly minimized through the use of wizards and the step-by-step process. However, it is possible that errors will occur.

Identifying Common Installation Problems

As most of you are aware, installations sometimes do get errors. You might encounter some of the following installation errors:

Media Errors   Media errors are caused by defective or damaged DVDs. To check the disc, put it into another computer and see if you can read it. Also check your disc for scratches or dirt—it may just need to be cleaned.

Insufficient Disk Space   Windows 10 needs at least 16 GB for the 32-bit OS and 20 GB for the 64-bit OS to execute properly. If the Setup program cannot verify that this space exists, the program will not let you continue.

Not Enough Memory   Make sure your computer has the minimum amount of memory required by Windows 10 (1 GB for 32-bit or 2 GB for 64-bit). Having insufficient memory may cause the installation to fail or blue-screen errors to occur after installation.

Not Enough Processing Power   Make sure your computer has the minimum processing power required by Windows 10 (1 GHz or faster processor or system-on-a-chip (SoC)). Having insufficient processing power may cause the installation to fail or blue-screen errors to occur after installation.

Hardware That Is Not on the HCL   If your hardware is not listed on the Hardware Compatibility List, Windows 10 may not recognize the hardware or the device may not work properly.

Hardware with No Driver Support   Windows 10 will not recognize hardware without driver support.

Hardware That Is Not Configured Properly   If your hardware is Plug and Play (PnP) compatible, Windows 10 should configure it automatically. If your hardware is not Plug and Play compatible, you will need to manually configure the hardware per the manufacturer's instructions.

Incorrect Product Key   Without a valid product key, the installation will not go past the Product Key screen. Make sure you have not typed in an incorrect key (check your Windows 10 installation folder or your computer case for this key).

Incorrect CPU Version   When installing or upgrading Windows10, the version of Windows 10 that is installed must match the CPU version. For example, if your system is a 32-bit system, you must use a 32-bit version of Windows 10. If your system is a 64-bit system, you can install either the 32-bit or 64-bit version of Windows 10.

Failure to Access TCP/IP Network Resources   If you install Windows 10 with typical settings, the computer is configured as a DHCP client. If there is no DHCP server to provide IP configuration information, the client will still generate an autoconfigured IP address but be unable to access network resources through TCP/IP if the other network clients are using DHCP addresses.

Installing Nonsupported Hard Drives   If your computer is using a hard disk that does not have a driver included on the Windows 10 media, you will receive an error message stating that the hard drive cannot be found. You should verify that the hard drive is properly connected and functional. You will need to obtain a disk driver for Windows 10 from the manufacturer and then specify the driver location by selecting the Load Driver option during partition selection.

Troubleshooting with Installation Log Files

When you install Windows 10, the Setup program creates several log files. You can view these logs to check for any problems during the installation process. Two log files are particularly useful for troubleshooting:

- The action log includes all of the actions that were performed during the setup process and a description of each action. These actions are listed in chronological order. The action log is stored as \Windows\panther\setupact.log.

- The error log includes any errors that occurred during the installation. For each error, there is a description and an indication of the severity of the error. This error log is stored as \Windows\panther\setuperr.log.

In Exercise 1.4, you will view the Windows 10 Setup logs to determine whether there were any problems with your Windows 10 installation.

EXERCISE 1.4

Troubleshooting Failed Installations with Setup Logs

1. Select Start ➢ This PC.

2. Double-click Local Disk (C:).

3. Double-click Windows.

4. Double-click Panther.

5. In the Windows folder, double-click the Setupact.log file to view your action log in Notepad. When you are finished viewing this file, close Notepad.

6. Double-click the Setuperr.log file to view your error file in Notepad. If no errors occurred during installation, this file will be empty. When you are finished viewing this file, close Notepad.

7. Close the directory window.

Supporting Multiple-Boot Options

You may want to install Windows 10 but still be able to run other operating systems. *Dual-booting* or multibooting allows your computer to boot multiple operating systems. Your computer will be automatically configured for dual-booting if there was a dual-boot–supported operating system on your computer prior to the Windows 10 installation, you didn't upgrade from that operating system, and you installed Windows 10 into a different partition.

One reason for dual-booting is to test various systems. If you have a limited number of computers in your test lab and you want to be able to test multiple configurations, you should dual-boot. For example, you might configure one computer to dual-boot with Windows 7, Windows 8/8.1, and Windows 10.

Here are some keys to successful dual-boot configurations:

- Make sure you have plenty of disk space.

- Windows 10 must be installed on a separate partition in order to dual-boot with other operating systems.

- Install older operating systems before installing newer operating systems. If you want to support dual-booting with Windows 7 and Windows 10, Windows 7 must be installed first. If you install Windows 10 first, you cannot install Windows 7 without ruining your Windows 10 configuration.

- Do not install Windows 10 on a compressed volume unless the volume was compressed using NTFS compression.

Once you have installed each operating system, you can choose the operating system that you will boot to during the boot process. You will see a boot-selection screen that asks you to choose which operating system you want to boot.

The Boot Configuration Data (BCD) store contains boot information parameters that were previously found in boot.ini in older versions of Windows. To edit the boot options in the BCD store, use the bcdedit utility, which can be launched only from a command prompt. To open a command prompt window, you can do the following:

1. Launch \Windows\system32\cmd.exe.

2. Open the Run command by pressing the [Windows] key + R and then entering **cmd**.

3. Type **cmd.exe** in the Search Programs And Files box and press Enter.

Once the command-prompt window is open, type **bcdedit** to launch the bcdedit utility. You can also type **bcdedit/?** to see all the different bcdedit commands. A few bcdedit commands may be needed when dual-booting a machine. Table 1.4 shows some of the bcdedit commands that may be needed when dual-booting.

TABLE 1.4   Bcdedit commands for dual-booting

Command	Explanation
/createstore	Creates a new empty boot configuration data store
/default	Allows you to specify which operating system will start when the time-out expires
/deletevalue	Allows you to delete a specified element from a boot entry
/displayorder	Shows the display order that the boot manager uses when showing the display order to the user
/export	Allows you to export the contents of the system store into a file
/import	Restores the system store by using the data file previously generated by using the /export option
/set	Allows you to set an entry option value
/store	Specifies the store to be used
/timeout	Specifies the amount of time used before the system boots into the default operating system

Using Windows Activation

Windows Activation is Microsoft's way of reducing software piracy. Unless you have a corporate license for Windows 10, you will need to perform post installation activation. This can be done online or through a telephone call. Windows 10 will attempt automatic activation three days after you log on to it for the first time. There is a grace period when you will be able to use the operating system without activation. After the grace period expires, a permanent watermark is displayed. Until the activation key is entered certain personalization settings are not configurable until Windows 10 is activated. When the grace period runs out, Windows will automatically lock you out of the system.

To access the Windows Activation screen, click the Start button and choose settings (the spoke icon). Scroll down to Update And Security and click on that link. On the left side, you will see a link for Activation. When you click on Activation, you will see the Activation screen (shown in Figure 1.19). Scroll down to the Activate Windows Now section. You may need to click the Change Product Key button and put in the license number that came with your Windows 10 copy. Once Windows 10 is activated, it will show that you are activated.

FIGURE 1.19   The Windows Activation Wizard screen

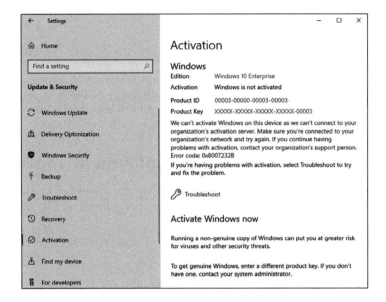

Understanding Automated Deployment Options

If you need to install Windows 10 on multiple computers, you could manually install the operating system on each computer. However, automating the deployment process will make your job easier, more efficient, and more cost effective if you have a large number of client computers on which to install Windows 10.

Windows 10 comes with several utilities that can be used for deploying and automating the Windows 10 installation. With access to multiple utilities with different functionality, administrators have increased flexibility in determining how to best deploy Windows 10 within a large corporate environment.

The following sections contain overviews of the automated deployment options, which will help you choose which solution is best for your requirements and environment. Each utility will then be covered in more detail throughout this chapter. The options for automated deployment of Windows 10 are as follows:

- Microsoft Deployment Toolkit (MDT)

- Unattended installation, or unattended setup, which uses `Setup.exe`

- Windows Automated Installation Kit (Windows AIK)
- Windows Assessment and Deployment Kit for Windows 10
- Windows Deployment Service (WDS), which requires Windows Server for deployment
- System Preparation Tool (Sysprep.exe), which is used to create images or clones
- Windows Autopilot

> Another option that you have to deploy Windows 10 is through System Center Configuration Manager (SCCM). Since SCCM is its own application, it is beyond the scope of this book. You can learn more about SCCM on the Microsoft website at http://www.microsoft.com.

An Overview of the Microsoft Deployment Toolkit

Microsoft released a deployment assistance toolset called the *Microsoft Deployment Toolkit (MDT)*. It is used to automate desktop and server deployment. The MDT provides an administrator with the following benefits:

- Administrative tools that allow for the deployment of desktops and servers through the use of a common console (see Figure 1.20)

FIGURE 1.20 Microsoft Deployment Toolkit console

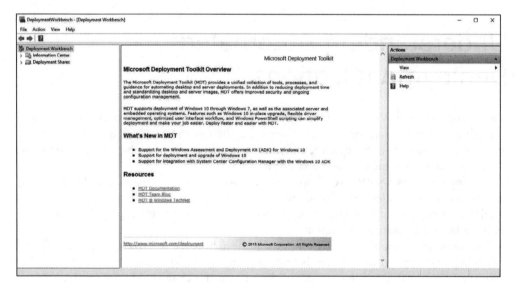

- Quicker deployments and the capabilities of having standardized desktop and server images and security
- Zero-touch deployments of Windows 10, Windows Server, and Windows 7/ 8/8.1

To install the MDT package onto your computer (regardless of the operating system being deployed), you must first meet the minimum requirements of MDT. These components need to be installed only on the computer where MDT is being installed:

- Windows 10, Windows 7, Windows 8, Windows 8.1, or Windows Server.
- The Windows Assessment and Deployment Kit (ADK) for Windows 10 is required for all deployment scenarios.
- System Center 2012 R2 Configuration Manager Service Pack 1 with the Windows ADK for Windows 10 is required for zero-touch installation (ZTI) and user-driven installation (UDI) scenarios.
- If you are using ZTI and/or UDI, you are allowed to add the MDT SQL database to any version of System Center Configuration Manager with SQL Technology; if you are using LTI, you must use a separately licensed SQL Server product to host your MDT SQL database.

 You can install MDT without installing Windows (ADK) first, but you will not be able to use the package fully until Windows (ADK) is installed.

In Exercise 1.5, you will download and install MDT. You can install MDT on the Windows 10 operating system machine that you installed earlier in this chapter. If you decide to install the MDT onto a server or production machine, I recommend that you perform a full backup before completing Exercise 1.5. Installing MDT will replace any previous version of MDT that the machine may currently be using.

EXERCISE 1.5

Downloading and Installing MDT

1. Download the MDT Update 1 utility from Microsoft's website (https://www.microsoft.com/en-us/download/details.aspx?id=54259).

2. Click the Download button.

3. You get a screen with the message "Choose the download you want." Choose the x64 or x86 version. Click Next.

4. A message box may appear asking if you want to run or save the MDT. I clicked the down arrow next to Save and saved the files into the downloads directory.

5. Double-click `MicrosoftDeploymentToolkit_xxx.exe` to start the installation.

6. At the Welcome screen, click Next as shown in Figure 1.21.

FIGURE 1.21   Microsoft Deployment Toolkit setup screen

7. At the License screen, click the I Accept The Terms In The License Agreement radio button and click Next.

8. At the Custom Setup screen, click the down arrow next to Microsoft Deployment Toolkit and choose Entire Feature Will Be Installed On Local Hard Drive. Click Next as shown in Figure 1.22.

FIGURE 1.22   Microsoft Deployment Toolkit Custom Setup screen

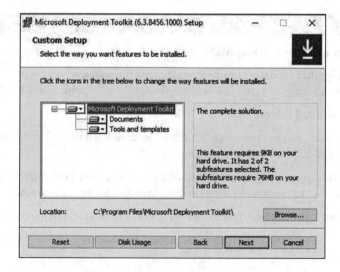

9. At the Customer Experience Improvement Program screen, choose if you want to participate or not and click Next.

10. At the Ready To Install screen, click the Install button.

11. If a User Account Control dialog box appears, click the Yes button.

12. When the installation completes, click the Finish button.

Now that you have installed MDT, you are going to configure the package. In Exercise 1.6, you will configure MDT and set up a distribution share and database. I am creating the MDT on a Windows Server so that we can distribute Windows 10. Make sure the Windows Assessment and Deployment Kit (ADK) for Windows 10 is installed because it is required for all deployment scenarios.

EXERCISE 1.6

Configuring MDT

1. Create a shared folder on your network called Distribution, and give the Everyone group full control to the folder for this exercise.

2. Open the MDT workbench by choosing Start ➤ then the down arrow ➤ Microsoft Development Toolkit ➤ Deployment Workbench.

3. If the User Account Control box appears, click Yes.

4. In the left-hand pane, click Deployment Shares, and then right-click the deployment shares and choose New Deployment Share.

5. The New Deployment Share Wizard begins (as shown in Figure 1.23). At the first screen, you will choose the directory where the deployments will be stored. Click the Browse button and choose the Distribution share that you created in step 1. Then click Next.

6. At the Share Name screen, accept the default, Distribution. Click Next.

7. At the Descriptive Name screen, accept the default description name (as shown in Figure 1.24) and click Next.

FIGURE 1.23   New Deployment Share Wizard screen

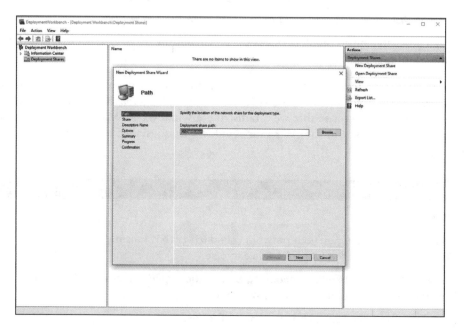

FIGURE 1.24   Descriptive Name screen

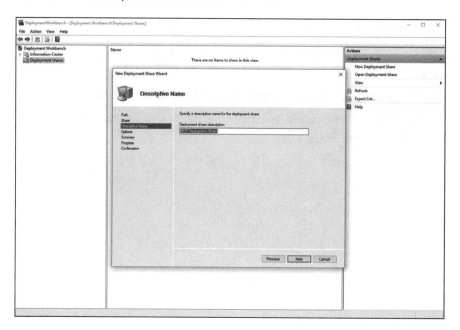

8. At the Options screen, make sure all check boxes are checked as shown in Figure 1.25.

FIGURE 1.25   Options screen

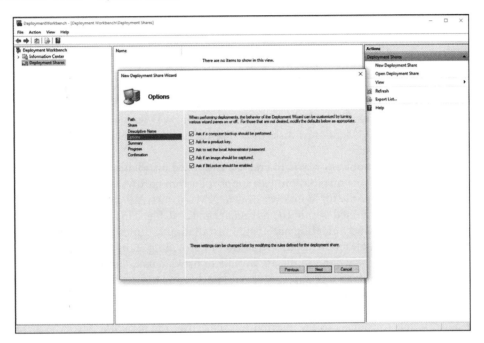

9. At the Summary screen, look over the options and choose the Next button.

10. The Installation will progress screen will show you how the installation is performing. Once it's finished, click the Finish button.

11. The new deployment share is set up and ready to start deploying. Now an operating system needs to be set up in the MDT for deployment.

12. Close the MDT workbench.

Now that you have seen how to install the MDT utility, let's take a look at some other ways to automatically install Windows 10.

An Overview of Unattended Installation

Unattended installation is a practical method of automating deployments when you have a large number of clients to install and the computers require different hardware and software configurations. Unattended installations allow you to create customized installations that are specific to your environment. Custom installations can support custom hardware and software installations.

Unattended installations utilize an answer file called `autounattend.xml` to provide configuration information during the installation process. Think about the Windows 10 installation from earlier in this chapter. You are asked for your locale, type of installation, and so on. The answer file allows these questions to be answered without user interaction. In addition to providing standard Windows 10 configuration information, the answer file can provide installation instructions for applications, additional language support, service packs, and device drivers.

With an unattended installation, you can use a distribution share to install Windows 10 on the target computers. You can also use a Windows 10 DVD with an answer file located on the root of the DVD, on a floppy disk, or on a universal flash device (UFD), such as an external USB flash drive.

Unattended installations allow you to create customized installations that are specific to your environment. Custom installations can support custom hardware and software installations. Since the answer file for Windows 10 is in XML format, all custom configuration information can be contained within the `autounattend.xml` file. This is different from past versions of Windows, where creating automated installation routines for custom installations required multiple files to be used. In addition to providing standard Windows 10 configuration information, you can use the answer file to provide installation instructions for applications, additional language support, service packs, and device drivers.

If you use a distribution share, it should contain the Windows 10 operating system image and the answer file to respond to installation configuration queries. The target computer must be able to connect to the distribution share over the network. After the distribution share and target computers are connected, you can initiate the installation process. Figure 1.26 illustrates the unattended installation process.

FIGURE 1.26   Unattended installation with distribution share and a target computer

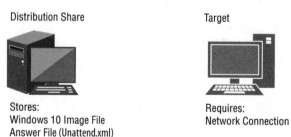

Distribution Share

Target

Stores:
Windows 10 Image File
Answer File (Unattend.xml)

Requires:
Network Connection

Advantages of Unattended Installation

In a midsize or large organization, it just makes sense to use automated setups. As stated earlier, it is nearly impossible to install Windows 10 one at a time on hundreds of machines.

But there are many advantages to using unattended installations as a method for automating Windows 10:

- Unattended installation saves time and money because users do not have to interactively respond to each installation query.

- It can be configured to provide automated query response while still selectively allowing users to provide specified input during installations.

- It can be used to install clean copies of Windows 10 or upgrade an existing operating system (providing it is on the list of permitted operating systems) to Windows 10.

- It can be expanded to include installation instructions for applications, additional language support, service packs, and device drivers.

- The physical media for Windows 10 does not need to be distributed to all computers on which it will be installed.

Disadvantages of Unattended Installation

As stated earlier, a manual installation is not practical for mass installations. But one of the biggest disadvantages to performing an unattended installation is that an administrator does not physically walk through the installation of Windows 10. A client operating system is one of the most important items that you will install onto a machine. As an IT manager and consultant, I have always felt better physically installing a client operating system. This way, if there are any glitches, I can see and deal with them immediately. If something happens during an unattended install, you may never know it, but the end user may experience small issues throughout the lifetime of the machine.

Two other disadvantages of using unattended installations as a method for automating Windows 10 installations are listed here:

- They require more initial setup than a standard installation of Windows 10.

- Someone must have access to each client computer and must initiate the unattended installation process on the client side.

An Overview of Windows Deployment Services

Windows Deployment Services (WDS) is a suite of components that allows you to remotely install Windows 10 on client computers.

A WDS server installs Windows 10 on the client computers, as illustrated in Figure 1.27. The WDS server must be configured with the Preboot Execution Environment (PXE) boot files, the images to be deployed to the client computers, and the answer file. WDS client computers must be PXE-capable. PXE is a technology that is used to boot to the network when no operating system or network configuration has been installed and configured on a client computer.

FIGURE 1.27   Windows Deployment Services (WDS) uses a WDS server and WDS clients.

WDS Server

Stores:
PXE Boot Files and Boot Images
Windows 10 Boot Images
Answer File(s)

WDS Client

Requires:
PXE-Compatible Boot

The WDS clients access the network with the help of a Dynamic Host Configuration Protocol (DHCP) server. This allows the WDS client to remotely install the operating system from the WDS server. The network environment must be configured with a DHCP server, a Domain Name System (DNS) server, NTFS volumes, and Active Directory to connect to the WDS server. No other client software is required to connect to the WDS server. Remote installation is a good choice for automatic deployment when you need to deploy to large numbers of computers and the client computers are PXE-compliant.

Advantages of WDS

The advantages of using WDS as a method for automating Windows 10 installations are as follows:

- Allows an IT department to remotely install Windows operating systems through the network. This advantage helps reduce the difficulty and IT man power cost compared to a manual installation.

- Allows an IT department to deploy multiple images for mixed environments including Windows 7, Windows 8/8.1, Windows 10, and Windows Server.

- Allows IT departments to use Windows setups including Windows Preinstallation Environment (Windows PE), .wim files, and image-based setups.

- WDS can use multicasting to allow for the transmitting and image data to communicate with each other.

- An IT department can create reference images using the Image Capture Wizard, which is an alternative to the ImageX tool.

- Allows an IT Administrator to install a driver package to the server and configure the drivers to be deployed to client computers at the same time the image is installed.

- Allows IT departments to standardize Windows 10 installations throughout a group or organization.

- The physical media for Windows 10 does not need to be distributed to all computers that will be installed.

- End-user installation deployment can be controlled through the Group Policy utility. For example, you can configure what choices a user can access or are automatically specified through the end-user Setup Wizard.

Disadvantages of WDS

The disadvantages of using WDS as a method for automating Windows 10 installations include the following:

- WDS can be used only if your network is running Windows Server 2008 and above with Active Directory installed.
- The clients that use WDS must be PXE-capable.

You can configure WDS on a Windows Server computer by using the Windows Deployment Services Configuration Wizard or by using the WDSUTIL command-line utility. Table 1.5 describes the WDSUTIL command-line options.

TABLE 1.5   WDSUTIL command-line options

WDSUTIL Option	Description
/initialize-server	Initializes the configuration of the WDS server
/uninitialized-server	Undoes any changes made during the initialization of the WDS server
/add	Adds images and devices to the WDS server
/convert-ripimage	Converts Remote Installation Preparation (RIPrep) images to WIM images
/remove	Removes images from the server
/set	Sets information in images, image groups, WDS servers, and WDS devices
/get	Gets information from images, image groups, WDS servers, and WDS devices
/new	Creates new capture images or discover images
/copy-image	Copies images from the image store
/export-image	Exports to WIM files images contained within the image store
/start	Starts WDS services
/stop	Stops WDS services
/disable	Disables WDS services
/enable	Enables WDS services

TABLE 1.5   WDSUTIL command-line options *(continued)*

WDSUTIL Option	Description
/approve-autoadddevices	Approves Auto-Add devices
/reject-autoadddevices	Rejects Auto-Add devices
/delete-autoadddevices	Deletes records from the Auto-Add database
/update	Uses a known-good resource to update a server resource

An Overview of the System Preparation Tool and Disk Imaging

The *System Preparation Tool,* or *Sysprep* (Sysprep.exe), is used to prepare a computer for disk imaging, and the disk image can then be captured using DISM (an imaging-management tool included with Windows 10) or third-party imaging software. Sysprep is a free utility that comes on all Windows operating systems. By default, the Sysprep utility can be found on Windows Server and Windows 10 operating systems in the \Windows\system32\sysprep directory.

Disk imaging is the process of taking a checkpoint of a computer and then using that checkpoint to create new computers, thus allowing for automated deployments. The reference, or source, computer has Windows 10 installed and is configured with the settings and applications that should be installed on the target computers. The image (checkpoints) is then created and can be transferred to other computers, thus installing the operating system, settings, and applications that were defined on the reference computer.

Using Imaging Software

Using the System Preparation Tool and disk imaging is a good choice (and the one most commonly used in the real world) for automatic deployment when you have a large number of computers with similar configuration requirements or machines that need to be rebuilt frequently.

For example, StormWind Studios, an online computer education company, reinstalls the same software every few weeks for new classes. Imaging is a fast and easy way to simplify the deployment process.

Most organizations use images to create new machines quickly and easily, but they also use them to reimage end users' machines that crash.

In most companies, end users will have space on a server (home folders) to allow them to store data. IT departments give our end users space on the server because this way we need to back up only the servers at night and not the end users' machines. If your end users place all of their important documents on the server, that information gets backed up.

Now, if we are also using images in our company and an end user's machine crashes, we just reload the image and they are back up and running in minutes. Since their documents are being saved on the server, they do not lose any of their information.

Many organizations use third-party imaging software (such as Ghost) instead of using Sysprep.exe and Image Capture Wizard. This is another good way of imaging your Windows 10 machines. Just make sure your third-party software supports the Windows 10 operating system.

To perform an unattended installation, the System Preparation Tool prepares the reference computer by stripping away any computer-specific data, such as the security identifier (SID), which is used to uniquely identify each computer on the network, any event logs, and any other unique system information. The System Preparation Tool also detects any Plug and Play devices that are installed and can adjust dynamically for any computers that have different hardware installed.

When the client computer starts an installation using a disk image, you can customize what is displayed on the Windows Welcome screen and the options that are displayed through the setup process. You can also fully automate when and how the Windows Welcome screen is displayed during the installation process by using the /oobe option with the System Preparation Tool and an answer file named oobe.xml.

Sysprep is a utility that is good only for setting up a new machine. You do not use Sysprep to image a computer for upgrading a current machine. There are a few switches that you can use in conjunction with Sysprep to configure the Sysprep utility for your specific needs. Table 1.6 shows you the important Sysprep switches and what they will do for you when used.

TABLE 1.6   Sysprep switches

Switch	Explanation
/pnp	Forces a mini-setup wizard to start at reboot so that all Plug and Play devices can be recognized.
/generalize	This allows Sysprep to remove all system-specific data from the Sysprep image. If you're running the GUI version of Sysprep, this is a check-box option.
/oobe	Initiates the Windows Welcome screen at the next reboot.

TABLE 1.6   Sysprep switches *(continued)*

Switch	Explanation
/audit	Initiates Sysprep in audit mode.
/nosidgen	Sysprep does not generate a new SID on the computer restart. Forces a mini-setup on restart.
/reboot	Stops and restarts the computer system.
/quiet	Runs without any confirmation dialog messages being displayed.
/mini	Tells Sysprep to run the mini-setup on the next reboot.

 Real World Scenario

The SID Problem with Deployment Software

For many years, when you had to create many machines that each had a Microsoft operating system on it, you would have to use files to help deploy the multiple systems.

Then, multiple third-party companies came out with software that allowed you to take a picture of the Microsoft operating system, and you could deploy that picture to other machines. One advantage of this is that all the software that is installed on the system could also be part of that picture. This was a great way to copy all the software on a machine over to another machine.

There was one major problem for years—*security identifier (SID)* numbers. All computers get assigned a unique SID that represents them on a domain network. The problem for a long time was that when you copied a machine to another machine, the SID number was also copied.

Microsoft released Sysprep many years ago, and that helped solve this problem. Sysprep would allow you to remove the SID number so that a third-party software package could move the image to another machine without issues. Many third-party image software products now also remove the SID numbers, but Sysprep was one of the first utilities to help solve this problem.

When you decide to use Sysprep to set up your images, there are a few rules that you must follow for Sysprep to work properly:

▪ You can use images to restart the Windows activation clock. The Windows activation clock starts to decrease as soon as Windows starts for the first time. You can restart the Windows activation clock only three times using Sysprep.

- The computer on which you're running Sysprep has to be a member of a workgroup. The machine can't be part of a domain. If the computer is a member of the domain, when you run Sysprep, the computer will automatically be removed from the domain.

- When installing the image, the system will prompt you for a product key. During the install you can use an answer file, which in turn will have all the information needed for the install, and you will not be prompted for any information.

- A third-party utility or Image Capture Wizard is required to deploy the image that is created from Sysprep.

- If you are using Sysprep to capture an NTFS partition, any files or folders that are encrypted will become corrupt and unreadable.

One advantage to Sysprep and Windows 10 is that you can use Sysprep to prepare a new machine for duplication. You can use Sysprep to image a Windows 10 machine. The following steps are necessary to image a new machine:

1. Install the Windows 10 operating system.

2. Install all components on the OS.

3. Run `sysprep /generalize` to get the Windows 10 system ready to be imaged.

When you image a computer using the Windows Sysprep utility, a Windows image (`.wim`) file is created. Most third-party imaging software products can work with the Windows image file.

Advantages of the System Preparation Tool

The following are advantages of using the System Preparation Tool as a method for automating Windows 10 installations:

- For large numbers of computers with similar hardware, it greatly reduces deployment time by copying the operating system, applications, and desktop settings from a reference computer to an image, which can then be deployed to multiple computers.

- Using disk imaging facilitates the standardization of desktops, administrative policies, and restrictions throughout an organization.

- Reference images can be copied across a network connection or through DVDs that are physically distributed to client computers.

Disadvantages of the System Preparation Tool

There are some disadvantages of using the System Preparation Tool as a method for automating Windows 10 installations:

- Image Capture Wizard, third-party imaging software, or hardware disk-duplication devices must be used for an image-based setup.

- The version of the System Preparation Tool that shipped with Windows 10 must be used. An older version of Sysprep cannot be used on a Windows 10 image.

- The System Preparation Tool will not detect any hardware that is not Plug and Play compliant.

Overview of the Windows Assessment and Deployment Kit

Another way to install Windows 10 is to use the *Windows Assessment and Deployment Kit (ADK)*. The Windows (ADK) is a set of utilities and documentation that allows an administrator to configure and deploy Windows operating systems. An administrator can use the Windows (ADK) to access the following utilities:

- Windows Configuration Designer

- Windows Assessment Toolkit

- Windows Performance Toolkit

The Windows (ADK) can be installed and configured on the following operating systems:

- Windows 10

- Windows 7 with SP1

- Windows 8/8.1

- Windows Server 2019

- Windows Server 2016

- Windows Server 2012 R2

- Windows Server 2012

- Windows Server 2008

- Windows Server 2008 R2

The Windows (ADK) is a good solution for organizations that need to customize the Windows deployment environments. The Windows (ADK) allows an administrator to have the flexibility needed for mass deployments of Windows operating systems. Since every organization's needs are different, the Windows (ADK) allows you to use all or just some of the deployment tools available. It allows you to manage deployments by using some additional tools.

Windows Configuration Designer   The tools included with this part of the Windows (ADK) will allow an administrator to easily create a provisioning package.

Windows Assessment Toolkit   When new Windows operating systems are installed, applications that ran on the previous version of Windows may not work properly. The Windows Assessment Toolkit allows an administrator to help solve these issues before they occur.

Windows Performance Toolkit   The Windows Performance Toolkit is a utility that will locate computers on a network and then perform a thorough inventory of them. This inventory can then be used to determine which machines can have Windows 10 installed.

Summary of Windows 10 Deployment Options

Table 1.7 summarizes the installation tools and files that are used with unattended and automated installations of Windows 10. Table 1.7 shows the associated installation method and a description of each tool.

TABLE 1.7   Summary of Windows 10 unattended deployment utilities

Tool or File	Automated Installation Option	Description
setup.exe	Unattended installation	Program used to initiate the installation process
autounattend.xml	Unattended installation	Answer file used to customize installation queries
Windows System Image Manager	Unattended installation	Program used to create answer files to be used for unattended installations
DISM.exe	DISM	Command-line utility that works in conjunction with Sysprep to create and manage Windows 10 image files for deployment
sysprep.exe	Sysprep	System Preparation Tool, which prepares a source reference computer that will be used in conjunction with a distribution share or with disk duplication through Image Capture Wizard, third-party software, or hardware disk-duplication devices

The Windows 10 installation utilities and resources relating to automated deployment are found in a variety of locations. Table 1.8 provides a quick reference for each utility or resource and its location.

TABLE 1.8   Location of Windows 10 deployment utilities and resources

Utility	Location
DISM.exe	Included with Windows 10; installed to %WINDIR%\system32\DISM
sysprep.exe	Included with Windows 10; installed to %WINDIR%\system32\sysprep
Windows System Image Manager	Installed with the Windows ADK; installed to C:\Program Files (x86)\Windows Kits\10\Assessment and Deployment Kit\ Deployment Tools\WSIM\ImgMgr.exe

Deploying Unattended Installations

You can deploy Windows 10 installations or upgrades through a Windows 10 distribution DVD or through a distribution server that contains Windows 10 images and associated files, such as autounattend.xml for unattended installations. Using a DVD can be advantageous if the computer on which you want to install Windows 10 is not connected to the network or is connected via a low-bandwidth network. It is also typically faster to install a Windows 10 image from DVD than to use a network connection.

Unattended installations rely on options configured in an answer file that is deployed with the Windows 10 image. Answer files are XML files that contain the settings that are typically supplied by the installer during attended installations of Windows 10. Answer files can also contain instructions for how programs and applications should be run.

The Windows Setup program is run to install or upgrade to Windows 10 from computers that are running compatible versions of Windows. In fact, Windows Setup is the basis for the other types of installation procedures I'll be discussing in this chapter, including unattended installations, WDS, and image-based installations.

The Windows Setup program (setup.exe) replaces winnt32.exe and winnt.exe, which are the setup programs used in versions of Windows prior to Windows Vista. Although it's a graphical tool, Windows Setup can be run from the command line. For example, you can use the following command to initiate an unattended installation of Windows 10:

setup.exe /unattend:answerfile

The Windows Setup program has several command-line options that can be applied. Table 1.9 describes the setup.exe command-line options.

TABLE 1.9   Setup.exe command-line options and descriptions

Setup.exe Option	Description
/1394debug: *channel* [baudrate:*baudrate*]	Enables kernel debugging over a FireWire (IEEE 1394) port for troubleshooting purposes. The [baudrate] optional parameter specifies the baud rate for data transfer during the debugging process.
/debug:port [*baudrate*:*baudrate*]	Enables kernel debugging over the specified port for troubleshooting purposes. The [baudrate] optional parameter specifies the baud rate for data transfer during the debugging process.
/DynamicUpdate {enable | disable}	Used to prevent a dynamic update from running during the installation process.

Setup.exe Option	Description
/emsport:{com1|com2|usebiossettings|off} [/emsbaudrate:*baudrate*]	Configures EMS to be enabled or disabled. The [baudrate] optional parameter specifies the baud rate for data transfer during the debugging process.
/m:*folder_name*	Used with Setup to specify that replacement files should be copied from the specified location. If the files are not present, Setup will use the default location.
/noreboot	Normally, when the down-level phase of Setup.exe is complete, the computer restarts. This option specifies that the computer should not restart so that you can execute another command prior to the restart.
/tempdrive:*drive letter*	Specifies the location that will be used to store the temporary files for Windows 10 and the installation partition for Windows 10.
/unattend:[*answerfile*]	Specifies that you will be using an unattended installation for Windows 10. The answerfile variable points to the custom answer file you will use for installation.

Using the System Preparation Tool to Prepare an Installation for Imaging

You can use disk images to install Windows 10 on computers that have similar hardware configurations. Also, if a computer is having technical difficulties, you can use a disk image to quickly restore it to a baseline configuration.

To create a disk image, you install Windows 10 on the source computer with the configuration that you want to copy and use the System Preparation Tool to prepare the installation for imaging. The source computer's configuration should also include any applications that should be installed on target computers.

Once you have prepared the installation for imaging, you can use imaging software such as Image Capture Wizard to create an image of the installation.

The System Preparation Tool (Sysprep.exe) is included with Windows 10, in the %WINDIR%\system32\sysprep directory. When you run this utility on the source computer, it strips out information that is unique for each computer, such as the SID. Table 1.10 defines the command options that you can use to customize the sysprep.exe operation.

TABLE 1.10   System Preparation Tool command-line options

Switch	Description
/audit	Configures the computer to restart into audit mode, which allows you to add drivers and applications to Windows or test the installation prior to deployment
/generalize	Removes any unique system information from the image, including the SID and log information
/oobe	Specifies that the Windows Welcome screen should be displayed when the computer reboots
/quiet	Runs the installation with no user interaction
/quit	Specifies that the System Preparation Tool should quit after the specified operations have been completed
/reboot	Restarts the target computer after the System Preparation Tool completes
/shutdown	Specifies that the computer should shut down after the specified operations have been completed
/unattend	Indicates the name and location of the answer file to use

In the following sections, you will learn how to create a disk image and how to copy and install from it.

Preparing a Windows 10 Installation

To run the System Preparation Tool and prepare an installation for imaging, take the following steps:

1. Install Windows 10 on a source computer. The computer should have a similar hardware configuration to that of the destination computer(s). The source computer should not be a member of a domain.

2. Log on to the source computer as Administrator and, if desired, install and configure any applications, files (such as newer versions of Plug and Play drivers), or custom settings (for example, a custom desktop) that will be applied to the target computer(s).

3. Verify that your image meets the specified configuration criteria and that all applications are properly installed and working.

4. Select Start ➤ This PC, and navigate to C:\%WINDIR%\System32\sysprep. Double-click the Sysprep application icon.

5. The Windows System Preparation Tool dialog box appears. Select the appropriate options for your configuration.

6. If configured to do so, Windows 10 will shut down after Sysprep is run. The next time it is rebooted, the setup process will begin as if the PC is brand new.

7. You will now be able to use imaging software to create an image of the computer to deploy to other computers.

In Exercise 1.7, you will use the System Preparation Tool to prepare the computer for disk imaging. The Sysprep utility must be run on a machine with a clean version of Windows 10. If you upgraded a Windows 7/8/8.1 machine to Windows 10, you will not be able to run the Sysprep utility.

EXERCISE 1.7

Prepare a System for Imaging by Using the System Preparation Tool

1. Log on to the source computer as Administrator and, if desired, install and configure any applications that should also be installed on the target computer.

2. Select Start ➤ This PC, and navigate to C:\%WINDIR%\System32\sysprep. Double-click the Sysprep application icon.

3. In the System Preparation Tool dialog box, select Enter System Out-Of-Box Experience (OOBE) in the system cleanup action.

4. Depending on the shutdown options you selected, the System Preparation Tool will quit, the computer will shut down, or the computer will be rebooted into setup mode, where you will need to configure the setup options. Choose the Reboot option. Click OK.

5. After the computer has been shut down, the administrator will need to image the machine. Administrators can use an image capturing software to capture the image.

Using the Deployment Image Servicing and Management Tool

Deployment Image Servicing and Management (DISM.exe) is a command-line utility that allows you to manipulate a Windows image. DISM also allows you to prepare a Windows PE image. DISM replaces multiple programs that were included with Windows 7/8/8.1. These programs include Package Manager (Pkgmgr.exe), PEimg, and Intlcfg. These tools have been consolidated into one tool (DISM.exe), and new functionality has been added to improve the experience for offline servicing.

When DISM was first released, it was primarily used for servicing and managing Windows images. But now DISM has become even more powerful, including capturing images and deploying images.

DISM provides additional functionality when used with Windows 10 and Windows Server. You can use DISM to do the following:

- Capture Windows images
- Copy and move Windows images
- Install Windows images
- Add, remove, and enumerate packages
- Add, remove, and enumerate drivers
- Enable or disable Windows features
- Apply changes to an Unattend.xml answer file
- Configure international settings
- Upgrade a Windows image to a different edition
- Prepare a Windows PE 3.0 image
- Works with all platforms (32-bit, 64-bit, and Itanium)
- Allows for the use of Package Manager scripts

Table 1.11 shows the different commands that can be used with DISM.exe.

TABLE 1.11   DISM.exe command-line commands

Command	Description
/Add-Driver	Adds third-party driver packages to an offline Windows image.
/Get-CurrentEdition	Displays the edition of the specified image.
/Get-Drivers	Displays basic information about driver packages in the online or offline image. By default, only third-party drivers will be listed.
/Get-DriverInfo	Displays detailed information about a specific driver package.
/Get-Help /?	Displays information about the option and the arguments.
/Get-TargetEditions	Displays a list of Windows editions that an image can be changed to.
/Remove-Driver	Removes third-party drivers from an offline image.
/Set-ProductKey:<productKey>	Can only be used to enter the product key for the current edition in an offline Windows image.
/Online /Enable-Feature /All /FeatureName:Microsoft-Hyper-V	This command allows you to install Hyper-V into a Windows image while it's an actual image.

Using Windows System Image Manager to Create Answer Files

Answer files are automated installation scripts used to answer the questions that appear during a normal Windows 10 installation. You can use answer files with Windows 10 unattended installations, disk image installations, or WDS installations. Setting up answer files allows you to easily deploy Windows 10 to computers that may not be configured in the same manner, with little or no user intervention. Because answer files are associated with image files, you can validate the settings within an answer file against the image file.

You can create answer files by using the Windows System Image Manager (Windows SIM) utility. There are several advantages to using Windows SIM to create answer files:

- You can easily create and edit answer files through a graphical interface, which reduces syntax errors.

- It simplifies the addition of user-specific or computer-specific configuration information.

- You can validate existing answer files against newly created images.

- You can include additional application and device drivers in the answer file.

In the following section, you will learn about options that can be configured through Windows SIM, how to create answer files with Windows SIM, how to format an answer file, and how to manually edit answer files.

Configuring Components through Windows System Image Manager

You can use Windows SIM to configure a wide variety of installation options. The following list defines which components can be configured through Windows SIM and gives a short description of each component:

auditSystem   Adds additional device drivers, specifies firewall settings, and applies a name to the system when the image is booted into audit mode. Audit mode is initiated by using the sysprep/audit command.

auditUser   Executes RunSynchronous or RunAsynchronous commands when the image is booted into audit mode. Audit mode is initiated by using the sysprep/audit command.

generalize   Removes system-specific information from an image so that the image can be used as a reference image. The settings specified in the generalize component will be applied only if the sysprep/generalize command is used.

offlineServicing   Specifies the language packs and packages to apply to an image prior to the image being extracted to the hard disk.

oobeSystem   Specifies the settings to apply to the computer the first time the computer is booted into the Windows Welcome screen, which is also known as the Out-Of-Box

Experience (OOBE). To boot to the Welcome screen, the sysprep/oobe command should be used.

specialize   Configures the specific settings for the target computer, such as network settings and domain information. This configuration pass is used in conjunction with the generalize configuration pass.

Windows PE   Sets the Windows PE specific configuration settings as well as several Windows Setup settings, such as partitioning and formatting the hard disk, selecting an image, and applying a product key.

Deploying with Windows Autopilot

So far, we have talked about automating the deployment of Windows 10 on-site. Now it's time to look at how to deploy Windows 10 machines from the cloud. Microsoft has introduced a new way to deploy Windows 10 by using Intune and Windows Autopilot.

Windows Autopilot is a group of multiple technologies that allow an administrator to set up and configure brand-new devices directly from the manufacturer. These devices can go directly into the production environment and when the user logs into Intune, the device will get automatically configured for your environment.

Administrators can also use Windows Autopilot to reconfigure, recover, and repurpose devices that are already in your corporate environment. This allows administrators to quickly and easily repurpose machines so that they can be assigned to different users. Since Windows Autopilot is a benefit with using Microsoft Intune, your IT department does not need to set up an onsite infrastructure to support this service. This helps reduce the cost of building machines for your IT department.

So, what does this actually mean to your IT department? Let's take a look at just a couple scenarios where Windows Autopilot can help your IT department quickly set up or repurpose Windows 10 devices.

When you purchase Windows 10 machines from different vendors, currently you need to make sure that you have custom images for each vendor. The reason for this is that each vendor puts in its own hardware and that hardware needs custom drivers to work properly. With Windows Autopilot, you can have the vendor send the machines directly to your remote users or IT department for immediate deployment.

When the user logs into Windows Azure with their email address and password, Windows Autopilot will automatically apply settings, policies, and applications and, if need be, even change the version of Windows 10 (for example, from Windows 10 Pro to Windows 10 Enterprise) on the machine. The machine will automatically be ready for use in your corporate environment without any need for the IT department to manually make any changes to the new machine.

Another scenario of using Windows Autopilot is when you need to repurpose machines within your organization. Currently, when many of us get a new machine for a user, we need to load an image onto that machine and set it up for that specific user. After the machine is given to the user, we normally take their machine, reimage it, and pass it on to someone with an older machine. This can result in a large chain of repurposed machines.

With Windows Autopilot, when a user gets a machine from another user, once they log into their Azure account, the machine can reload a clean operating system with all of the policies and applications that they need to do their job. The IT department doesn't need to reimage machines before they are redeployed.

After the IT department deploys or repurposes the Windows 10 machines, those machines can then be managed by using Microsoft Intune, System Center Configuration Manager, Windows Update for Business, and other compatible tools. Windows Autopilot allows your organization to complete the following tasks:

- Join Windows 10 devices automatically to Azure Active Directory (Azure AD) or to your on-site Active Directory (via Hybrid Azure AD Join).

- Automatically enroll your Windows 10 devices into MDM services, such as Microsoft Intune (this requires an Azure AD Premium subscription).

- Restrict the creation of the Administrator account.

- Build and automatically assign Windows 10 devices to configuration groups based on the Windows 10 device profile.

- Customizable OOBE content that is specific to your organization.

Windows Autopilot Requirements

So now that you understand the benefits of using Windows Autopilot, let's take a look at what's required so that you can use Windows Autopilot in your organization.

First off, and most importantly, Windows Autopilot depends on the version and specific capabilities of Windows 10. Secondly, you will need to have an Azure subscription set up with Azure Active Directory. Finally, you will need to add the Mobile Device Management (MDM) services along with Intune to your Azure subscription so that you can set up and manage Windows Autopilot.

Hardware Requirements

If an administrator wants to deploy a new machine directly from a vendor using Windows Autopilot, a unique hardware ID for the device needs to be captured and uploaded. This step can be done directly by the hardware vendor, but if an administrator needs to get this information manually, they can do this through a data gathering process that collects the device data. For this to be done, the version of Windows 10 must be version 1703 or later.

The hardware ID (commonly called a hardware hash) contains data details about the Windows 10 device. This data includes the manufacturer information (including the model), the device's serial number, the hard drive's serial number, and many other factors that are used to uniquely identify the device.

To manually gather this information, an administrator can use Microsoft System Center Configuration Manager (version 1802 or higher). System Center Configuration Manager automatically collects the hardware hashes for existing Windows 10 systems as long as the Windows 10 systems are using Windows 10 version 1703 and higher. After all of the hash information is collected, the data can be exported from System Center Configuration Manager into a CSV file.

Once you have met the hardware requirements, we need to look at the software requirements of Windows 10.

Software Requirements

So as stated above, one of the main requirements for Windows Autopilot is Windows 10. Windows 10 must meet the following minimum requirements:

- Windows 10 version 1703 (Semi-Annual Channel) or higher.

- Windows 10 must be one of the following editions in order to use Windows Autopilot:

  - Windows 10 Pro

  - Windows 10 Pro Education

  - Windows 10 Pro for Workstations

  - Windows 10 Enterprise

  - Windows 10 Education

  - Windows 10 Enterprise 2019 LTSC

Besides meeting the minimum software requirements, your organization must also meet minimum networking requirements

Networking Requirements

Windows Autopilot depends on multiple Microsoft cloud–based subscriptions. These include an Azure subscription setup with Azure Active Directory. Your organization is going to have to also subscribe to MDM services along with using Microsoft Intune.

After your organization sets up the Microsoft cloud–based subscriptions, you will need to ensure that the proper access to these services have been configured. Now this access may change based on how your Azure subscription is set up. For example, if you are using a hybrid setup (where you have an onsite network and an Azure network working together), you need to make sure that your firewall and DNS settings are set up properly. If you are using just an Azure network, then you need to make sure that access to the Azure network is set up properly.

Since Windows Autopilot requires access to Internet-based services, you need to ensure that the following settings are set up as a minimum:

- Administrators must properly configure DNS name resolution for their Internet DNS names.

- Firewalls must allow all hosts to have access to port 80 (HTTP), 443 (HTTPS), and 123 (UDP/NTP).

- If your organization requires that users authenticate before gaining Internet access, white-list access may be needed so your users can access the required services.

After you have met the required software and hardware configuration, the next step is to set up Windows Autopilot profiles.

Windows Autopilot Profiles

Windows Autopilot profiles allow an administrator to choose how the Windows 10 system will be set up and configured on Azure AD and Intune. This allows your organization to set up different options depending on the requirements needed for configuring the Windows 10 devices. The following Windows Autopilot profiles are available:

Skip Cortana, OneDrive and OEM Registration Setup Pages   Any device that registers with Windows Autopilot will automatically skip the Cortana, OneDrive, and OEM registration setup pages during the out-of-box experience (OOBE) process.

Automatically Set Up for Work or School   Any device that registers with Windows Autopilot will automatically be configured as a work or school device. Because of this, these questions will not be asked during the OOBE process.

Sign In Experience with Company Branding   Instead of presenting your user with a generic Azure Active Directory sign-in page, any device that registers with Windows Autopilot will automatically be presented with a customized sign-in page. This page can be configured with the organization's name, logon, and additional help text, as configured in Azure Active Directory.

Skip Privacy Settings   Any device that registers with Windows Autopilot will not be asked about privacy settings during the Windows 10 OOBE process. This setting is used if the organization is going to configure these privacy settings using Intune.

Disable Local Admin Account Creation on the Device   Organizations can decide whether the user who is registering with Windows Autopilot will have the ability to have administrator access once the process is finished.

Skip End User License Agreement   If your organization is using Windows 10 version 1709 or later, organizations can allow users to skip the End User License Agreement (EULA) page during the OOBE process. When an organization chooses this profile setting, the organization accepts the EULA terms on their user's behalf.

Disable Windows Consumer Features   If your organization is using Windows 10 version 1803 or later, organizations have the ability to disable certain Windows features. For example, the Windows 10 device would not automatically install any additional Microsoft Store apps once the user first signs into the Windows 10 device.

If you decide that you want to use PowerShell when configuring Windows Autopilot, after the software and hardware requirements are met, you can use the `Install-Module WindowsAutopilotIntune` cmdlet to configure Windows Autopilot.

Understanding Windows Updates

One task that is very important to any IT department is keeping the Windows operating systems up-to-date. This can happen in many different ways, depending on your infrastructure setup. If you are using an onsite network only, your users can update their own machines or you can set up a server to help you out.

Windows Update is a utility that can connect to the Microsoft update website, connect to your Azure network, or connect to a local onsite update server called a Windows Server Update Services (WSUS) server. Windows Update is used to ensure that the Windows 10 operating system (along with other Microsoft products) has the most up-to-date versions of Microsoft operating system files or software.

Some of the common update categories associated with Windows Update are as follows:

- Security updates
- Critical updates
- Service packs
- Drivers
- Product/Software updates
- Windows Store

To truly understand updates, you need to understand how the update process works with Microsoft. Microsoft normally releases updates to their products on the second Tuesday of the month (this is why we use the term Patch Tuesdays). But before that update gets released to the public, it has already been tested at Microsoft.

It all starts with the Windows engineering team adding new features and functionality to Windows using product cycles. These product cycles are comprised from three phases; development, testing, and release.

After the new Windows 10 features or functionality are developed, Microsoft employees test these updates out themselves on their own Windows 10 machines. This is referred to as "selfhost testing."

After the updates get tested at Microsoft, they then get released to the public. With Windows 10, Microsoft has introduced new ways to service updates. Microsoft's new servicing options are referred to as Semi-Annual Channel, Long-Term Servicing Branch (LTSB), and Windows Insider. Table 1.12 (taken directly from Microsoft's website) shows the different servicing options and the benefits of those options.

TABLE 1.12 Servicing options

From this channel	To this channel	You need to
Windows Insider Program	Semi-Annual Channel (Targeted)	Wait for the final Semi-Annual Channel release.
	Semi-Annual Channel	Not directly possible, because Windows Insider Program devices are automatically upgraded to the Semi-Annual Channel (Targeted) release at the end of the development cycle.
	Long-Term Servicing Channel	Not directly possible (requires wipe-and-load).
Semi-Annual Channel (Targeted)	Insider	Use the Settings app to enroll the device in the Windows Insider Program.
	Semi-Annual Channel	Select the **Defer upgrade** setting, or move the PC to a target group or flight that will not receive the next upgrade until it is business ready. Note that this change will not have any immediate impact; it only prevents the installation of the next Semi-Annual Channel release.
	Long-Term Servicing Channel	Not directly possible (requires wipe-and-load).
Semi-Annual Channel	Insider	Use the Settings app to enroll the device in the Windows Insider Program.
	Semi-Annual Channel (Targeted)	Disable the **Defer upgrade** setting, or move the device to a target group or flight that will receive the latest Current Semi-Annual Channel release.
	Long-Term Servicing Channel	Not directly possible (requires wipe-and-load).

TABLE 1.12   Servicing options *(continued)*

From this channel	To this channel	You need to
Long-Term Servicing Channel	Insider	Use media to upgrade to the latest Windows Insider Program build.
	Semi-Annual Channel (Targeted)	Use media to upgrade. Note that the Semi-Annual Channel build must be a later build.
	Semi-Annual Channel	Use media to upgrade. Note that the Semi-Annual Channel build must be a later build.

Windows Update Process

There are multiple ways a user can receive updates. The user can get updates directly from Microsoft. This is done by the user using the Updates section of Windows settings. This is how most of us get our updates at home. But this is a process that doesn't work well in a business environment. The reason for this is that if you have hundreds of users, they are all connecting directly with Microsoft and receiving the same updates. This can take up a lot of Internet bandwidth and the IT department has very little control over what updates get installed.

When it comes to company-based updates, there are better options. Administrators can set up either Group Policy Objects (GPOs) or Azure MDM solutions (such as Microsoft Intune) to configure the Windows Update for Business settings that control how and when Windows 10 devices are updated and which updates get accepted by the IT department. Windows Update for Business updates are updates that you receive from your Microsoft cloud-based services (MDM and Intune).

Administrators can also set up a Microsoft Windows Server Update Service (WSUS) server. WSUS runs on a Windows server, and that server goes out to the Microsoft website and downloads the updates for your Windows clients. This allows client machines to receive their updates from a server that is controlled by the IT department.

    WSUS is discussed in detail in *MCSA Windows Server 2016 Complete Study Guide: Exam 70-740, Exam 70-741, Exam 70-742, and Exam 70-743, 2nd Edition*, by William Panek (Wiley, 2018).

Using Windows Update for Business

Windows Update for Business allows an IT administrator to keep their organization's Windows 10 devices up-to-date with the latest Microsoft security defenses and Windows features by using Microsoft Azure. Windows Update for Business allows your Windows 10 systems to connect to Microsoft's Windows Update service.

Administrators have the ability to configure Windows Update for Business by using Group Policies or MDM solutions to configure the Windows Update for Business settings. These settings will control how and when Windows 10 devices are updated.

So, what does this mean for your organization? Administrators have total control over how updates are delivered and which updates will be delivered. Administrators can do this best by doing reliability and performance testing on a small group of systems (including just a single system for testing) before allowing updates to roll out to all of the computers in their organization. By testing updates, administrators can determine which updates will work best for their company.

Windows Update for Business Update Types

Windows Update for Business allows an organization to choose which updates an organization wants delivered to their Windows 10 systems. Administrators can do this by setting up management policies to help choose which updates they want delivered to their users. The following are different types of updates that Administrators can deploy to their Windows 10 devices:

Feature Updates   These updates were previously referred to as upgrades. Feature Updates not only contain security updates and revisions, but they also include major feature additions and changes. Feature Updates are released semi-annually in the spring and in the fall.

Quality Updates   Quality Updates are normally operating system updates that are usually released the second Tuesday of each month. Sometimes these updates, depending on their importance, can actually be released at any time. Quality Updates include security updates, critical updates, and driver updates.

Windows Update for Business also deploys non-Windows operating system updates (for example, Visual Studio) as part of the Quality Updates deployment.

Driver Updates   Driver Updates are updates for third-party devices that apply to your Windows 10 systems. For example, you may be using a printer that Microsoft Windows 10 has a driver for; these drivers get updated as part of the Driver Updates process. Administrators have the ability to enable or disable Driver Updates by using Windows Update for Business policies.

Microsoft Product Updates   Microsoft Product Updates are updates for Microsoft application or software products like Office. Administrators have the ability to enable or disable Microsoft Product Updates by using Windows Update for Business policies.

Deferring Updates

Windows Update for Business allows administrators to defer updates from being installed for a specific period of time. Administrators can defer the installation of both Feature Updates and Quality Updates for a specific period of time, but that specific period of time starts as soon as those updates are first made available through the Windows Update service.

Administrators can use this time to test and validate the updates before they are pushed to all of your Windows 10 devices. The way deferrals work is by allowing administrators to specify the amount of time after an update is released before it is offered to your Windows 10 devices.

For example, if an administrator decides to defer Feature Updates for 365 days, the Windows 10 devices will not install any Feature Update before the 365 days expire. Administrators can defer Feature Updates by using the *Select when Preview Builds and Feature Updates are Received* policy.

Table 1.13 shows you the different updates that can be deferred and the maximum time that they can be deferred for.

TABLE 1.13   Maximum Update Deferral

Update	Maximum Deferral
Feature Updates	365 days
Quality Updates	30 days
Non-deferrable	None

Pausing an Update

Administrators also have the ability to pause an update if they discover an issue while they are deploying Feature Updates or Quality Updates. Administrators can choose to pause the update for up to 35 days. This helps prevent other Windows 10 devices from experiencing the same issues.

If the administrator pauses the installation of a Feature Update, then Quality Updates are still deployed and vice versa. When an administrator sets a pause time period for an update, the pause time is calculated from the start date that the administrator sets.

To pause a Feature Update, the administrator uses the *Select when Preview Builds and Feature Updates are Received* policy. To pause a Quality Update, the administrator uses the *Select when Quality Updates are Received* policy.

Selecting Branch Readiness Level for Feature Updates

Windows Update for Business allows administrators to choose which channel of Feature Updates they want to receive. Currently Microsoft offers branch readiness level options to organizations for pre-release and released updates. The following options are included:

- Windows Insider Program for Business prerelease updates. These updates include Windows Insider Fast, Windows Insider Slow, and Windows Insider Release Preview.

- Semi-Annual Channel for released updates

Prior to version 1903 of Windows 10, there are only two channels for released updates: Semi-Annual Channel and Semi-Annual Channel (Targeted). Versions of Windows 10 released after version 1903 get a single release channel: Semi-Annual Channel.

Administrators have the ability to configure the branch readiness level by configuring the *Select when Preview Builds and Feature Updates are Received* policy. But if an administrator wants to manage pre-release builds, they need to enable preview builds by configuring the *Manage preview Builds* policy.

Monitoring Windows Updates

Administrators have the ability to monitor which Windows 10 computers are receiving their updates by using the Update Compliance utility. The Update Compliance utility lets administrators see a complete view of Windows 10 operating system updates Administrators can view which operating systems are meeting compliances, how the update deployments are progressing, and any errors that may have occurred on the Windows 10 devices.

The Update Compliance utility uses multiple factors to show you a complete view of the update process. These factors include diagnostic data from the installation progress, Windows Update configuration settings, and additional data (for example, Windows Defender Antivirus diagnostic data). This service is included free with your Azure subscription and there is no need to set up any additional infrastructure requirements.

Update Compliance Prerequisites

To use the Update Compliance utility, your organization must meet some prerequisites:

- Only Windows 10 Professional, Education, and Enterprise editions can be used with the Update Compliance utility. Update Compliance only gathers data for the standard desktop Windows 10 version. The Update Compliance utility is not currently compatible with other operating systems like Windows Server, Surface Hub, or IoT.

- Windows 10 devices must be on the Semi-Annual Channel and the Long-Term Servicing Channel. The Update Compliance utility will show administrators Windows Insider Preview devices. But currently Windows Insider Preview devices will not have any detailed deployment information.

- The Update Compliance utility requires at minimum the Basic level of diagnostic data and a Commercial ID to be enabled on the Windows 10 device.

- Administrators must opt in to the Windows Analytics to see device names for versions of Windows 10 version 1803 or higher.

- If administrators want to use the Windows Defender Status, Windows 10 devices must be E3 licensed and have Cloud Protection enabled. E5-licensed devices should use Windows Defender ATP instead.

- Administrators must add the Update Compliance utility to their Azure subscription. To do this, the administrator must log in to the Azure portal and select + Create A Resource. At the search for window, type **Update Compliance**. At the bottom of the screen, select the Create button to add the Update Compliance utility to your Azure subscription.

Summary

This chapter started with a discussion of the features included with Windows 10. We also took a look at installing Windows 10. Installation is an easy process, but you must first make sure the machine is compatible with the Windows 10 operating system.

There are two main ways to install Windows 10: upgrade or clean install. You can upgrade a Windows 7 or Windows 8/8.1 machine to Windows 10.

I discussed automated installation of Windows 10. Installing Windows 10 through an automated process is an effective way to install the Windows 10 operating system on multiple computers.

There are several methods for automated installation: unattended installations, Windows Deployment Services (WDS), Windows Assessment and Deployment Kit (ADK), third-party applications, unattended installations, and using the System Preparation Tool along with Image Capture Wizard.

Windows Deployment Services (WDS) is a suite of components that allows you to remotely install Windows 10 on client computers.

The Windows (ADK) is a set of utilities and documentation that allows an administrator to configure and deploy Windows operating systems.

You can use unattended answer files to automatically respond to the queries that are generated during the normal installation process.

You can also prepare an installation for imaging by using the System Preparation Tool (sysprep.exe) and creating a disk image by using the Image Capture Wizard utility or a third-party utility.

Microsoft Deployment Toolkit (MDT) is a way of automating desktop and server deployment. With the MDT, an administrator can deploy desktops and servers through the use of a common console, which allows for quicker deployments, having standardized desktop and server images and security and zero-touch deployments of Windows 10, Windows 8, Windows 7, and Windows Server.

I also talked about installing Windows 10 devices using Intune and Windows Autopilot. I explained how Windows Autopilot is used and configured and the requirements needed to use Windows Autopilot. I also explained the different profiles that you can use with Windows Autopilot.

After the Windows 10 installation is complete, you'll want to make sure all updates and service packs are installed. You can use Windows Update to complete that task on-site. I finally explained how to setup and configure cloud-based updates by using Windows Update for Business. I talked about how you can use The Update Compliance utility to get reporting data on how updates are being delivered to your Windows 10 devices.

Exam Essentials

Understand the Windows 10 hardware requirements.   The minimum hardware requirements to run Windows 10 properly are 1 gigahertz (GHz) or faster processor or SoC, 1 gigabyte (GB) for 32-bit or 2 GB for 64-bit of RAM, 16 GB for 32-bit OS or 20 GB for

64-bit OS of hard drive space, DirectX 9 or later with WDDM 1.0 video driver, and a DVD-R/W drive or compatible network interface card.

Understand how to complete a clean install.   If your machine meets the minimum hardware requirements, you can install Windows 10. There are a few different ways to install Windows 10 onto a computer. You can use the installation disk or USB, install it over a network, or install it from an image.

Understand how to complete an upgrade.   You can't upgrade a Windows Vista machine to Windows 10. To complete an upgrade on a Windows 7 or Windows 8/8.1 machine, insert the Windows 10 DVD into the Windows machine or connect to the Windows 10 files over the network and complete an upgrade on the computer.

You can't upgrade a Windows XP machine directly to Windows 10. If the machine is running Windows XP, you have to use a migration tool to migrate all the user data from Windows XP to a Windows 10 machine.

Know the difference between the various unattended installation methods.   Understand the various options available for unattended installations of Windows 10 and when it is appropriate to use each installation method.

Understand the features and uses of WDS.   Know when it is appropriate to use WDS to manage unattended installations. Be able to list the requirements for setting up WDS servers and WDS clients. Be able to complete an unattended installation using WDS.

Be able to use disk images for unattended installations.   Know how to perform unattended installations of Windows 10 using the System Preparation Tool and disk images.

Understand the Microsoft Deployment Toolkit (MDT).   Know that the MDT is a way of automating desktop and server deployment. Understand that the MDT allows an administrator to deploy desktops and servers through the use of a common console.

Be able to use Windows Autopilot.   Windows Autopilot is a group of multiple technologies that allow an administrator to set up and configure brand-new devices, repurpose current machines, and even recover corporate machines.

Understand how to receive updates.   You need to understand how to set up and receive Microsoft updates for Windows 10, Microsoft products, and the Windows Store. Make sure you know the different settings for configuring advanced update options.

Understand Windows Update for Business.   You need to understand how to set up and receive Microsoft updates for Windows 10 using Windows Update for Business in Azure. Make sure you know the different settings for configuring Windows Update for Business options.

Review Questions

1. You are the network administrator for a large communications company. You have 25 computers that currently run Windows 7. These computers have the following configurations:

   - A single MBR disk
   - A disabled TPM chip
   - Disabled hardware virtualization
   - UEFI firmware running in BIOS mode
   - Enabled Data Execution Prevention (DEP)

   You plan to upgrade the computers to Windows 10. You need to ensure that the computers can use Secure Boot. Which two actions should you perform? (Choose two).

   A. Convert the MBR disk to a GPT disk.

   B. Enable the TPM chip.

   C. Disable DEP.

   D. Enable hardware virtualization.

   E. Convert the firmware from BIOS to UEFI.

2. You are the network administrator for StormWind Studios. Your network contains an Active Directory domain. The domain contains 300 computers that run Windows 10.

   You have both an on-site Active Directory network and a Microsoft Azure Active Directory (Azure AD) with Microsoft Intune. You need to automatically register all the existing computers to the Azure AD network and also enroll all of the computers in Intune. What should you use?

   A. Use a DNS Autodiscover address record.

   B. Use a Windows Autopilot deployment profile.

   C. Use an Autodiscover service connection point (SCP).

   D. Set up a Group Policy Object (GPO).

3. You are the network administrator for a large company. You have 2 computers that run Windows 7. Computer 1 has a 32-bit CPU that runs Windows 7 Enterprise. Computer 2 has a 64-bit CPU that runs Windows 7 Enterprise. You plan to perform an in-place upgrade to the 64-bit version of Windows 10. Which computers can you upgrade to the 64-bit version of Windows 10?

   A. Computer1 only

   B. Computer2 only

   C. Computer1 and Computer2

   D. Neither

4. You are the network administrator for your organization. You have a reference computer that runs Windows 10. You need to create and deploy an image of the Windows 10 computer. You create an answer file named `answer.xml`. You have to make sure that the installation applies the answer file after you deploy the image. Which command should you run before you capture the image?

    A. `dism.exe /append answer.xml /check`

    B. `dism.exe /mount answer.xml /verify`

    C. `sysprep.exe /reboot /audit /unattend:answer.xml`

    D. `sysprep.exe /generalize /oobe /unattend:answer.xml`

5. You have a Windows 10 Windows Image (WIM) that is mounted. You need to view the list of third-party drivers installed on the WIM. What should you do?

    A. Run DISM and specify the `/get-drivers` parameter.

    B. Run `Driverquery.exe` and use the `/si` parameter.

    C. From Device Manager, view all hidden drivers.

    D. From Windows Explorer, open the mount folder.

6. You have computers that run Windows 10 Pro. The computers are joined to Microsoft Azure Active Directory (Azure AD) and enrolled in Microsoft Intune. You need to upgrade the computers to Windows 10 Enterprise. What should you configure in Intune?

    A. A device enrollment policy

    B. A device cleanup rule

    C. A device compliance policy

    D. A Windows Autopilot device profile

7. You are the network administrator for a large organization. You are in charge of developing a plan to install 200 Windows 10 computers in your company's data center. You decide to use WDS. You are using a Windows Server 2012 R2 domain and have verified that your network meets the requirements for using WDS. What command-line utility should you use to configure the WDS server?

    A. `dism`

    B. `wdsutil`

    C. `setup.exe`

    D. The WDS icon in Control Panel

8. Will is the network manager for a large company. He has been tasked with creating a deployment plan to automate installations for 100 computers that need to have Windows 10 installed. Will wants to use WDS for the installations. To fully automate the installations, he needs to create an answer file. Will does not want to create the answer files with a text editor. What other program can he use to create unattended answer files via a GUI interface?

    A. DISM

    B. Answer Manager

    C. Windows System Image Manager

    D. System Preparation Tool

9. You are using WDS to install 20 Windows 10 computers. When the clients attempt to use WDS, they are not able to complete the unattended installation. You suspect that the WDS server has not been configured to respond to client requests. Which one of the following utilities would you use to configure the WDS server to respond to client requests?

 A. Active Directory Users and Computers

 B. Active Directory Users and Groups

 C. WDS MMC snap-in

 D. WDSMAN

10. You want to install a group of 25 computers using disk images created in conjunction with the System Preparation Tool. Your plan is to create an image from a reference computer and then copy the image to all the machines. You do not want to create an SID on the destination computer when you use the image. Which sysprep.exe command-line option should you use to set this up?

 A. /specialize

 B. /generalize

 C. /oobe

 D. /quiet

Chapter

2

Managing Authentication

MICROSOFT EXAM OBJECTIVES COVERED IN THIS CHAPTER:

✓ **Manage device authentication**

- Manage authentication policies; manage sign-on options; perform Azure AD join.

✓ **Manage user profiles**

- Configure user profiles; configure Enterprise State Roaming in Azure AD; configure sync settings; implement Folder Redirection (including OneDrive).

Now that you understand how to create a Windows 10 device, it's time to work with Active Directory. There are different ways to set up Active Directory. Administrators can set up Active Directory on their local networks or in an Azure virtual machine. But you can also set up Active Directory within the Azure desktop.

For all of you administrators that currently work on an Active Directory network, Azure Active Directory is not really the Active Directory that we all know. It is a database that controls access, and yes, you can join computers to an Azure Active Directory network but that's almost where the similarities stop.

So I think the best way to talk about Active Directory in this chapter is to talk about what it does and how Azure Active Directory differs from that. Then I think the features and limitations of Azure Active Directory will be a lot clearer.

Active Directory vs. Azure Active Directory

One of the most confusing things that Microsoft can do at times is name a new feature or service similarly to a feature or service that already exists. This is what happened here with Active Directory and Azure Active Directory.

A perfect example of this is Universal Group Membership Caching (UGMC). UGMC has NOTHING to do with Universal Groups. Universal Groups are a type of group and UGMC helps a site, with no Global Catalog, with logins. But because they both have the words Universal Groups, people think that they are connected.

Azure Active Directory is not the Active Directory that most of us use on a daily basis. This might be overstating it a bit. Think of Azure Active Directory as Active Directory lite. So let's look at Active Directory and then look at Azure Active Directory so that you can see the differences between the two.

Understanding Active Directory

There are different ways that you can setup a network. If all of the machines can work both as clients and servers, this type of network is referred to as a Workgroup or Peer-to-Peer network. The downside of this type of network is that it is too small and that each computer has its own authentication database. This means that every user has to have an account on every computer. This can lead to all types of issues and it is also a very difficult network to manage.

This is where Active Directory comes in. Active Directory at its core is just a database. It's a single database that all of your users can belong to. This makes it much easier to manage a network and it also allows an administrator to have better control over the users and their permissions.

Active Directory is built on the database standard called Directory Services. Directory Services got its "claim to fame" with Novell. Novell used Directory Services to control access to their networks. When Microsoft decided to move their network over to Directory Services, they decided to name their version Active Directory.

Active Directory networks are grouped together in units known as Domains (as shown as triangles). A domain is a logical grouping of objects into a distributed database. Some of these objects are user accounts, group accounts, and published objects (folders and printers).

It is very important to understand that domains are a logical grouping of objects. Logical is the key word in this description. Domains are logical, not physical. For example, Microsoft.com is a worldwide entity. Not all of the domain users are located in Redmond, Washington. They are scattered all over the world.

Active Directory can be a local version by loading Active Directory onto an on-site server or setting up Active Directory in a virtual machine on Azure. But Active Directory is Active Directory no matter how you set it up. It's a database that you setup to help control access to your network. No matter if that network is on-site or in a VM in the cloud.

One of the advantages to using domains is the ability to have a *child domain*, which is a subdomain of another domain. You can build child domains based on physical locations, departments, and so forth.

Child domains give you greater scalability. Active Directory child domains give an administrator the flexibility to design a structure that meets an organization's needs. For example, you may have a site located in other states or countries. Creating a child domain for that office allows that office to be an independent domain, and thus they can have their own security and domain settings. One or more domains that follow the same contiguous namespace are called a tree. So if my domain name is Stormwind.com and the child domains are NH.Stormwind.com, Arizona.Stormwind.com, and Florida.Stormwind.com, this would be a tree. All domains here follow the Stormwind.com namespace.

Another Active Directory advantage is the ability to extend the Active Directory schema. The Active Directory schema contains all the objects and attributes of the database. For example, when you create a new user in Active Directory, the system asks you to fill in the user's first name, last name, username, password, and so forth. These fields are the attributes of the user object, and the way that the system knows to prompt for these fields is that the user object has these specific attributes assigned to it within the Active Directory schema. An administrator has the ability to change or expand these fields based on organizational needs.

Let's take a look at some of the advantages of Active Directory.

Active Directory Certificate Services   Active Directory Certificate Services (AD CS) provides a customizable set of services that allows you to issue and manage public key infrastructure (PKI) certificates. These certificates can be used in software security systems that employ public key technologies.

Active Directory Domain Services   Active Directory Domain Services (AD DS) includes new features that make deploying domain controllers simpler and lets you implement them faster. AD DS also makes the domain controllers more flexible, both to audit and to authorize access to files. Moreover, AD DS has been designed to make performing administrative tasks easier through consistent graphical and scripted management experiences.

Active Directory Rights Management Services   Active Directory Rights Management Services (AD RMS) provides management and development tools that let you work with industry security technologies, including encryption, certificates, and authentication. Using these technologies allows organizations to create reliable information protection solutions.

Kerberos Authentication   Windows Server uses the Kerberos authentication protocol and extensions for password-based and public-key authentication. The Kerberos client is installed as a security support provider (SSP), and it can be accessed through the Security Support Provider Interface (SSPI).

Kerberos Constrained Delegation   Kerberos constrained delegation (KCD) is an authentication protocol that administrators can setup for delegating client credentials for specific service accounts. For example, KCD may be a requirement for services in SharePoint 2019. If you are planning on using SharePoint 2019 Analysis Services and Power Pivot data, you will need to configure KCD. KCD allows a service account to impersonate another service account and this allows access to specific resources.

Managed Service Accounts   The *Managed Service Accounts* is a Windows Server account that is managed by Active Directory. Regular service accounts are accounts that are created to run specific services such as Exchange and SQL Server. Normally when an administrator creates a service account, it's up to that administrator to maintain the account (including changing the password). Managed Service Accounts are accounts that administrators create but the accounts are managed by Active Directory (including password changes). To create Managed Service Accounts, you must use the `New-ADServiceAccount` PowerShell command. You must use PowerShell in order to create a Managed Service Account.

Group Managed Service Accounts   The group Managed Service Account (gMSA) provides the same functionality within the domain as Managed Service Accounts, but gMSAs extend their functionality over multiple servers. These accounts are very useful when a service account needs to work with multiple servers as with a server farm (for Network Load Balancing).

There are times when the authentication process requires that all instances of a service use the same service account. This is where gMSAs are used. Once group Managed Service Accounts are used, Windows Server will automatically manage the password for the service account. The network administrator will no longer be responsible for managing the service account password.

Security Auditing   Security auditing gives an organization the ability to help maintain the security of an enterprise. By using security audits, you can verify authorized or unauthorized access to machines, resources, applications, and services. One of the best advantages of security audits is to verify regulatory compliance.

TLS/SSL (Schannel SSP)   Schannel is a security support provider (SSP) that uses the Secure Sockets Layer (SSL) and Transport Layer Security (TLS) Internet standard authentication protocols together. The Security Support Provider Interface (SSPI) is an API used by Windows systems to allow security-related functionality, including authentication.

Windows Deployment Services   Windows Deployment Services allows an administrator to install Windows operating systems remotely. Administrators can use Windows Deployment Services to set up new computers by using a network-based installation.

Now when it comes to setting up Active Directory on-site or on a virtual machine, that server becomes a Domain Controller. Microsoft only has three server types; Domain Controller, Member Server, or Stand Alone Server. So it's important that you understand how each server works. So let's take a look at servers and what types of Microsoft servers you can have.

Server   A *server* is a machine that users connect to so they can access resources located on that machine. These resources can be files, printers, applications, and so forth. Usually, the type of server is dependent on the resource that the user needs. For example, a print server is a server that controls printers. A file server contains files. Application servers can run applications for the users. Sometimes you will hear a server referred to by the specific application that it may be running. For example, someone may say, "That's our SQL server" or "We have an Exchange server."

Domain Controller   This is a server that contains a replica of the Active Directory database. As mentioned earlier in this chapter, Active Directory is the database that contains all the objects in your network. A *domain controller* is a server that contains this database. All domain controllers are equal in a Windows Server network and each can both read from and write to the directory database. Some domain controllers may contain extra roles, but they all have the same copy of Active Directory.

Member Server   A *member server* is a server that is a member of a domain-based network but does not contain a copy of Active Directory. For example, it is recommended by Microsoft that a Microsoft Exchange server be loaded on a member server instead of a domain controller. Both domain controllers and member servers can act as file, print, or application servers. Your choice of server type depends on whether you need that server to have a replica of Active Directory.

Stand-Alone Server   A *stand-alone server* is not a member of a domain. Many organizations may use this type of server for virtualization. For example, say you load Windows Server with Hyper-V (Microsoft's virtualization server) on a stand-alone server. You can then create virtual machines that act as domain controllers to run the network.

Another component of a Microsoft network is a Global Catalog. The *Global Catalog* is a database of all Active Directory objects in a forest with only a subset of the object attributes.

In other words, the Global Catalog is a partial representation of the Active Directory objects. Think of the Global Catalog as an index. If you needed to look something up in this Windows 10 book, you would go to the index and find what page you need to turn to. You would not just randomly look through the book for the information. This is the same purpose the Global Catalog serves in your Active Directory forest. When you need to find a resource in the forest (user, published printer, and so forth), you can search the Global Catalog to find its location.

Domain controllers need to use a Global Catalog to help with user authentication. Global Catalogs are a requirement on an Active Directory domain. All domain controllers can be Global Catalogs, but this is not always a good practice. Your network should have at least two Global Catalogs for redundancy, but too many can cause too much Global Catalog replication traffic unless you have a single-domain model.

Read-Only Domain Controllers

Windows Server supports another type of domain controller called the *read-only domain controller (RODC)*. This is a full copy of the Active Directory database without the ability to write to Active Directory. The RODC gives an organization the ability to install a domain controller in a location (on site or off site) where security is a concern.

RODCs need to get their Active Directory database from another domain controller. So if you have a network with no domain controllers set up yet for the domain, the RODC option will not be available (the option will be grayed out). Implementing an RODC is the same as adding another domain controller to a domain. The installation is exactly the same except that when you get to the screen to choose Domain Controller options, you check the box for RODC. Again, this is ONLY available if there are other domain controllers already in the domain.

Installing Active Directory On-Site or in Azure

Before you install Active Directory into your network, you must first make sure that your network and the server meet some minimum requirements. Table 2.1 will show you the requirements needed for Active Directory.

TABLE 2.1   Active Directory requirements

Requirement	Description
Adprep	When adding the first Windows Server domain controller to an existing Active Directory domain, Adprep commands run automatically as needed.
Credentials	When installing a new AD DS forest, the administrator must be set to local Administrator on the first server. To install an additional domain controller in an existing domain, you need to be a member of the Domain Admins group.
DNS	Domain Name System needs to be installed for Active Directory to function properly. You can install DNS during the Active Directory installation.

Requirement	Description
NTFS	The Windows Server drives that store the database, log files, and SYSVOL folder must be placed on a volume that is formatted with the NTFS file system.
RODCs	Read-only domain controllers can be installed as long as another domain controller (Windows Server 2008 or newer) already exists on the domain. Also, the forest functional level must be at least Windows Server 2003.
TCP/IP	You must configure the appropriate TCP/IP settings on your domain, and you must configure the DNS server addresses.

The Installation Process

Windows Server computers are configured as either member servers (if they are joined to a domain) or stand-alone servers (if they are part of a workgroup). The process of converting a server to a domain controller is known as *promotion*. Through the use of a simple and intuitive wizard in Server Manager, system administrators can quickly configure servers to be domain controllers after installation. Administrators also have the ability to promote domain controllers using Windows PowerShell.

The first step in installing Active Directory is promoting a Windows Server computer to a domain controller. The first domain controller in an environment serves as the starting point for the forest, trees, domains, and the operations master roles.

Exercise 2.1 shows the steps you need to follow to promote an existing Windows Server computer to a domain controller. To complete the steps in this exercise, you must have already installed and configured a Windows Server computer. I am using a Windows Server 2016 computer for this exercise. You also need a DNS server that supports SRV records. If you do not have a DNS server available, the Active Directory Installation Wizard automatically configures one for you. I would recommend that you do this lab on a test box. This lab is needed later so that I can show you how to connect your on-site setup with Azure.

EXERCISE 2.1

Setting Up an On-Site Domain Controller

1. Install the Active Directory Domain Services by clicking the Add Roles And Features link in Server Manager's Dashboard view.

2. At the Before You Begin screen, click Next.

3. The Select installation Type screen will be next. Make sure that the Role-Based radio button is selected and click Next.

4. At the Select Destination Server screen, choose the local machine. Click Next.

5. At the Select Server Roles screen, click the check box for Active Directory Domain Services.

6. After you check the Active Directory Domain Services box, a pop-up menu will appear asking you to install additional features. Click the Add Features button.

7. Click Next.

8. At the Select Features screen, accept the defaults and click Next.

9. Click Next at the information screen.

10. Click the Install button at the Confirmation Installation screen.

11. The Installation Progress screen will show you how the installation is progressing.

12. After the installation is complete, click the Close button.

13. On the left-side window, click the AD DS link.

14. Click the More link next to Configuration Required For Active Directory Domain Services.

15. Under the Post-Deployment Configuration section, click the Promote This Server To A Domain Controller link.

16. At this point, you will configure this domain controller. You are going to install a new domain controller in a new domain in a new forest. At the Deployment Configuration screen, choose the Add A New Forest radio button. You then need to add a root domain name. In this exercise, I will use StormWindAD.com (see Figure 2.1). Click Next.

FIGURE 2.1 New Forest screen

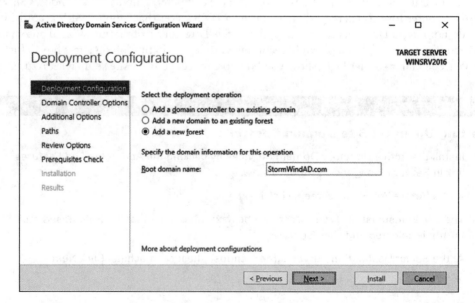

17. At the Domain Controller Options screen, set the following options (see Figure 2.2):

- Function levels: Windows Server 2016 (for both)

- Verify that the DNS and Global Catalog check boxes are checked. Notice that the RODC check box is grayed out. This is because RODCs need to get their Active Directory database from another domain controller. Since this is the first domain controller in the forest, RODCs are not possible. If you need an RODC, complete the previous steps on a member server in a domain where domain controllers already exist.

- Password: **P@ssw0rd**

  Then click Next.

FIGURE 2.2   Domain Controller Options screen

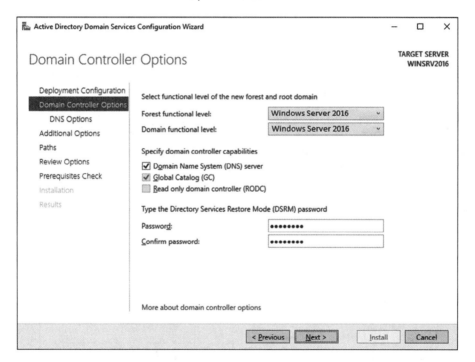

18. At the DNS screen, click Next.

19. At the Additional Options screen, accept the default NetBIOS domain name and click Next.

20. At the Paths screen, accept the default file locations and click Next.

21. At the Review Options screen (see Figure 2.3), verify your settings and click Next. At this screen, there is a View Script button. This button allows you to grab a PowerShell script based on the features you have just set up.

EXERCISE 2.1 *(continued)*

FIGURE 2.3   Review Options screen

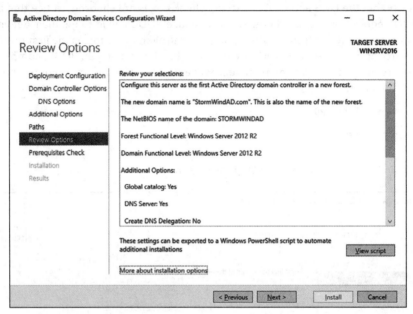

22. At the Prerequisites Check screen, click the Install button (as long as there are no errors). Warnings are OK just as long as there are no errors (see Figure 2.4).

FIGURE 2.4   Prerequisites Check screen

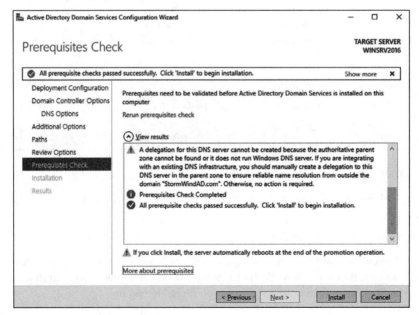

23. After the installation completes, the machine will automatically reboot. Log in as the administrator.

24. Close Server Manager.

25. Click the Start button on the keyboard and choose Administrative Tools.

26. You should see new MMC snap-ins for Active Directory.

27. Close the Administrative Tools window.

Using Active Directory Administrative Tools

After a server has been promoted to a domain controller, you will see that various tools are added to the Administrative Tools program group, including the following:

Active Directory Administrative Center This is a *Microsoft Management Console (MMC)* snap-in that allows you to accomplish many Active Directory tasks from one central location. This MMC snap-in allows you to manage your directory services objects, including doing the following tasks:

- Reset user passwords
- Create or manage user accounts
- Create or manage groups
- Create or manage computer accounts
- Create or manage organizational units (OUs) and containers
- Connect to one or several domains or domain controllers in the same instance of Active Directory Administrative Center
- Filter Active Directory data

Active Directory Domains and Trusts Use this tool to view and change information related to the various domains in an Active Directory environment. This MMC snap-in also allows you to set up shortcut trusts.

Active Directory Sites and Services Use this tool to create and manage Active Directory sites and services to map to an organization's physical network infrastructure.

Active Directory Users and Computers User and computer management is fundamental for an Active Directory environment. The Active Directory Users and Computers tool allows you to set machine- and user-specific settings across the domain. This tool is discussed throughout this book.

Active Directory Module for Windows PowerShell *Windows PowerShell* is a command-line shell and scripting language. The Active Directory Module for Windows PowerShell is a group of cmdlets used to manage your Active Directory domains, Active Directory Lightweight Directory Services (AD LDS) configuration sets, and Active Directory Database Mounting Tool instances in a single, self-contained package. The Active

Directory Module for Windows PowerShell is a normal PowerShell window. The only difference is that the Active Directory PowerShell module is pre-loaded when you choose the Active Directory Module for Windows PowerShell.

A good way to make sure that Active Directory is accessible and functioning properly is to run the Active Directory Users and Computers tool. When you open the tool, you should see a configuration similar to that shown in Figure 2.5. Specifically, you should make sure the name of the domain you created appears in the list. You should also click the Domain Controllers folder and make sure that the name of your local server appears in the right pane. If your configuration passes these two checks, Active Directory is present and configured.

FIGURE 2.5 Viewing Active Directory information using the Active Directory Users and Computers tool

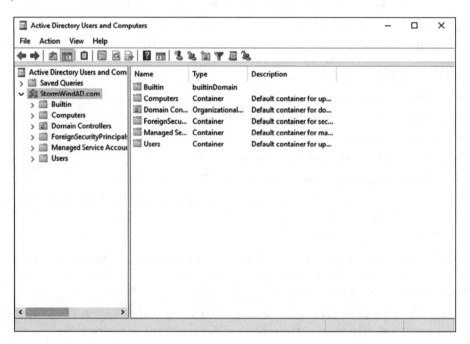

Understanding Azure Active Directory

So now that you understand how to install Active Directory on your on-site network, it's time to see how to configure your Azure Active Directory. One big misconception is that Azure Active Directory is set up and configured the same way that your on-site Active Directory is set up. The advantage of Azure Active Directory is that there is no installation. As soon as you set up your Azure subscription, Azure Active Directory is ready to go.

So before we begin setting up your Azure Active Directory, let's take a look at some of the features that Azure Active Directory delivers. The following features are just some of the features available in Azure AD managed domains.

Simple Deployment   Administrators can easily enable Azure AD Domain Services for their Azure AD directory. Managed domains include cloud-only user accounts and user accounts synchronized from an on-premises directory.

Domain-Join   Administrators have the ability to easily join computers to the Azure domain. Administrators can even combine the Azure domain with Windows 10 so that the clients can automatically join the domain with automated domain joining tools.

Setting Domain Names   Azure administrators have the ability to create custom domain names (for example, WillPanek.com) that are either verified or unverified with the Azure AD Domain Service wizards. Administrators can also create domain names using the Microsoft domain suffix of onmicrosoft.com. So if you want, you can create a domain of WillPanek.onmicrosoft.com. So as an administrator, you have a lot of flexibility when creating domain names for your organization.

AD Account Lockout Protection   Administrators can set up password protection with account lockout protection. If a user enters an improper password five times within two (2) minutes, the user account is locked out for 30 minutes. The nice advantage of this is that the user account will automatically unlock after the 30 minutes are up.

Group Policy Support   Azure administrators have the ability to create and use built-in GPOs for both the user and computer containers. This gives administrators the ability to enforce company compliances for security policies. Administrators can create custom GPOs that can be assigned to Organizational Units (OUs) and this in turn will help administrators manage and enforce company policies.

For example, you can set a GPO up so that your users will use Folder Redirection. Folder Redirection allows a user to place a file in one folder but it gets redirected to another (this includes OneDrive).

To use a Group Policy to redirect OneDrive, you need the OneDrive sync to be at least build 18.111.0603.0004 or later. You can see the OneDrive build number in the About tab of the OneDrive settings.

The Group Policy Object for "OneDrive Known Folder Move" won't work if an administrator has already set up a Windows Folder Redirection policy to redirect a user's Documents, Pictures, or Desktop folders to a storage location other than OneDrive. If this has been done, the administrator must first remove the Redirection Group Policy Object that has already been created. The redirection for OneDrive doesn't affect the Music and Videos folders. So, an administrator can keep them redirected with the Windows Group Policy object that is already created.

Azure AD Integration   One of the nice advantages of Azure is that administrators do not need to manage or configure Azure AD replication. Azure user accounts, group membership, or even user passwords are automatically replicated between Azure AD and Azure AD Domain Services. Azure AD tenant information is automatically replicated and synchronized to your onsite or Azure AD domains.

NTLM and Kerberos Authentication Support   Some applications, like Exchange, require Windows integrated authentication. Since Azure AD supports NTLM and Kerberos support, any service or application that needs to work with NTLM and Kerberos will work within the Azure AD domain.

LDAP Integration   Administrators have the ability to use any application, service, or LDAP security measure with Azure AD. LDAP is an industry standard and any LDAP-compatible application or feature can be integrated with your Azure AD network.

DNS Support   Administrators have the ability to set up, configure, and integrate DNS with their Azure network. DNS is a hostname resolution service and Azure allows administrators to easily configure DNS with many of the same DNS administration tools that they are currently familiar with.

Working with Organizational Units   Organizational Units (OUs) are Active Directory storage containers that administrators can use to manage users, computers, and groups accounts. One of the nice advantages of using OUs is the ability to set policies on each individual OU. So administrators have the ability to set different policies for different OUs and this gives an organization better control on how policies are administered.

High Availability   One of the most important requirements for any IT department is the ability to keep their network up and running. Some organizations require minimum downtime requirements. This means that your organization can only be down for a certain amount of time per year. Azure AD Domain Services offers an organization the ability to setup high availability for your Azure domains.

This feature guarantees higher service resiliency and uptime. With built-in health monitoring, Azure offers automatic failure recovery by spinning up a new instance to take over for any failed instances. This feature provides automatic and continued services for your organization's Azure network.

Management Tools Support   Administrators have the ability to use the same tools that they are familiar with for managing their current domains. The Active Directory Administrative Center and Active Directory PowerShell utilities can be used when managing their Azure AD domains.

Azure AD Questions and Answers

The following section is questions and answers about features and functionality of Azure Active Directory. The text was taken directly from Microsoft's website (`https://docs .microsoft.com/en-us/azure/active-directory-domain-services/active-directory -ds-faqs`). I recommend that you visit this page often for updates about features and Services.

Q. Can I create multiple managed domains for a single Azure AD directory?

Answer: No. You can only create a single managed domain serviced by Azure AD Domain Services for a single Azure AD directory.

Q. Can I enable Azure AD Domain Services in an Azure Resource Manager virtual network?

Answer: Yes. Azure AD Domain Services can be enabled in an Azure Resource Manager virtual network. Classic Azure virtual networks are no longer supported for creating new managed domains.

Q. Can I migrate my existing managed domain from a classic virtual network to a Resource Manager virtual network?

Answer: Not currently. Microsoft will deliver a mechanism to migrate your existing managed domain from a classic virtual network to a Resource Manager virtual network in the future.

Q. Can I enable Azure AD Domain Services in an Azure CSP (Cloud Solution Provider) subscription?

Answer: Yes. You can enable Azure AD Domain Services in Azure CSP subscriptions.

Q. Can I enable Azure AD Domain Services in a federated Azure AD directory? I do not synchronize password hashes to Azure AD. Can I enable Azure AD Domain Services for this directory?

Answer: No. Azure AD Domain Services needs access to the password hashes of user accounts, to authenticate users via NTLM or Kerberos. In a federated directory, password hashes are not stored in the Azure AD directory. Therefore, Azure AD Domain Services does not work with such Azure AD directories.

Q. Can I make Azure AD Domain Services available in multiple virtual networks within my subscription?

Answer: The service itself does not directly support this scenario. Your managed domain is available in only one virtual network at a time. However, you may configure connectivity between multiple virtual networks to expose Azure AD Domain Services to other virtual networks. See how you can connect virtual networks in Azure.

Q. Can I enable Azure AD Domain Services using PowerShell?

Answer: Yes. You can enable Azure AD Domain Services using PowerShell.

Q. Can I enable Azure AD Domain Services using a Resource Manager Template?

Answer: No, it is not currently possible to enable Azure AD Domain Services using a template. Instead use PowerShell to enable Azure AD Domain Services using PowerShell.

Q. Can I add domain controllers to an Azure AD Domain Services managed domain?

Answer: No. The domain provided by Azure AD Domain Services is a managed domain. You do not need to provision, configure, or otherwise manage domain controllers for this domain—these management activities are provided as a service by Microsoft. Therefore, you cannot add additional domain controllers (read-write or read-only) for the managed domain.

Q. Can guest users invited to my directory use Azure AD Domain Services?

Answer: No. Guest users invited to your Azure AD directory using the Azure AD B2B invite process are synchronized into your Azure AD Domain Services managed domain. However, passwords for these users are not stored in your Azure AD directory. Therefore, Azure AD Domain Services has no way to sync NTLM and Kerberos hashes for these users into your managed domain. As a result, such users cannot log in to the managed domain or join computers to the managed domain.

Q. Can I connect to the domain controller for my managed domain using Remote Desktop?

Answer: No. You do not have permissions to connect to domain controllers for the managed domain via Remote Desktop. Members of the AAD DC Administrators group can administer the managed domain using AD administration tools such as the Active Directory Administration Center (ADAC) or AD PowerShell. These tools are installed using the Remote Server Administration Tools feature on a Windows server joined to the managed domain.

Q. I've enabled Azure AD Domain Services. What user account do I use to domain-join machines to this domain?

Answer: Members of the administrative group AAD DC Administrators can domain-join machines. Additionally, members of this group are granted remote desktop access to machines that have been joined to the domain.

Q. Do I have domain administrator privileges for the managed domain provided by Azure AD Domain Services?

Answer: No. You are not granted administrative privileges on the managed domain. Both Domain Administrator and Enterprise Administrator privileges are not available for you to use within the domain. Members of the domain administrator or enterprise administrator groups in your on-premises Active Directory are also not granted domain/enterprise administrator privileges on the managed domain.

Q. Can I modify group memberships using LDAP or other AD administrative tools on managed domains?

Answer: No. Group memberships cannot be modified on domains serviced by Azure AD Domain Services. The same applies for user attributes. You may however change group memberships or user attributes either in Azure AD or on your on-premises domain. Such changes are automatically synchronized to Azure AD Domain Services.

Q. How long does it take for changes I make to my Azure AD directory to be visible in my managed domain?

Answer: Changes made in your Azure AD directory using either the Azure AD UI or PowerShell are synchronized to your managed domain. This synchronization process runs in the background. Once initial synchronization is complete, it typically takes about 20 minutes for changes made in Azure AD to be reflected in your managed domain.

Q. Can I extend the schema of the managed domain provided by Azure AD Domain Services?

Answer: No. The schema is administered by Microsoft for the managed domain. Schema extensions are not supported by Azure AD Domain Services.

Q. Can I modify or add DNS records in my managed domain?

Answer: Yes. Members of the AAD DC Administrators group are granted DNS Administrator privileges, to modify DNS records in the managed domain. They can use the DNS Manager console on a machine running Windows Server joined to the managed domain, to manage DNS. To use the DNS Manager console, install DNS Server Tools, which is part of the Remote Server Administration Tools optional feature on the server. More information on utilities for administering, monitoring and troubleshooting DNS is available on TechNet.

Q. What is the password lifetime policy on a managed domain?

Answer: The default password lifetime on an Azure AD Domain Services managed domain is 90 days. This password lifetime is not synchronized with the password lifetime configured in Azure AD. Therefore, you may have a situation where users' passwords expire in your managed domain, but are still valid in Azure AD. In such scenarios, users need to change their password in Azure AD and the new password will synchronize to your managed domain. Additionally, the password-does-not-expire and user-must-change-password-at-next-logon attributes for user accounts are not synchronized to your managed domain.

Q. Does Azure AD Domain Services provide AD account lockout protection?

Answer: Yes. Five invalid password attempts within 2 minutes on the managed domain cause a user account to be locked out for 30 minutes. After 30 minutes, the user account is automatically unlocked. Invalid password attempts on the managed domain do not lock out the user account in Azure AD. The user account is locked out only within your Azure AD Domain Services managed domain.

Q. Can I failover Azure AD Domain Services to another region for a DR event?

Answer: No. Azure AD Domain Services does not currently provide a geo-redundant deployment model. It is limited to a single virtual network in an Azure region. If you want to utilize multiple Azure regions, you need to run your Active Directory Domain Controllers on Azure IaaS VMs.

Q. Can I get Azure AD Domain Services as part of Enterprise Mobility Suite (EMS)? Do I need Azure AD Premium to use Azure AD Domain Services?

Answer: No. Azure AD Domain Services is a pay-as-you-go Azure service and is not part of EMS. Azure AD Domain Services can be used with all editions of Azure AD (Free, Basic, and, Premium). You are billed on an hourly basis, depending on usage.

Managing Azure AD

So now that we have looked at some of the features of Azure AD along with the common questions and answers about Azure AD, it's time to go through the Azure AD Dashboard. Figure 2.6 shows you the Azure AD Dashboard (you get to the Azure AD dashboard by clicking on Azure AD on the left side menu of the main dashboard). Let's take a look at some of the different options on the left side starting with Overview.

FIGURE 2.6   Viewing the Azure AD Dashboard

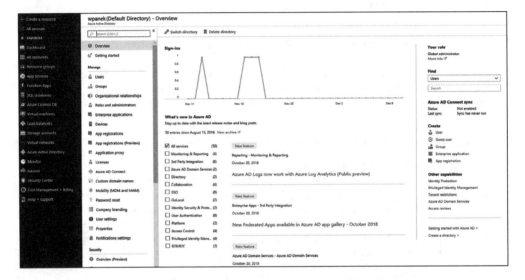

Overview

The Overview section of the Azure AD Dashboard is the figure you are looking at in Figure 2.6. The first thing you will notice in the center of the screen is the default Azure AD directory and the number of Sign-ins on Azure.

Below the Sign-ins section are all the different services that you have with Azure AD. You can click on the All services check box to see every service or you can click on an individual service and see the details of just those services on Azure AD.

On the right-hand side, you can see the role that your user is currently logged in as and you can also search for individual objects in the Find section.

Also, on the right-hand side you can add Users, Guest users, Groups, Enterprise applications, and App registrations. Below that you will see that you can access Other capabilities like Identity Protection, Privilege Identity Management, Tenant restrictions, Azure AD Domain Services, and Access reviews.

Below that section, you can view Getting started with Azure AD and you have the ability to Create a directory.

Getting Started

The Getting Started section (on the left side window under Overview) allows you to view videos and resources about how to accomplish tasks in Azure AD.

Users

The Users section (under Manage) on the left side allows you to view all of your current Azure AD user accounts (see Figure 2.7). Under the Users section, an administrator can also create New users, New guest users, Reset passwords, Delete users, Multi-Factor Authentication, Refresh your screen, or set up your columns.

FIGURE 2.7   Viewing User Section

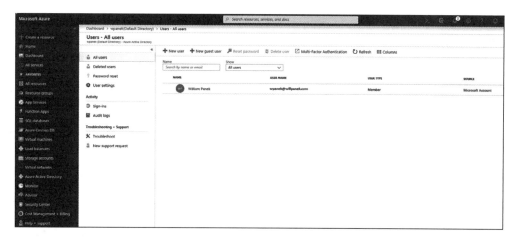

Another task that can be created in the User's section is the ability to manipulate the user's settings. The User Settings link allows you to setup how the user can launch and view applications, how the user can register applications, and if the user can access the Azure AD administration portal. Administrators can also manage External user and access panel control from the settings section.

The User section also allows administrators to see how often the user is logging into Azure (this allows you to perform an access review) and administrators can also get audit information about the user account. Finally, in the User section, you can also troubleshoot user issues and also open a support ticket with Microsoft for additional help.

Groups

The Groups section allows an administrator to create and manage groups (see Figure 2.8). In the Groups section, you can create new groups, manage group settings for all groups, manage group membership, and delete groups. Administrators can also do auditing on groups along with troubleshooting group issues or opening a support ticket with Microsoft for additional help.

FIGURE 2.8   Viewing Group Section

Organizational Relationships

The Organizational Relationships section allows you to work with user accounts from other organizations. The Organizational relationship section also allows you to invite users who already own an Azure Active Directory account or a Microsoft Account. If they have one of these account types already setup, they can automatically sign in without any further configuration from an Administrator.

In the Settings section of Organizational relationships (see Figure 2.9), Administrators can setup what guest accounts can do regarding Azure. For example, an Administrator can decide if guest user access is limited or if users can invite other users to use your organization's Azure network. Finally, you can setup Collaboration restrictions (which domains you can invite users from) for your guest user accounts.

FIGURE 2.9   Viewing the Settings Section of Organizational Relationships

The Lifecycle Management section of Organizational relationships also allows an Administrator to setup Terms of use agreements while also allowing Administrators to have auditing of their guest users. Finally, Administrators can troubleshoot issues or opening a support ticket with Microsoft for additional help.

Roles and Administrators

The Roles and Administrators section allows you to see all of the available Azure AD roles and what each role does. In Table 2.2, I will show you the different roles that are available and what each role does in Azure AD.

Azure AD Roles

When you are in the Azure AD Roles and Administrators section, you can click on any of these roles to see who currently has this role in your organization.

TABLE 2.2   Azure Roles

Role	Description of Role Permission
Application administrator	This role allows you to create and manage all aspects of app registrations and enterprise apps.
Application developer	This role allows you to create application registrations independent of the "Users can register applications" setting.
Billing administrator	This role allows you to perform common billing related tasks like updating payment information.
Cloud application administrator	This role allows you to create and manage all aspects of app registrations and enterprise apps except App Proxy.
Cloud device administrator	This role allows you to have full access to manage devices in Azure AD.
Compliance administrator	This role allows you to read and manage compliance configuration and reports in Azure AD and Office 365.
Conditional Access administrator	This role allows you to manage conditional access capabilities.
Customer LockBox access approver	This role allows you to approve Microsoft support requests to access customer organizational data.
Desktop Analytics administrator	This role allows you to access and manage Desktop management tools and services.

TABLE 2.2   Azure Roles *(continued)*

Role	Description of Role Permission
Dynamics 365 administrator	This role allows you to manage all aspects of the Dynamics 365 product.
Exchange administrator	This role allows you to manage all aspects of the Exchange product.
Global administrator	This role allows you to manage all aspects of Azure AD and Microsoft services that use Azure AD identities.
Guest inviter	This role allows you to invite guest users independent of the "members can invite guests" setting.
Information Protection administrator	This role allows you to manage all aspects of the Azure Information Protection product.
Intune administrator	This role allows you to manage all aspects of the Intune product.
License administrator	This role allows you to have the ability to assign, remove, and update license assignments.
Message center reader	This role allows you to read messages and updates for their organization in Office 365 Message Center only.
Password administrator	This role allows you to reset passwords for non-administrators and Helpdesk Administrators.
Power BI administrator	This role allows you to manage all aspects of the Power BI product.
Privileged role administrator	This role allows you to manage role assignments in Azure AD and all aspects of Privileged Identity Management.
Reports reader	This role allows you to read sign-in and audit reports.
Security administrator	This role allows you to read security information and reports and manage configuration in Azure AD and Office 365.
Security reader	This role allows you to read security information and reports in Azure AD and Office 365.
Service administrator	This role allows you to read service health information and manage support tickets.
SharePoint administrator	This role allows you to manage all aspects of the SharePoint service.

Role	Description of Role Permission
Skype for Business administrator	This role allows you to manage all aspects of the Skype for Business product.
Teams Communications Administrator	This role allows you to manage calling and meetings features within the Microsoft Teams service.
Teams Communications Support Engineer	This role allows you to troubleshoot communications issues within Teams using advanced tools.
Teams Communications Support Specialist	This role allows you to troubleshoot communications issues within Teams using basic tools.
Teams Service Administrator	This role allows you to manage the Microsoft Teams service.
User administrator	This role allows you to manage all aspects of users and groups, including resetting passwords for limited admins.

Enterprise applications

The Enterprise applications section allows an Administrator to view, setup, and configure your organization's Enterprise applications (see Figure 2.10). Administrators can also setup an Application proxy within the Enterprise Applications section. An Application proxy allows an Administrator to provide single sign-on (SSO) and secure remote access for web applications hosted on your on-premise network.

FIGURE 2.10   Viewing the Enterprise Applications Section

The Enterprise applications section also allows an Administrator to setup user settings for your Enterprise applications. These settings include users giving consent to applications accessing data on their company networks, users adding applications to their Access panel, and if users can only see Office 365 in the O365 portal.

The Enterprise applications section allows an Administrator to also setup Conditional access (setting up application policies), seeing who has logged into the applications, and auditing. Administrators can also troubleshoot application issues or opening a support ticket with Microsoft for additional help.

Application Menu Options

In the main Azure AD dashboard, there are three other menu options on the left hand side that have to do with Enterprise Applications. All three of these options (App registrations, App registrations (Preview), and Application Proxy) can be accessed in the Enterprise Applications section or directly using the Azure AD dashboard menu. Either link gets you to the same settings. Because of this, I will not add them below while explaining the Azure AD menu options.

Devices

The Devices section allows an Azure AD Administrator to setup which devices can access Azure AD. Administrators can also setup device settings and device roaming settings (Enterprise State Roaming). Finally, Administrators can do auditing and troubleshooting from the Device section.

Licenses

The Licenses section allows you to view purchased licensing for additional Azure AD components. If you purchase additional Azure AD components (for example: Azure Active Directory Premium P2 or Enterprise Mobility + Security E5), those additional components will show up in the Licenses section. You can also see if there are any licensing issues in this section.

The Licenses section also allows you to view additional components that are available and what those components do. Administrators can also view auditing and get troubleshooting from this section.

Azure AD Connect

Azure AD Connect (see Figure 2.11) allows an Administrator to integrate their Azure AD with your Windows Server AD or another directory on your network. One of the nice advantages of the Azure AD Connect section is that it allows an Administrator to download and install Azure AD Connect by using the Download link.

FIGURE 2.11   Viewing the Azure AD Connect Section

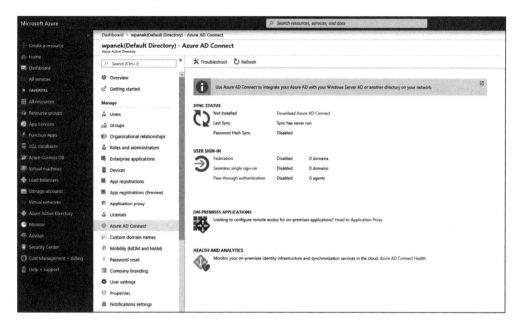

Azure AD Connect helps you integrate your on-premises Active Directory with Azure AD. This allows your users to be more productive by giving those users access to both cloud and on-premises resources by using a common user account for accessing both networks. By using Azure AD Connect, users and organizations can take advantage of the following features:

- Users can have a common hybrid identity that allows them to access on-site or cloud based services that use both Windows Server Active Directory and Azure Active Directory.

- Administrators have the ability to provide conditional access based on their device and user identity, network location, application resource, and multifactor authentication.

- Users can use this common identity in Azure AD, Office 365, Intune, SaaS apps, and third-party applications.

- Developers can create applications that use the common identity model thus integrating applications into on-site Active Directory or cloud based Azure applications.

To use Azure AD Connect, your on-site network must be using Windows Server 2008, Windows Server 2008 R2, Windows Server 2012, Windows Server 2012 R2, Windows Server 2016, and/or Windows Server 2019.

The Azure AD Connect section allows you to setup how your users will seamlessly pass through between both networks. Administrators can setup seamless connections by using a

Federation server (including Active Directory Federation Services (AD FS)), Seamless single sign-on, or Pass-through authentication.

Custom Domain Names

The Custom Domain Names section allows you to add and verify new domain names (see Figure 2.12). When you first build your Azure subscription, your new Azure AD tenant comes with an initial domain name (for example, willpanek.onmicrosoft.com).

FIGURE 2.12 Viewing the Custom Domain Names section

Administrators can't change or delete the initial domain name that is created, but they do have the ability to add their organization's domain names to the list of supported names. Adding custom domain names allows an administrator to create user names that are familiar to their users, such as wpanek@willpanek.com.

Mobility (MDM and MAM)

One feature that many organizations have started to implement is the ability for their employees to bring in their own devices to work (Bring Your Own Device, or BYOD). Because of this, Microsoft has tools like Mobile Device Management (MDM) and Mobile Application Management (MAM) to help IT administrators manage corporate data on personal devices.

Also, many organizations have started issuing devices like tablets to their employees, and many companies do not mind personal use of those devices. These are reasons Microsoft has implemented mobility tools into its Azure AD networks.

Windows 10 devices (either personal or corporate) have the ability to be connected to a corporate Azure AD network either by using the Windows 10 Settings app or through any of the Universal Windows Platform (UWP) apps.

Windows 10 Mobile Devices

When a user connects their personal device to a corporate network, the user should understand that corporate policies may affect their devices and settings.

Password Reset

The Password Reset section allows an administrator to determine if they want to enable self-service password reset (SSPR). If an organization decides to enable this feature, users will be able to reset their own passwords or unlock their accounts.

An administrator can allow all accounts to use SSPR (see Figure 2.13) or they can just choose certain groups that will have the ability to do SSPR.

FIGURE 2.13   Setting the self-service password reset

In the Password Reset section, administrators can also choose to use authentication methods. Authentication methods allow an organization to verify that the user is who they say they are. Methods for this include verification by mobile app notification, mobile app code, email, mobile phone, office phone, or security question. Administrators can choose between a single verification or multiple verifications.

Administrators can also require registrations when a user logs into Azure AD and can also set up password resets so that the user is notified if their password changes. Administrators can also choose to be notified when administrator passwords are reset.

Also, in the Password Reset section, admins can choose to enable a custom helpdesk link for users and finally you can configure password changes to be replicated back to an Active Directory network. Administrators can perform auditing and troubleshooting from the Password Reset section.

Company Branding

The Company Branding section allows an organization to set up custom text and graphics that your users will see when they sign in to Azure Active Directory.

Properties

The Properties section allows an Azure AD administrator to change the Default Directory properties. These settings include the Default Directory name, language, technical contact email, global privacy contact, privacy statement URL, and access management person for Azure.

Notifications Settings

The Notifications settings section (see Figure 2.14) allows an administrator to set up how often and what types of notifications they should receive. The Notifications settings section allows you to choose if you receive emails for Weekly status and educational content, service notifications, new features availability, and product research. Administrators also have the ability to set the Administrator email in the Notifications settings section.

FIGURE 2.14 Configuring the notifications settings

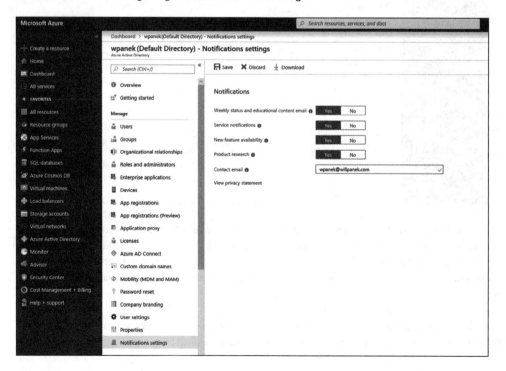

Security Overview (Preview)

The Overview (Preview) section (under the Security header on left side) allows an administrator to view an Overview of your security policies and security issues. Security is a big part of Azure AD because unlike an On-site network, the Azure AD network can be accessed from anywhere in the world. So making sure your Azure AD security is strong is a very important task for any Azure Administrator.

The Overview (Preview) allows an Administrator to view if there are any risky user accounts (deemed by Microsoft), configured user risk policies, new risky sign-ins, and sign-in risk remediation policies.

Identity Secure Score (Preview)

The Identity Secure Score section allows an Administrator to view their Azure AD Identity Secure Score. The Identity Secure Score is an indicator for how aligned Azure AD is with Microsoft's best practices recommendations for your organization's security setup.

The Identity Secure Score is an integer number between 1 and 248. The higher the number, the better your security settings align with Microsoft's recommendations. The score helps an organization objectively measure their identity security position, plan for identity security improvements, and review the successful implementation of your organization's improvements.

On this Identity Secure Score dashboard, an organization will be able to view your organization's score, comparison graph, trend graph, and a list of identity security best practices.

So the way this works is that Azure views your security configuration every 48 hours. Its then takes what it sees and compares your organization's settings against Microsoft's best practices. Based on that evaluation, your organization's security score is calculated. Based on that security score, an administrator can adjust their security settings and policies to make improvements.

Conditional Access

The Conditional Access section (see Figure 2.15) allows an Azure AD Administrator to set security policies. When it comes to Azure, one of the biggest concerns for organizations is cloud based security. Azure allows users to access their networks from anywhere in the world and from almost any device. Because of this, just securing resource access is not enough. This is where Conditional Access Policies come into play.

Conditional Access policies allow an organization to set how resources are accessed using access control decisions (who have access to resources) through Azure AD. Setting up Conditional Access policies allows an organization to have automated access control decisions based on the policies that your organization sets. Some of the situations that Conditional Access policies can help with are sign-in risk, network location risk, device management, and client applications.

FIGURE 2.15   Conditional Access Policies section

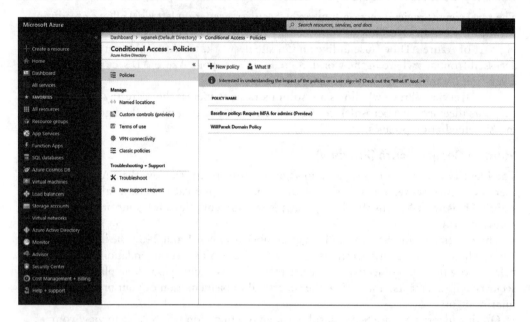

Configuring Objects

Now that we have looked at some of the different sections within Azure AD, let's look at how to create objects like users and groups.

User accounts allow employees to log into the Azure network. In Exercise 2.2, I will show you how to create a user account in Azure AD.

EXERCISE 2.2

Creating an Azure AD User Account

1. Log into the Azure portal at https://azure.microsoft.com.

2. Click on the Azure Active Directory link.

3. Under Manage, click the Users link.

4. Click the link +New User.

5. Type in the name of your user and a username. For this lab, I used George Washington as my user's name and GWashington@wpanek.onmicrosoft.com as the username (see Figure 2.16).

6. Click on Profile and put in the user's name and job information. Click the OK button when done filling in the profile information.

7. We are not going to add this user to a group yet. Make sure the Directory role is set to User.

FIGURE 2.16   New User information

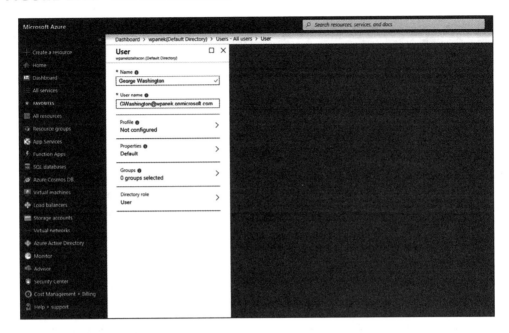

8. You can click on the Show Password box to see the temporary password assigned. Then click the Create button.

9. You should now see your user account (see Figure 2.17). If you would like to change any user information, double click on the user account and make changes. Be sure to save any changes that are made.

FIGURE 2.17   New User Created

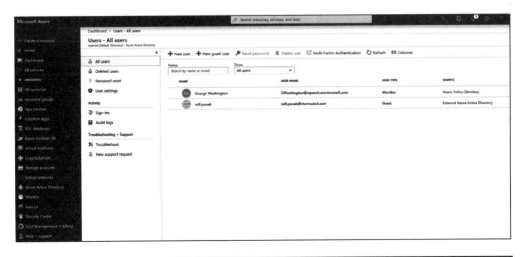

In Exercise 2.3, I will show you how to create a group in Azure AD.

EXERCISE 2.3

Creating an Azure AD Group Account

1. Log into the Azure portal at https://azure.microsoft.com.

2. Click on the Azure Active Directory link.

3. Under Manage, click the Groups link.

4. Click on the link +New Group.

5. Under the Group Type pull down, choose Security. Security groups are the group type you use when you want the group to be assigned to resources. Office 365 groups allow users to collaborate with other users by giving them access to a shared mailbox, calendar, files, SharePoint site, and more.

6. In the Group Name box, type the name of your group. I used Marketing for my group name.

7. In the Group Description field, type a description for your group.

8. In the Membership Type pull down, choose Assigned. Assigned groups allow an administrator to add specific users to be members of the group and to have unique permissions. Dynamic user groups allow an administrator to use dynamic group rules to automatically add and remove members. Dynamic device groups allow an administrator to use dynamic group rules to automatically add and remove devices.

9. Click the Create button.

Self-Service Password Reset

As stated earlier, the Password Reset section allows an Administrator to determine if they want to enable Self-service password resets (SSPR). If an organization decides to enable this feature, users will be able to reset their own passwords or unlock their accounts.

An Administrator can allow all accounts to use the SSPR or they can just choose certain groups that will have the ability to do SSPR. To setup SSPR, the following Prerequisites must be met:

- An Azure AD tenant subscription with the minimum of at least one trial license enabled.

- Global Administrator account that can be used to enable SSPR.

- A non-administrator test account with a password that you know.

- A pilot group account to test with the non-administrator test account (the user account needs to be a member of this group).

In Exercise 2.4, I will show you how to setup the Self-Service Password Reset option in Azure Active Directory. To complete this exercise, you must have created a user and group in Exercise 3.2 and Exercise 3.3.

EXERCISE 2.4

Setting Up Self-Service Password Reset

1. From your existing Azure AD tenant, click the Azure Active Directory.

2. Select Password Reset.

3. From the Properties page, under the option Self Service Password Reset Enabled, choose the Selected option (see Figure 2.18).

FIGURE 2.18   Choosing the Selected option

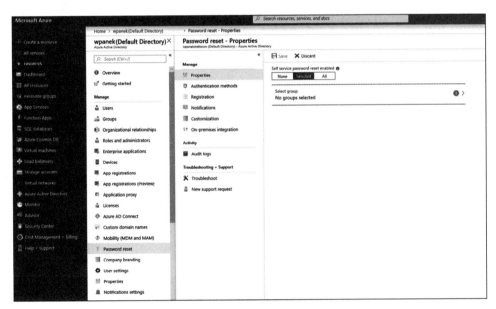

4. From Select group, choose your pilot group.

5. Click Save.

6. From the Authentication methods page, make the following choices and then click Save:

   Number of methods required to reset: 1

   Methods available to users:

   Mobile phone

   Office phone

EXERCISE 2.4 *(continued)*

7. From the Registration page, make the following choices:

   Require users to register when they sign in: Yes

   Set the number of days before users are asked to
   reconfirm their authentication information: 365

In Exercise 2.5, I will show you how to test the Self-Service Password Reset option. For this exercise to be completed, you must have completed the previous exercise (Exercise 2.4). This test must be done with a normal user account. You can't run this test using an administrator account.

EXERCISE 2.5

Testing the Self-Service Password Reset

1. Open a new browser window in InPrivate or incognito mode, and browse to `https://aka.ms/ssprsetup`.

2. Sign in with a non-administrator test user, and register your authentication phone.

3. Once complete, click the button marked Looks Good and close the browser window.

4. Open a new browser window in InPrivate or incognito mode, and browse to `https://aka.ms/sspr`.

5. Enter your non-administrator test user's user ID, the characters from the CAPTCHA, and then click Next.

6. Follow the verification steps to reset your password.

Configuring Azure AD Identity Protection

One feature that can help any organization protect themselves is to add and configure Azure AD Identity Protection. Azure Active Directory Identity Protection is a feature of the Azure AD Premium P2 edition. Azure AD Identity Protection allows an organization to:

- Identify possible vulnerabilities that can affect your organization's identities
- Setup automated reactions to detected suspicious actions
- Identify suspicious events and take proper action to resolve those events

Azure AD Identity Protection allows an Azure Administrator to use the same type of protection that Microsoft uses to protect and secure users' identities.

One of the most common security breaches that hackers use to gain access to an organization is by stealing and using a current user's identity. In recent years, hackers have used more effective ways of stealing user data by using common attacks like phishing for data and hacking into third party organizations.

For an organization, detecting a compromised user account is no easy task. Azure AD helps an organization by using an adaptive learning algorithm and heuristics to determine irregularities and suspicious events. Once these events are recognized, Identity Protection produces a report and generates an alert that allows an Azure Administrator to view the issues and take appropriate actions to stop the attack.

There are advantages of using Identity Protection because Identity Protection is more than just a monitoring and reporting utility. Identity Protection allows an Azure Administrator to create policies that automatically detect and respond to events that meet a specific risk level. These policies can automatically stop the hack by blocking the user account and require that the user's password gets reset. During the password reset, multi-factor user authentication is then enforced.

To use Azure AD Identity Protection, an organization needs to add the service to their Azure subscription. In Exercise 2.6, I will show you how to add Azure AD Identity Protection.

EXERCISE 2.6

Adding Azure AD Identity Protection

1. Log into the Azure portal at https://azure.microsoft.com.

2. Click Marketplace.

3. Click Identity.

4. Click on Azure AD Identity Protection (see Figure 2.19).

FIGURE 2.19   Choosing Azure AD Identity Protection

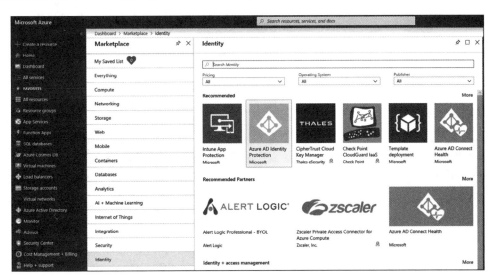

5. When the Azure AD Identity Protection information page appears, click the Create button.

6. If a page appears showing that the Directory is Default Directory, you can choose a different directory you want this added to and then click Create. If the default directory is fine, don't click Create.

7. You should see a message (see Figure 2.20) that states that the Default Directory is protected. Click on that message to open the Azure AD Identity Protection dashboard. If this message does not appear, click the Create button and then click Azure Active Directory on left side. On the right side under Your Role, you should see a section called Other Capabilities. Click Identity Protection to see this message. This is also how you can access the Identity Protection dashboard later.

FIGURE 2.20   Clicking the message to open the Identity Protection Dashboard

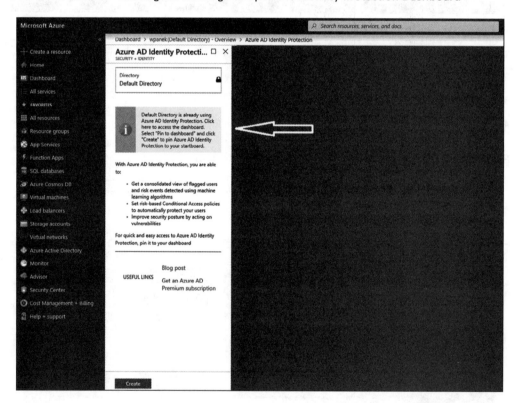

8. At this point, you should be seeing the Azure AD Identity Protection dashboard (as seen in Figure 2.21). Take a few minutes and look at the different sections within the

dashboard. Under the Investigation section, click on Users Flagged For Risk, Risk Events, and Vulnerabilities.

FIGURE 2.21   Identity Protection Dashboard

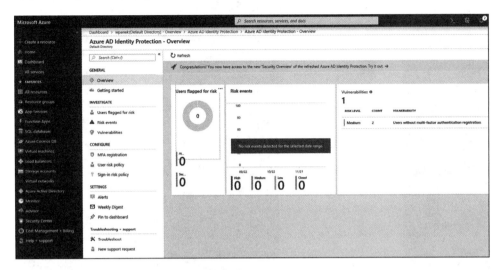

9. Under the Configure section, click User Risk Policy.

10. Under Users, make sure all users are selected.

11. Click Set Condition. Under User Risk, choose Select A Risk Level. Choose Medium And Above. Click the Select button. Choose the Done button.

12. Under Controls, select Choose Select a control. Under Select The Controls To Be Enforced, choose Allow Access and make sure the check box for Require Password Change is selected. Click the Select button.

13. Under Enforce Policy, choose On if you want to enforce this policy. If you do not want this policy to go live, do not choose On.

14. Click the Save button.

15. You can also set a sign-in risk policy by clicking on Sign-in Risk Policy. Under Users, choose All Users. Under Conditions, choose Medium And Above. Under Controls, Access, make sure you choose Allow Access and choose the Require Multi-factor Authentication check box. Choose either On or Off for Enforce Policy (choose Off if you just want to see how the policy is created) and then click the Save button.

16. Under Settings, click Alerts. Choose the level of risk you want to set. For this lab, I am choosing Medium. Click the link under Emails Are Sent To The Following Users and choose who the alerts should be sent to. Click the Add button and choose an email address. Then click the Done button (as seen in Figure 2.22). Click the Save button.

FIGURE 2.22   Setting an email for alerts

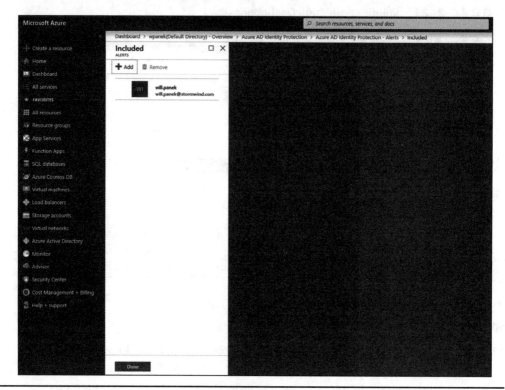

Managing Hybrid Networks

One nice feature of using both an on-site and Azure network is that Microsoft has many different tools to help you connect both networks. Connecting both networks is important so that users can seamlessly move between the two networks.

Microsoft's identity solutions extend your organization's on-site network with the Azure network features. These solutions create a common user identity for authentication and authorization to all resources. The advantage is that the users can access these resources no matter where they reside. This is what Microsoft refers to as *hybrid identity*.

To properly set up your hybrid identity, one of the following authentication methods can be used. Which one you decide to use is all depended on your environment scenario. The three available methods are:

▪   Password hash synchronization (PHS)

▪   Pass-through Authentication (PTA)

▪   Federation

So, what is the real advantage of setting up both networks using one of these methods? When you choose one of the authentication methods, you are providing your users with *Single Sign-On (SSO)* capabilities. Single sign-on allows your users to sign in once but have access to resources on both networks. This is what gives your users seamless access to all resources. So let's take a look at some of the available Identity solutions.

Password Hash Synchronization with Azure AD

One of the hybrid identity sign-in methods that you can use is called *Password hash synchronization*. Azure AD and your on-site Active Directory synchronize with each other by using a hash value. The hash value is created based on the user's password. This way the two systems can stay in sync with each other. Azure AD Connect is also required for this setup to function properly.

Password hash synchronization is a feature that is part of the Azure AD Connect sync and it allows you to log into Azure AD applications like O365. The advantage is that your users log into their account using their on-site username and password. This helps users because it reduces the number of username and passwords that they need to know.

Another advantage to your organization is that they can use password hash synchronization as a backup sign-on method if your organization decides to use Federation services with Active Directory Federation Services (AD FS). To setup password hash synchronization, your environment needs to implement the following:

- Azure AD Connect.
- Directory synchronization between your on-site Active Directory and your Azure AD instance.
- Have password hash synchronization enabled.

Azure Active Directory Pass-through Authentication

Another option for allowing your users to sign in to both on-site and cloud based applications using the same passwords is *Azure AD Pass-through Authentication*. Organizations can use Azure AD Pass-through Authentication instead of using Azure AD Password Hash Synchronization. The organizational benefits for using Azure AD Pass-through Authentication is the ability to enforce on-site Active Directory security and password policies.

Azure AD Pass-through Authentication utilizes an agent installed onto an on-premise server. This allows Azure Active Directory to validate the username and password directly on one of the on-premise Active Directory Domain Controllers.

This will help your organization with costs because your IT support desk will not be inundated by user's calls trying to remember their different passwords. This will help lower your IT department budget for total cost of ownership (TCO). Less calls to support means less support people needed. Some of the key benefits to using Azure AD Pass-through Authentication are as follows:

- Better User Experience
  - Users can use the same account password to sign into both your Azure AD and On-Site AD networks.

- Users don't need to talk to IT as often to reset passwords for multiple accounts.
- Azure AD allows your users to do their own password management using the Self-Service Password Management tools.

- Easy Deployment
  - There is no need to deploy a large infrastructure on-site. Azure AD network can handle most of your networking services.
  - Less budgeting needed for on-site IT departments. Since your Azure AD and your on-site AD can easily integrate with each other, there is no need for large IT departments on-site.

- Security
  - One nice advantage is that on-site passwords will never be stored in the Azure cloud.
  - Users' accounts are protected using Azure AD Conditional Access policies. These policies include Multi-Factor Authentication (MFA), filtering for brute force password attacks, and stopping legacy authentication.
  - The Azure agent will only allow outbound connections from within your network. The advantage of this means that you are not required to load an agent on your perimeter network.
  - With the use of certificate-based authentication, organizations get secure connections between the Azure agent and Azure AD.

- Highly Available
  - By installing additional Azure agents onto on-site servers, you can get high availability of Azure sign-in requests.

Federation with Azure AD

To understand what Federation can do for your organization, you must first understand Trusts. Federation, along with Active Directory Federation Services (AD FS), are just Trusts on steroids. Understanding what a Trust can do for your organization will help you understand why we use Federation services.

Understanding Trusts

Trust relationships make it easier to share security information and network resources between domains. As was already mentioned, standard transitive two-way trusts are automatically created between the domains in a tree and between each of the trees in a forest. Figure 2.23 shows an example of the default trust relationships in an Active Directory forest.

FIGURE 2.23   Default trusts in an Active Directory forest

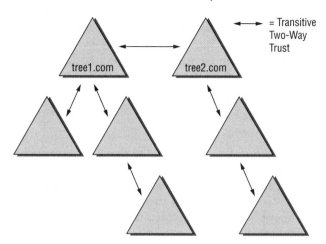

When configuring trusts, you need to consider two main characteristics:

Transitive Trusts   By default, Active Directory trusts are *transitive trusts*. The simplest way to understand transitive relationships is through this example: if Domain A trusts Domain B and Domain B trusts Domain C, then Domain A implicitly trusts Domain C. If you need to apply a tighter level of security, trusts can be configured as intransitive.

One-Way vs. Two-Way   Trusts can be configured as one-way or two-way relationships. The default operation is to create *two-way trusts* or *bidirectional trusts*. This makes it easier to manage trust relationships by reducing the trusts you must create. In some cases, however, you might decide against two-way trusts. In one-way relationships, the trusting domain allows resources to be shared with the trusted domain but not the other way around.

When domains are added together to form trees and forests, an automatic transitive two-way trust is created between them. Although the default trust relationships work well for most organizations, there are some reasons you might want to manage trusts manually:

- You may want to remove trusts between domains if you are absolutely sure you do not want resources to be shared between domains.

- Because of security concerns, you may need to keep resources isolated.

In addition to the default trust types, you can configure the following types of special trusts:

External Trusts   You use *external trusts* to provide access to resources on a Windows NT 4 domain or forest that cannot use a forest trust. Windows NT 4 domains cannot benefit from the other trust types that are used in Windows Server 2016. Thus, in some cases, external trusts could be your only option. External trusts are always nontransitive, but they can be established in a one-way or two-way configuration.

Default SID Filtering on External Trusts   When you set up an external trust, remember that it is possible for hackers to compromise a domain controller in a trusted domain. If this trust is compromised, a hacker can use the security identifier (SID) history attribute to associate SIDs with new user accounts, granting themselves unauthorized rights (this is called an *elevation-of-privileges attack*). To help prevent this type of attack, Windows Server 2016 automatically enables SID filter quarantining on all external trusts. SID filtering allows the domain controllers in the trusting domain (the domain with the resources) to remove all SID history attributes that are not members of the trusted domain.

Realm Trusts   *Realm trusts* are similar to external trusts. You use them to connect to a non-Windows domain that uses Kerberos authentication. Realm trusts can be transitive or nontransitive, one-way or two-way.

Cross-Forest Trusts   *Cross-forest trusts* are used to share resources between forests. They have been used since Windows Server 2000 domains and cannot be nontransitive, but you can establish them in a one-way or a two-way configuration. Authentication requests in either forest can reach the other forest in a two-way cross-forest trust. If you want one forest to trust another forest, you must set it (at a minimum) to at least the forest function level of Windows Server 2003.

Selective Authentication vs. Forest-wide Authentication   Forest-wide authentication on a forest trust means that users of the trusted forest can access all of the resources of the trusting forest. Selective authentication means that users cannot authenticate to a domain controller or resource server in the trusting forest unless they are explicitly allowed to do so.

Shortcut Trusts   In some cases, you may actually want to create direct trusts between two domains that implicitly trust each other. Such a trust is sometimes referred to as a *shortcut trust*, and it can improve the speed at which resources are accessed across many different domains. Let's say you have a forest, as shown in Figure 2.24.

FIGURE 2.24   Example of a forest

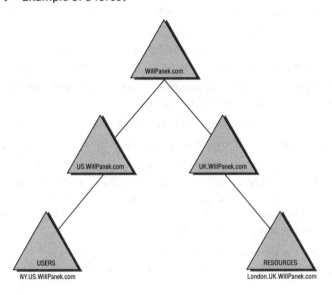

Users in the NY.us.WillPanek.com domain can access resources in the London.uk .WillPanek.com domain, but the users have to authenticate using the parent domains to gain access (NY.us.WillPanek.com to us.WillPanek.com to WillPanek.com to uk.WillPanek .com to finally reach London.uk.WillPanek.com). This process can be slow. An administrator can set up a one-way trust from London.uk.WillPanek.com (trusting domain) to NY.us.WillPanek.com (trusted domain) so that the users can access the resources directly.

> Perhaps the most important aspect to remember regarding trusts is that creating them only *allows* you to share resources between domains. The trust does not grant any permissions between domains by itself. Once a trust has been established, however, system administrators can easily assign the necessary permissions.

Understanding Federation

So now that you understand trusts, it's easier to understand Federation services because Federation is just a group of domains that have an established trust. These domains can be between sites or between separate organizations.

Remember, even though it's your company on Azure, Azure is owned by Microsoft. So you are technically setting up a trust between your company and Microsoft's network (onmicrosoft.com).

When setting up Federation, the trust level can be set to whatever the organization needs for their users. You do not need to just give open access to everyone. Also, Federation is just the mechanism to allow access across the trust. You still need to setup user's permissions to your resources.

When you setup authentication and authorization, using Federation, between your on-site network and Azure AD, all user authentications happen on-site. This allows an organization to have better levels of access control.

Federation services use claims that are passed to the application (resource) from the user domain after the user has initially authenticated. The username and password are never passed. Instead the application (resource) trusts the organization and this authenticates the user's claims.

Common Identity Scenarios

Table 2.3 was taken directly from Microsoft's website and it shows some of the common hybrid identity and access management scenarios along with Microsoft's recommendations as to which hybrid identity option would be suitable for each.

Understanding the Identity Table

In the following table, the three headers are abbreviated. Column 2, PHS and SSO, stands for Password hash synchronization with single sign-on. Column 3, PTA and SSO, stands for Pass-through authentication and single sign-on. Finally, Column 4 stands for Federated single sign-on using Active Directory Federation Services.

TABLE 2.3   Common Identity Scenarios and Recommendations

Scenario	PHS and SSO	PTA and SSO	AD FS
Sync new user, contact, and group accounts created in my on-premises Active Directory to the cloud automatically.	X	X	X
Set up my tenant for Office 365 hybrid scenarios.	X	X	X
Enable my users to sign in and access cloud services using their on-premises password.	X	X	X
Implement single sign-on using corporate credentials.	X	X	X
Ensure no password hashes are stored in the cloud.		X	X
Enable cloud multi-factor authentication solutions.		X	X
Enable on-premises multi-factor authentication solutions.			X
Support smartcard authentication for my users.			X
Display password expiry notifications in the Office portal and on the Windows 10 Desktop.			X

Azure AD Connect

Once you decide that you want your on-site network to be integrated with Azure AD, you need to install a component that allows both versions of Active Directory to work together. That component is called Azure AD Connect.

Azure AD Connect is a Microsoft utility that allows you to setup a hybrid design between Azure AD and your on-site AD. It provides some of the following features:

▪ Password hash synchronization

▪ Pass-through Authentication

- Federation integration
- Synchronization
- Health Monitoring

Azure AD Connect Health Monitoring

Azure AD Connect Health Monitoring is a way that an administrator can monitor their on-site identity infrastructure and maintain a constant connection to all of your Azure services.

To access the Azure AD Connect Health information, an administrator would need to connect to the Azure AD Connect Health portal. The portal can be used to view alerts, usage information, performance monitoring, and other key information. The Azure AD Connect Health portal gives you a one stop shop for all of your Azure AD Connect monitoring.

Installing Azure AD Connect

Before you can install Azure AD Connect, you need to make sure that your infrastructure and your Azure network have some prerequisites setup. The following is a list of requirements for installing Azure AD Connect:

- Azure AD
- On-site Active Directory
- Azure AD Connect server
- SQL Server database used by Azure AD Connect
- Azure AD Global Administrator account
- Enterprise Administrator account
- Connectivity between networks
- PowerShell and .Net Framework setup
- Enabled TLS 1.2 for Azure AD Connect

In Exercise 2.7, I will show you how to download and install Azure AD connect. To complete this exercise, you must have an on-site version of AD that can be connected to Azure.

EXERCISE 2.7

Installing Azure AD Connect

1. Log into the Azure portal at https://azure.microsoft.com.

2. Click on Azure Active Directory.

3. Click on Azure AD Connect.

4. Click the Download Azure AD Connect link.

5. Click on the Download button.

6. When the download box appears, choose to download the AzureADConnect.msi file to a network location. Once the download is complete, close the download box.

7. Log into the server (where you wish to install Azure AD Connect) as the local administrator.

8. Navigate to the AzureADConnect.msi file and double-click on the file to start the install.

9. On the Welcome screen, select the box to agree to the license terms and then click Continue.

10. On the Express Settings page, click Use Express Settings.

11. On the Connect To Azure AD page, enter the Azure Global administrator's username and password and then click Next.

12. The Connect To AD DS page will appear. Enter the username and password for an onsite enterprise admin and then click Next.

13. The Azure AD sign-in configuration page will appear. Review every domain marked Not Added and Not Verified. Make sure domains are verified in Azure AD. Once the domains are verified in Azure, click the Refresh symbol. If you need to verify your domains, go into Azure Active Directory, and then select Custom Domain Names. Enter the domain names for your onsite domain.

14. On the Ready to configure page, click Install.

15. When the installation completes, click Exit.

16. After the installation has completed, you will need to sign off and sign in again before you can use or set up any other services.

Azure VPN Gateway

As I have stated throughout this book, most (if not all) companies will have both an on-site network and an Azure network. Because of this, you will need to know how to connect both networks together. This is where you would use a Site-to-Site VPN (virtual private network) gateway connection.

Site-to-Site VPN gateway connections allow you to connect both networks together over a secure IPsec/IKE (Internet Key Exchange) VPN tunnel. To make this type of connection between networks, you need to have a VPN device located on-site. This VPN device will require a public IP address on the external side (the side facing the Internet) of the device.

To use a Site-to-Site VPN connection, you must meet the following requirements:

- Compatible VPN device with an administrator who can configure the device.

- An external public IP address for that VPN device.

- Knowledge of your on-site IP configuration and subnetting. None of your on-site IP subnets can overlap your Azure virtual network subnets.

Example Values for Site-to-Site VPN Connection

To help IT people better understand and configure Site-to-Site VPN connections, Microsoft released example values on their website. These example values can be used to setup a test environment or they can be used to help you better understand what values are needed to setup a Site-to-Site VPN connection.

Site-to-Site VPN Connection Examples
The following examples were taken directly from Microsoft's website, `https://docs.microsoft.com/en-us/azure/vpn-gateway/vpn-gateway-howto-site-to-site-resource-manager-portal`:

- VNet Name: TestVNet1

- Address Space: 10.1.0.0/16

- Subscription: The subscription you want to use

- Resource Group: TestRG1

- Location: East US

- Subnet: FrontEnd: 10.1.0.0/24, BackEnd: 10.1.1.0/24 (optional for this exercise)

- Gateway Subnet name: GatewaySubnet (this will auto-fill in the portal)

- Gateway Subnet address range: 10.1.255.0/27

- DNS Server: 8.8.8.8—Optional. The IP address of your DNS server.

- Virtual Network Gateway Name: VNet1GW

- Public IP: VNet1GWIP

- VPN Type: Route-based

- Connection Type: Site-to-site (IPsec)

- Gateway Type: VPN

- Local Network Gateway Name: Site1

- Connection Name: VNet1toSite1

- Shared Key: For this example, we use abc123. But you can use whatever is compatible with your VPN hardware. The important thing is that the values match on both sides of the connection.

Creating the VPN Gateway

Now that you have an understanding of why you would need a VPN gateway, let's look at what it takes to create a VPN gateway. Since every VPN device is different, I will show you how to create the actual Site-to-Site VPN connection in Exercise 2.8. You need to have someone create the connection on the VPN device.

EXERCISE 2.8

Creating the Site-to-Site VPN Connection

1. Log into the Azure portal at `https://azure.microsoft.com`.

2. On the left side of the portal page, click + Create A Resource and then type **Virtual Network Gateway** in the search box. In the Results section, click Virtual Network Gateway (as seen in Figure 2.25).

FIGURE 2.25 Choosing Virtual Network Gateway

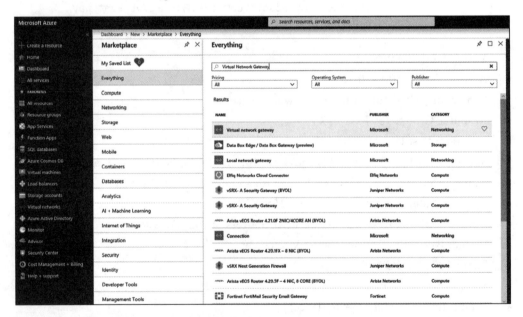

3. On the Virtual Network Gateway page, click the Create button.

4. On the Create Virtual Network Gateway page, enter the values for your virtual network gateway settings.

   - **Name:** This is the name of your gateway object.

   - **Gateway Type:** Select VPN. VPN gateways use the VPN type.

   - **VPN Type:** Choose the VPN type that fits your configuration. Route-based VPNs are the most common type.

- **SKU**: Select your gateway SKU. This will depend on the VPN type you select.

- **Enable Active-Active Mode**: If you are creating an active-active gateway configuration, choose this check box. If you are not creating an active-active gateway configuration, leave this check box unselected.

- **Location**: Choose your appropriate geographical location.

- **Virtual Network**: Choose the virtual network you want for this gateway.

- **Gateway Subnet Address Range**: This setting will only be seen if you did not already create a gateway subnet for your virtual network. If you did create a valid gateway subnet, this setting will not appear.

- **Public IP Address**: This setting specifies the public IP address that gets associated to the VPN gateway. Make sure Create New is the selected radio button and type a name for your public IP address.

- Unless your configuration specifically requires BGP ASN, leave this configuration's check box unchecked. If BGP ASN is required, the default setting for ASN is 65515. You can change this if needed.

5. Click Create. The settings will be validated and you'll see the "Deploying Virtual network gateway" message on the dashboard. This can take up to 45 minutes. Refresh your portal page to see the current status.

Creating the Local Network Gateway

The next step that we must complete is creating the local network gateway. The local network gateway refers to your on-site network. What you need to do is give your on-site network a name that Azure can use to access that network.

After you name the on-site network on Azure, you then need to tell Azure what IP address that it needs to use to access the on-site VPN device. You also need to specify the IP address prefix (that is located on your on-site location) that will be used to route traffic through the VPN gateway and to the VPN device.

In Exercise 2.9, I will show you how to setup the local network gateway. To complete this exercise, you need to know the IP address information for your on-site test or live network.

EXERCISE 2.9

Creating the Local Network Gateway

1. Log into the Azure portal https://azure.microsoft.com.

2. On the left side of the portal page, click the + Create A Resource and then type **Local network gateway** in the search box. In the Results section, click Local network gateway (as seen in Figure 2.26).

FIGURE 2.26 Choosing a Local network gateway

3. On the Local network gateway page, click the Create button.

4. On the Create Local Network Gateway page, enter the values for your local network gateway settings.

   - **Name**: Specify the name of your local network gateway.

   - **IP address**: This is the public IP address of the VPN device.

   - **Address Space**: This is the IP address ranges for the local network.

   - **Configure BGP settings**: Use this setting when configuring BGP. Otherwise, don't check this checkbox.

   - **Subscription**: Verify your current Azure subscription is showing.

   - **Resource Group**: You can create a new resource group or choose one that you have already created.

   - **Location**: Choose your appropriate geographical location.

5. Click the Create button.

Once you have finished creating the VPN connection, you will need to configure the company's VPN device. As stated above, Site-to-Site connections require a VPN device. Once the VPN device is configured properly, your Site-to-Site communications are completed.

Understanding ExpressRoute

ExpressRoute allows you to setup another way to connect your two networks. ExpressRoute allows you to connect your internal network to your external network using a private connection provided by your connection provider. Using ExpressRoute allows you to connect your internal network with any or all of the different Microsoft networks including Azure, Office 365, and Dynamics 365.

Since the connection is through your connection provider and not the internet, ExpressRoute is a much faster, more reliable, better security, and lower latencies connection over the Internet.

Implementing Active Directory Federation Services

Active Directory Federation Services (AD FS) demands a great deal of preparation and planning to ensure a successful implementation. The type of certificate authority used to sign the AD FS server's certificate must be planned. The SSL encryption level must be negotiated with the partnering organization. For instance, how much Active Directory information should be shared with the partnering organization? What should the DNS structure look like to support federation communications? You must explore all of these questions before implementing AD FS. In the following sections, I will discuss how to deploy AD FS and the configurations used to set up a federated partnership between your on-site network and Azure AD.

What Is a Claim?

A *claim* is an identifiable element (email address, username, password, and so on) that a trusted source asserts about an identity, such as, for example, the SID of a user or computer. An identity can contain more than one claim, and any combination of those claims can be used to authorize access to resources.

Windows Server extends the authorization identity beyond using the SID for identity and enables administrators to configure authorization based on claims published in Active Directory.

Today, the claims-based identity model brings us to cloud-based authentication. One analogy to the claim-based model is the old airport check-in procedure:

1. You first check in at the ticket counter.

2. You present a suitable form of ID (driver's license, passport, credit card, and so on). After verifying that your picture ID matches your face (authentication), the agent pulls up your flight information and verifies that you've paid for a ticket (authorization).

3. You receive a boarding pass (token). The boarding pass lets the gate agents know your name and frequent flyer number (authentication and personalization), your flight number and seating priority (authorization), and more. The boarding pass has bar-code information (certificate) with a boarding serial number proving that the boarding pass was issued by the airline and not a (self-signed) forgery.

Active Directory Federation Services is Microsoft's claims-based identity solution, providing browser-based clients (internal or external to your network) with transparent access to one or more protected Internet-facing applications.

When an application is hosted in a different network than the user accounts, users are occasionally prompted for secondary credentials when they attempt to access the application. These secondary credentials represent the identity of the users in the domain where the application is hosted. The web server hosting the application usually requires these credentials to make the most proper authorization decision.

AD FS makes secondary accounts and their credentials unnecessary by providing trust relationships that send a user's digital identity and access rights to trusted partners. In a federated environment, each organization continues to manage its own identities, but each organization can also securely send and accept identities from other organizations. This seamless process is referred to as *single sign-on (SSO)*.

Windows Server AD FS federation servers can extract Windows authorization claims from a user's authorization token that is created when the user authenticates to the AD FS federation server. AD FS inserts these claims into its claim pipeline for processing. You can configure Windows authorization claims to pass through the pipeline as is, or you can configure AD FS to transform Windows authorization claims into a different or well-known claim type.

Claims Provider

A *claims provider* is a federation server that processes trusted identity claims requests. A federation server processes requests to issue, manage, and validate security tokens. Security tokens consist of a collection of identity claims, such as a user's name or role or an anonymous identifier. A federation server can issue tokens in several formats. In addition, a federation server can protect the contents of security tokens in transmission with an X.509 certificate.

For example, when a StormWind user needs access to Fabrikam's web application, the StormWind user must request claims from the StormWind AD FS server claims provider. The claim is transformed into an encrypted security token, which is then sent to Fabrikam's AD FS server.

Relying Party

A *relying party* is a federation server that receives security tokens from a trusted federation partner claims provider. In turn, the relying party issues new security tokens that a local relying party application consumes. In the prior example, Fabrikam is the relying party that relies on the StormWind's claims provider to validate the user's claim. By using a relying-party federation server in conjunction with a claims provider, organizations can offer web single sign-on to users from partner organizations. In this scenario, each organization manages its own identity stores.

Endpoints

Endpoints provide access to the federation server functionality of AD FS, such as token issuance, information card issuance, and the publishing of federation metadata. Based on the type of endpoint, you can enable or disable the endpoint or control whether the endpoint is published to AD FS proxies.

Table 2.4 describes the property fields that distinguish the various built-in endpoints that AD FS exposes. The table includes the types of endpoints and their methods of client authentication. Table 2.5 describes the AD FS security modes.

TABLE 2.4 AD FS Endpoints

Name	Description
WS-Trust 1.3	An endpoint built on a standard Simple Object Access Protocol (SOAP)–based protocol for issuing security tokens.
WS-Trust 2005	An endpoint built on a prestandard, SOAP-based protocol for issuing security tokens.
WS-Federation Passive/SAML Web SSO	An endpoint published to support protocols that redirect web browser clients to issue security tokens.
Federation Metadata	A standard-formatted endpoint for exchanging metadata about a claims provider or a relying party.
SAML Artifact Resolution	An endpoint built on a subset of the Security Assertion Markup Language (SAML) version 2.0 protocol that describes how a relying party can access a token directly from a claims provider.
WS-Trust WSDL	An endpoint that publishes WS-Trust Web Services Definition Language (WSDL) containing the metadata that the federation service must be able to accept from other federation servers.
SAML Token (Asymmetric)	The client accepts a SAML token with an asymmetric key.

TABLE 2.5   AD FS Security Modes

Name	Description
Transport	The client credentials are included at the transport layer. Confidentiality is pre-served at the transport layer (Secure Sockets Layer [SSL]).
Mixed	The client credentials are included in the header of a SOAP message. Confidentiality is preserved at the transport layer (SSL).
Message	The client credentials are included in the header of a SOAP message. Confidentiality is preserved by encryption inside the SOAP message.

Claim Descriptions

Claim descriptions are claim types based on an entity's or user's attribute like a user's email address, common name or UPN. AD FS publishes these claims types in the federation metadata and most common claim descriptions are pre-configured in the AD FS Management snap-in.

The claim descriptions are published to federation metadata which is stored in the AD FS configuration database. The claim descriptions include a claim type URI, name, publishing state, and description.

Claim Rules

Claim rules define how AD FS processes a claim. The most common rule is using a user's email address as a valid claim. The email address claim is validated through the partner's Active Directory email attribute for the user's account. If there is a match, the claim is accepted as valid.

Claim rules can quickly evolve into more complex rules with more attributes such as a user's employee ID or department. The key goal of claim rules is to process the claim in a manner that validates the user's claim and to assemble a user's profile information based on a sufficient number of attributes to place the user into a role or group.

The Attribute Store

Attribute stores are the repositories containing claim values. AD FS natively supports Active Directory by default as an attribute store. SQL Server, AD LDS, and custom attribute stores are also supported.

AD FS Role Services

The AD FS server role includes federation, proxy, and web agent services. These services enable the following:

- Web SSO
- Federated web-based resources

- Customizing the access experience
- Managing authorization to access applications

Based on your organization's requirements, you can deploy servers running any one of the following AD FS role services:

Active Directory Federation Service   Microsoft federation solution for accepting and issuing claims based token for users to experience a single sign-on to a partnered web application.

Federation Service Proxy   The Federation Service Proxy forwards user claims over the internet or DMZ using WS-Federation Passive Requestor Profile (WS-F PRP) protocols to the internal AD FS farm. Only the user credential data is forwarded to the Federation Service. All other datagram packets are dropped.

Claims-Aware Agent   The claims-aware agent resides on a web server with a claims-aware application to enable the Microsoft ASP.NET application to accept AD FS security token claims.

Windows Token-Based Agent   The Windows token-based agent resides on a web server with a Windows NT token-based application to translate an AD FS security token to an impersonation-level Windows NT token-based authentication.

AD FS in Windows Server 2016

The Active Directory Federation Services role in Windows Server 2016 introduced the following new features:

- HTTP.SYS
- Server Manager integration
- AD FS deployment cmdlets in the AD FS module for Windows PowerShell
- Interoperability with Windows authorization claims
- Web proxy service

HTTP.SYS

Prior AD FS versions relied on IIS components for the AD FS claim functions. Microsoft has improved the overall claims handling performance and SSO customization by building the AD FS 3.0 code on top of the standard kernel mode driver—HTTP.SYS. This approach also avoids the huge security "no-no" of hosting IIS on an AD FS server.

The classic netsh HTTP command can be entered to query and configure HTTP.SYS. The AD FS proxy server introduces interesting deployment nuisances and "gotchas" with HTTP.SYS, which I will discuss in the section "Web Proxy Service."

Improved Installation Experience

The installation experience for Active Directory Federation Services 3.0 was cumbersome, requiring multiple hotfixes as well as .NET Framework 3.5, Windows PowerShell, and the

Windows Identity Foundation SDK. Windows Server 2016's AD FS role includes all of the software you need to run AD FS for an improved installation experience.

Web Proxy Service

The kernel mode (HTTP.SYS) in Windows Server 2016 includes server name indication (SNI) support configuration. I strongly recommend verifying that your current load balancer/reverse proxy firmware supports SNI. This prerequisite is a sore spot for most AD FS 3.0 upgrade projects in the field. Therefore, it's worthwhile checking the following:

- Your preferred load balancer/device needs to support SNI.

- Clients and user agents need to support SNI and should not become locked out of authentication.

- All SSL termination endpoints vulnerable to the recent heartbleed bug (http://heartbleed.com) need to be patched, exposing OpenSSL libraries and certificates.

AD FS Dependency Changes in Windows Server 2016

Active Directory Federation Services was built on a claim-based identity framework called *Windows Identity Foundation (WIF)*. Prior to Windows Server 2016, WIF was distributed in a software development kit and the .NET runtime. WIF is currently integrated into version 4.5 of the .NET Framework, which ships with Windows Server 2016.

Windows Identity Foundation

WIF is a set of .NET Framework classes; it is a framework for implementing claims-based identity for applications. Any web application or web service that uses .NET Framework version 4.5 or newer can run WIF.

New Claims Model and Principal Object

Claims are at the core of .NET Framework 4.5. The base claim classes (`Claim`, `ClaimsIdentity`, `ClaimsPrincipal`, `ClaimTypes`, and `ClaimValueTypes`) all live directly in `mscorlib`. Interfaces are no longer necessary to plug claims in the .NET identity system. `WindowsPrincipal`, `GenericPrincipal`, and `RolePrincipal` now inherit from `ClaimsPrincipal`, `WindowsIdentity`, and `GenericIdentity`, and `FormsIdentity` now inherits from `ClaimsIdentity`. In short, every principal class will now serve claims. The integration classes and interfaces (`WindowsClaimsIdentity`, `WindowsClaimsPrincipal`, `IClaimsPrincipal`, and `IClaimsIdentity`) have thus been removed. The `ClaimsIdentity` object model also contains various improvements, which makes it easier to query the identity's claims collection.

As you climb further up "Mount Federation," you will realize that not all vendor SAML flavors are compatible, and configuration challenges can bring even the most seasoned system integrators to their knees. SAML deserves an entire book, so to avoid this chapter reaching encyclopedia size, I will touch on just a few pointers.

AD FS negotiates SAML authentication in order of security strength from the weakest to the strongest, as shown in Table 2.6. The default mode, Kerberos, is considered the strongest method. The authentication precedence can be tuned by executing the PowerShell command Set-AD FSProperties -AuthenticationContextOrder to select an order to meet your organization's security requirements.

TABLE 2.6   SAML-supported authentication methods

Authentication Method	Authentication Context Class URI
Username/password	urn:oasis:names:tc:SAML:3.0:ac:classes:Password
Password-protected transport	urn:oasis:names:tc:SAML:3.0:ac:classes:PasswordProtectedTransport
Transport Layer Security (TLS) Client	urn:oasis:names:tc:SAML:3.0:ac:classes:TLSClient
X.509 certificate	urn:oasis:names:tc:SAML:3.0:ac:classes:X509
Integrated Windows authentication	urn:federation:authentication:windows
Kerberos	urn:oasis:names:tc:SAML:3.0:classes:Kerberos

Configuring a Web Application Proxy

One of the advantages of using the Remote Access role service in Windows Server is the Web Application Proxy. Normally, your users access applications on the Internet from your corporate network. The *Web Application Proxy* reverses this feature, and it allows your corporate users to access applications from any device outside the network.

Administrators can choose which applications to provide reverse proxy features, and this allows administrators the ability to give access selectively to corporate users for the application they want to set up for the Web Application Proxy service.

The Web Application Proxy feature allows applications running on servers inside the corporate network to be accessed by any device outside the corporate network. The process of allowing an application to be available to users outside of the corporate network is known as *publishing*.

Web Application Proxy works differently than a normal VPN solution because when an administrator publishes applications through Web Application Proxy, end users get access only to applications that the administrator published. Administrators have the ability to deploy the Web Application Proxy alongside a VPN as part of the Remote Access deployment for an organization.

Web Application Proxy can function as an AD FS proxy, and it also preauthenticates access to web applications using Active Directory Federation Services (AD FS).

Publishing Applications

One disadvantage to corporate networks is that the machines that access the network are normally devices issued by the organization. That's where Web Application Proxy publishing can help.

Web Application Proxy allows an administrator to publish an organization's applications, thus allowing corporate end users the ability to access the applications from their own devices. This is becoming a big trend in the computer industry called *Bring Your Own Device (BYOD)*.

In today's technology world, users are buying and using many of their own devices, even for business work. Because of this, users are comfortable with their own devices. Web Application Proxy allows an organization to set up applications and enable their corporate users to use these applications with the devices the users already own, including computers, tablets, and smartphones.

The client side is easy to use as long as the end user has a standard browser or Office client. End users can also use apps from the Microsoft Windows Store that allow the client system to connect to the Web Application Proxy.

Configuring Pass-through Authentication

Now when setting up the Web Application Proxy (see Figure 2.27) so that your users can access applications, you must have some kind of security or everyone with a device would be able to access and use your applications.

FIGURE 2.27   Example of Web Application Proxy setup

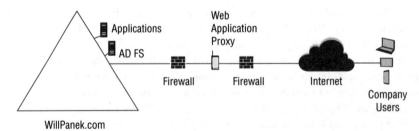

Because of this, Active Directory Federation Services (AD FS) should be deployed with a Web Application Proxy. AD FS gives you features such as single sign-on (SSO). Single sign-on allows you to log in one time with a set of credentials and use that set of credentials to access the applications over and over. To use a Web Application Proxy, you should set your firewall to allow for ports 443 and 49443.

When an administrator publishes an application using the Web Application Proxy, the method that users and devices use for authentication is known as preauthentication. The Web Application Proxy allows for two forms of preauthentication:

AD FS Preauthentication   AD FS preauthentication requires the user to authenticate directly with the AD FS server. After the AD FS authentication happens, the Web Application Proxy then redirects the user to the published web application. This guarantees that traffic to your published web applications is authenticated before a user can access it.

Pass-through Preauthentication   When using Pass-through Preauthentication, a user is not required to enter credentials before they are allowed to connect to published web applications.

Pass-through Authentication is truly a great benefit for your end users. Think of having a network where a user has to log in every time that user wants to access an application. The more times you make your end users log into an application, the more chances there are that the end user will encounter possible issues. Pass-through Authentication works in the following way:

1. The client enters a URL address on their device, and the client system attempts to access the published web application.

2. The Web Application Proxy sends the request to the web server.

3. If the backend server needs the user to authenticate, the end user needs to enter their credentials only once.

4. After the server authenticates the credentials, the client has access to the published web application.

To access applications easily that are published by the Web Application Proxy and use the AD FS preauthentication, end users need to use one of the following types of clients:

- Any HTTP client that supports redirection (web browsers). When Web Application Proxy receives an incoming message, the Web Application Proxy redirects the user to an authentication server and then back to the original web address authenticated.

- Rich clients that use HTTP basic.

- Clients that use MS-OFBA (Microsoft Office Forms Bases Authentication) protocol.

- Clients that use the Web Authentication Broker for authentication like Windows Store apps and RESTful applications.

Active Directory Federation Services Installation

I will now describe how to install and deploy Active Directory Federation Services roles on computers running Windows Server (see Exercise 2.10). I am using a Windows Server 2016 server for this exercise. You will learn about the following:

- Deploying AD FS role services using Windows PowerShell

- Supporting upgrade scenarios for AD FS

EXERCISE 2.10

Installing the AD FS Role on a Computer Using Server Manager

1. Start Server Manager.

2. Click Manage and click Add Roles And Features. Click Next.

3. The Add Roles And Features Wizard shows the Before You Begin screen. Click Next.

4. Click Role-Based Or Feature-Based Installation on the Select Installation Type screen. Click Next.

5. Click the server on which you want to install Active Directory Federation Services from the Server Pool list on the Select Destination Server screen. Click Next.

6. Select the Active Directory Federation Services check box on the Select Server Roles screen. Server Manager will prompt you to add other features associated with this role, such as management tools. Leave the default selections. Click Add Features to close the dialog.

7. Click Next on the Select Server Roles screen.

8. Click Next on the Select Features screen.

9. Server Manager shows the Active Directory Federation Services screen. This screen displays simple role introduction and important AD FS configuration information. Click Next.

10. From the Select Server Roles screen, select the check box next to the AD FS role services to install on the computer. Click Next.

11. Server Manager prompts you to add other features associated with this role, such as management tools. Leave the default selections. Click Add Features to close the dialog.

12. Read the Confirm Installation Selections screen. This screen provides a list of roles, role services, and features that the current installation prepares on the computer. Click Install to begin the installation.

Role Installation Using Windows PowerShell

To view the installation state of AD FS using Windows PowerShell, open an elevated Windows PowerShell console, type the following command, and press Enter:

```
Get-WindowsFeature "adfs*","*fed*"
```

Upgrading to Windows AD FS

Windows Server AD FS role supports upgrading version 3.0 of Active Directory Federation Services. You cannot upgrade versions of AD FS prior to version 3.0 using Windows Server.

Table 2.7 represents the support upgrade matrix for the AD FS role in Windows Server.

TABLE 2.7   Support upgrade matrix for the AD FS role in Windows Server

AD FS and Operating System Version	Windows Server 2016 / 2019 Upgrade Supported
AD FS 3.0 running on Windows Server 2008	Yes
AD FS 3.0 running on Windows Server 2008 R2	Yes
AD FS 3.0 Proxy running on Windows Server 2008	Yes
AD FS 3.0 Proxy running on Windows Server 2008 R2	Yes
AD FS 1.1 running on Windows Server 2008	No
AD FS 1.1 running on Windows Server 2008 R2	No
AD FS 1.1 Proxy running on Windows Server 2008	No
AD FS 1.1 Proxy running on Windows Server 2008 R2	No
AD FS 1.1 Web Agents on Windows Server 2008 or Windows Server 2008 R2	Yes

Configuring Active Directory Federation Services

Windows Server (should be Windows Server 2012 R2 or higher for full benefits) delineates role installation and role deployment. Role installations make staged role services and features available for deployment. Role deployment enables you to configure the role service, which enables the role service in your environment. AD FS in Windows Server uses the same deployment tools as AD FS 3.0. However, an entry point to start these tools is included in Server Manager. Server Manager indicates that one or more role services are eligible for deployment by showing an exclamation point inside a yellow triangle on the Action Flag notification.

AD FS Graphical Deployment

The AD FS Management snap-in link in Windows Server Manager is how you perform the initial configuration for the AD FS roles using the graphical interface. Administrators can also use PowerShell commands to install and configure AD FS.

Alternatively, you can start the AD FS management console using the AD FS Management tile on the Start screen. The Start screen tile points to the `Microsoft` `.IdentityServer.msc` file located in the `C:\windows\adfs` folder.

To configure AD FS, select Start ➤ Run and type `FsConfigWizard.exe`; alternatively, click the `FsConfigWizard.exe` file located in the `C:\windows\adfs` folder.

Exercise 2.11 uses the AD FS Federation Server Configuration Wizard. To complete this exercise, you'll need an active SSL certificate assigned to the server and a managed service account for the AD FS service.

EXERCISE 2.11

Configuring the AD FS Role on the Computer Using Server Manager

1. Select Create The First Federation Server In The Federation Server Farm.

2. Select the administrative account with permissions to configure the AD FS server and click Next.

3. Select the server certificate from the SSL certificate drop-down list.

4. Select the AD FS service name from the drop-down list.

5. Type **ADFS-Test** in the federation service's Display Name field and click Next.

6. Select Create A Database On This Server Using Windows Internal Database and click Next.

7. Click Next on the Review Options screen.

8. If the prerequisites check is successful, click Configure on the Prerequisite Check screen.

9. If the Result screen displays "This Server was successfully configured," you can click Close.

Deployment Using Windows PowerShell

Windows Server includes the Active Directory Federation Services module for Windows PowerShell when you install the AD FS role using Server Manager. The AD FS module for Windows PowerShell includes five new cmdlets to deploy the AD FS role:

- `Add-AdfsProxy`
- `Add-AdfsFarmNode`
- `Export-AdfsDeploymentSQLScript`
- `Install-AdfsStand-alone`
- `Install-AdfsFarm`

These AD FS cmdlets provide the same functionality as the command-line version of the AD FS Federation Server Configuration Wizard, `fsconfig` `.exe`. The AD FS role in Windows Server includes `fsconfig.exe` to remain compatible with previously authored deployment scripts. New deployments should take advantage of the deployment cmdlets included in the AD FS module for Windows PowerShell.

Add-AdfsProxy   Configures a server as a federation server proxy.

FederationServiceName   Specifies the name of the federation service for which a server proxies requests.

FederationServiceTrustCredentials   Specifies the credentials of the Active Directory identity that is authorized to register new federation server proxies. By default, this is the account under which the federation service runs or an account that is a member of the Administrators group on the federation server.

ForwardProxy   Specifies the DNS name and port of an HTTP proxy that this federation server proxy uses to obtain access to the federation service.

`Add-AdfsFarmNode`   Adds this computer to an existing federation server farm.

CertificateThumbprint   Specifies the value of the certificate thumbprint of the certificate that should be used in the SSL binding of the default website in IIS. This value should match the thumbprint of a valid certificate in the Local Computer certificate store.

OverwriteConfiguration   Must be used to remove an existing AD FS configuration database and overwrite it with a new database.

SQLConnectionString   Specifies the SQL Server database that will store the AD FS configuration settings. If not specified, AD FS uses Windows Internal Database to store configuration settings.

ServiceAccountCredential   Specifies the Active Directory account under which the AD FS service runs. All nodes in the farm must have the same service account.

PrimaryComputerName   Specifies the name of the primary federation server in the farm that this computer will join.

PrimaryComputerPort   Specifies the value of the HTTP port that this computer uses to connect with the primary computer in order to synchronize configuration settings. Specify a value for this parameter only if the HTTP port on the primary computer is not 80.

Active Directory Federation Services Certificates

There are three types of certificates used by an AD FS implementation:

- Service communications
- Token decrypting
- Token signing

The service communications certificate is required for communication with web clients over SSL and with Web Application Proxy services using Windows Communication Foundation (WCF) components. This certificate is specified at configuration time for AD FS.

The token decrypting certificate is required to decrypt claims and tokens received by the federation service. The public key for the decrypting certificate is usually shared with relying parties and others to encrypt the claims and tokens using the certificate.

The token signing certificate is required to sign all claims and tokens created by the server. You can have multiple token encrypting and signing certificates for an implementation, and new ones can be added within the AD FS management tool.

Relying-Party Trust

The federation service name originates from the SSL certificate used for AD FS. The SSL certificate can be template based and needs to be enrolled and used by IIS.

The next step in setting up AD FS is to configure a relying-party trust. A relying-party trust can be configured with a URL acquired from the relying party. The URL contains the federation metadata used to complete the federation trust configuration. The federation metadata may also be exported to a file that can then be imported into the relying-party trust. There is also a manual option for configuring a relying-party trust.

See Table 2.8 for the Federation Metadata fields.

TABLE 2.8   Federation Metadata Fields

Field	Description
Display Name	This is the friendly display name given to this relying party trust.
Profile	Select AD FS Profile for the standard Windows Server 2012 AD FS, or select AD FS 1.0 And 1.1 Profile for AD FS configurations that need to work with older versions of AD FS.
Certificate	This is the optional certificate file from the relying party for token encryption.
URL	This is the URL for the relying party. WS-Federation Passive Protocol URL or SAML 2.0 WebSSO protocols are supported.
Identifiers	This is the unique identifier used for this trust.
Authorization Rules	Selecting this permits all users to access the relying party or denies all users access to the relying party, depending on the needs of this trust.

Configuring Claims Provider and Transform Claims Rules

Claims provider trust rules are configured within the AD FS management console and are configured on a per-trust basis. Planning claims rules involves determining what claims are needed by the relying party to complete the authentication and authorization process and which users will need access to the relying-party trust. The relying party determines what claims need to be received and trusted from the claims provider.

Trust rules start with templates as the basis for the rule. There are different types of claims templates depending on the type of rule being used. The claims rule templates for transforms are described in Table 2.9.

TABLE 2.9 Transform claims rule templates

Template	Description
Send LDAP Attributes as Claims	Attributes found in an LDAP directory (such as Active Directory) can be used as part of the claim.
Send Group Membership as Claim	The group memberships of the logged-in user are sent as part of the claim.
Transform an Incoming Claim	This is used for configuring a rule to change an incoming claim. Changes include both the type and the value of an incoming claim.
Pass Through or Filter an Incoming Claim	This performs an action such as pass-through or filter on an incoming claim based on certain criteria, as defined in the rule.
Send Claims Using a Custom Rule	This creates a rule that's not covered by a predefined template, such as an LDAP attribute generated with a custom LDAP filter.

Defining Windows Authorization Claims in AD FS

Windows Server stores information that describes Windows authorization claims in the configuration partition of Active Directory. Windows refers to this information as *claim types*; however, Active Directory Federation Services typically refers to this information as claim descriptions. There are more than 40 new claim descriptions available in the AD FS Windows Server release.

The Active Directory Federation Services role included in Windows Server lets you configure AD FS to include Windows authorization claims in the AD FS claim pipeline. To simplify this configuration, you can create *claim descriptions* in AD FS. Claim types in Windows authorization claims are analogous to claim descriptions in AD FS. The Windows authorization claim ID maps to the AD FS claim description's claim identifier.

To simplify AD FS configuration using Windows authorization claims, create a claim description in AD FS for each Windows authorization claim you intend to deploy in AD FS.

Create Claim Pass-Through and Transformation Rules

You need to configure a claim rule with the Active Directory Claims Provider Trusts Wizard to insert Windows authorization claims into the AD FS claims pipeline.

Creating a claim description makes it easier to select the incoming claim type. Alternatively, you can type the claim type ID directly in the Incoming Claim Type list. A *pass-through claim rule* enables the Windows authorization claim to enter the AD FS claim pipeline. A pass-through claim leaves the claim type ID intact. Therefore, the pass-through claim ID begins with ad://ext, whereas most claim description URIs begin with http://. In addition, you can create a claim transformation claim rule on the Active Directory Claim Provider Trust Wizard to transform a Windows authorization claim into a well-known claim description.

Creating a claim provider trust claim rule enables the Windows authorization claim to enter the AD FS claim pipeline. However, this does not ensure that AD FS sends the Windows authorization claim. AD FS claim processing begins with the claim's provider. This allows the claim to enter the pipeline. Claim processing continues for the targeted relying party—first with the issuance authorization rules and then with the issuance transform rules.

You can configure Windows authorization claims in claims rules configured on a relying party. By default, a relying party does not have any issuance transform rules. Therefore, AD FS drops all claims in the pipeline destined for a relying party when the relying party does not have any rules that pass incoming claims. Additionally, issuance authorization rules determine whether a user can receive claims for a relying party and, therefore, access the relying party.

Choose the claim types from the list of inbound rules created in the Active Directory claims provider trust that you want to send to the designated relying party. Then create rules that continue to pass the selected claim types through the pipeline to the relying party. Alternatively, you can create a rule that passes all the inbound claims to the relying party.

The AD FS role in Windows Server cannot provide claim information when the incoming authentication is not Kerberos. Clients must authenticate to AD FS using Kerberos authentication. If Windows authorization claims are not entering the AD FS claim pipeline, then make sure the client authenticates to AD FS using Kerberos and the correct service principal name is registered on the computer/service account.

Enabling AD FS to Use Compound Authentication for Device Claims: Compound Authentication

Windows Server enhances Kerberos authentication by introducing compound authentication. Compound authentication enables a Kerberos TGS request to include two identities: the identity of the user and the identity of the user's device. Windows accomplishes compound authentication by extending Kerberos Flexible Authentication Secure Tunneling (FAST) or Kerberos armoring.

During normal Kerberos authentication, the Kerberos client requesting authentication for a service sends the ticket-granting service (TGS) a request for that service. Using Kerberos armoring, the TGS exchange is armored using the user's ticket-granting ticket (TGT). Prior to sending the ticket-granting service reply (TGS-REP) to the client, the KDC checks the 0x00020000 bit in the value of the msDS-SupportedEncryptionTypes attribute of the security principal's object running the service. An enabled bit means that the service can accept compound authentication. The KDC sends the TGS-REP, which includes the service's ability to support compound authentication.

The Kerberos client receives the ticket-granting service TGS-REP that includes compound authentication information. The Kerberos client then sends another ticket-granting service request (TGS-REQ), with the difference being that this TGS-REQ is armored with the device's TGT rather than the user. This allows the KDC to retrieve authentication information about the principal and the device.

The Active Directory Federation Services role included in Windows Server automatically enables compound authentication when creating an AD FS web farm. During the creation of the first node in the farm, the AD FS configuration wizard enables the compound authentication bit on the msDS-SupportedEncryptionTypes attribute on the account that you designate to run the AD FS service. If you change the service account, then you must manually enable compound authentication by running the Set-ADUser -compoundIdentitySupported:$true Windows PowerShell cmdlet.

In Exercise 2.12, you will learn how to configure multi-factor authentication.

EXERCISE 2.12

Configuring Multi-factor Authentication

1. In the AD FS Management Console, traverse to Trust Relationships And Relying Party Trusts.

2. Select the relying party trust that represents your sample application (claimapp) and then either by using the Actions pane or by right-clicking this relying party trust, select Edit Claim Rules.

3. In the Edit Claim Rules For Claimapp window, select the Issuance Authorization Rules tab and click Add Rule.

4. In the Add Issuance Authorization Claim Rule Wizard, on the Select Rule Template screen, select Permit Or Deny Users Based On An Incoming Claim Rule Template and click Next.

5. On the Configure Rule screen, complete all of the following tasks and click Finish.

    a. Enter a name for the claim rule, for example **TestRule**.

    b. Select Group SID As Incoming Claim Type.

    c. Click Browse, type in **Finance** for the name of your AD test group, and resolve it for the Incoming Claim Value field.

    d. Select the Deny Access To Users With This Incoming Claim option.

    e. In the Edit Claim Rules For Claimapp window, make sure to delete the Permit Access To All Users rule that was created by default when you created this relying-party trust.

Verify Multifactor Access Control Mechanism

In this phase, you will verify the multi-factor access control policy that you set up in the previous phase. You can use the following procedure to verify that a test AD user can access your sample application because the test account belongs to the Finance group. Conversely, you will use the procedure to verify that AD users who do not belong to the Finance group cannot access the sample application.

1. On your client computer, open a browser window and navigate to your sample application. I am showing you an example of an application link below and what it should look like. But you must make sure that Webserv1 (in our example) is set up to successfully see a response: `https://webserv1.contoso.com/claimapp`. This action automatically redirects the request to the federation server, and you are prompted to sign in with a username and password.

2. Type in the credentials of a test AD account to be granted access to the application.

3. Type in the credentials of another test AD account that does not belong to the Finance group.

At this point, because of the access control policy that you set up in the previous steps, an access denied message is displayed for an AD account that does not belong to the Finance group. The default message text is "You are not authorized to access this site. Click here to sign out, and sign in again or contact your administrator for permissions." However, this text is fully customizable.

Using PowerShell Commands

In the following table (Table 2.10), I will show you some of the PowerShell commands available for Azure Active Directory. You must be using a newer version of PowerShell on your on-site servers or client machines. If you run into any issues trying to run these commands, please check out a newer version of Microsoft PowerShell on Microsoft's website.

TABLE 2.10   PowerShell commands for Azure Active Directory

Command	Description
Add-AzureADAdministrativeUnitMember	This command allows an Azure admin to add an administrative unit member.
Add-AzureADApplicationPolicy	Administrators can use this command to add an application policy.

Command	Description
Add-AzureADScopedRoleMembership	This command allows an Azure admin to add a scoped role membership to an administrative unit.
Add-AzureADServicePrincipalPolicy	Administrators can use this command to add a service principal policy.
Get-AzureADAdministrativeUnit	This command allows an Azure admin to view an administrative unit.
Get-AzureADAdministrativeUnitMember	Administrators can use this command to view a member of an administrative unit.
Get-AzureADApplicationPolicy	This command allows an Azure admin to view an application policy.
Get-AzureADDirectorySetting	Administrators can use this command to view a directory setting.
Get-AzureADDirectorySettingTemplate	This command allows an Azure admin to view a directory setting template.
Get-AzureADObjectSetting	Administrators can use this command to view an object setting.
Get-AzureADPolicy	This command allows an Azure admin to view a policy.
Get-AzureADPolicyAppliedObject	Administrators can use this command to view the objects to which a policy is applied.
Get-AzureADScopedRoleMembership	This command allows an Azure admin to view a scoped role membership from an administrative unit.
Get-AzureADServicePrincipalPolicy	Administrators can use this command to view the service principal policy.
New-AzureADAdministrativeUnit	This command allows an Azure admin to create an administrative unit.
New-AzureADDirectorySetting	Administrators can use this command to create a directory settings object.

TABLE 2.10 PowerShell commands for Azure Active Directory *(continued)*

Command	Description
New-AzureADObjectSetting	This command allows an Azure admin to create a settings object.
New-AzureADPolicy	Administrators can use this command to create a policy.
Remove-AzureADAdministrativeUnit	This command allows an Azure admin to remove an administrative unit.
Remove-AzureADAdministrativeUnitMember	Administrators can use this command to remove an administrative unit member.
Remove-AzureADDirectorySetting	This command allows an Azure admin to delete a directory setting in Azure Active Directory.
Remove-AzureADObjectSetting	Administrators can use this command to delete settings in Azure Active Directory.
Remove-AzureADPolicy	This command allows an Azure admin to delete a policy.
Remove-AzureADScopedRoleMembership	Administrators can use this command to remove a scoped role membership.
Set-AzureADDirectorySetting	Updates a directory setting in Azure Active Directory.
Set-AzureADObjectSetting	This command allows an Azure admin to update object settings.
Set-AzureADPolicy	Administrators can use this command to update a policy.
sGet-AzureADApplicationProxy ConnectorGroupMembers	Retrieve the members of an Application Proxy connector group

In Table 2.11, I will show you some of the PowerShell commands available for Azure and AD FS. You must be using a newer version of PowerShell on your on-site servers or client machines. If you run into any issues trying to run these commands, please check out a newer version of Microsoft PowerShell on Microsoft's website.

TABLE 2.11 PowerShell commands for Azure and AD FS

Command	Description
Add-AdfsAttributeStore	Administrators can use this command to add an attribute store to the Federation Service.
Add-AdfsCertificate	This command allows an administrator to add a new certificate to the AD FS server for signing, decrypting, or securing communications.
Add-AdfsClaimsProviderTrust	Administrators can use this command to add a new claims provider trust to the Federation Service.
Add-AdfsClient	This command allows an admin to register an OAuth 2.0 client with AD FS.
Add-AdfsFarmNode	Administrators can use this command to add a computer to an existing federation server farm.
Add-AdfsNativeClientApplication	This command allows an admin to add a native client application role to an application in AD FS.
Add-AdfsServerApplication	Administrators can use this command to add a server application role to an application in AD FS.
Disable-AdfsCertificateAuthority	This command allows an admin to disable a certificate authority.
Disable-AdfsLocalClaimsProviderTrust	This command allows an administrator to disable a local claims provider trust.
Disable-AdfsRelyingPartyTrust	Administrators can use this command to disable a relying party trust of the Federation Service.
Enable-AdfsApplicationGroup	This command allows an administrator to enable an application group in AD FS.
Enable-AdfsClaimsProviderTrust	Administrators can use this command to enable a claims provider trust in the Federation Service.

TABLE 2.11   PowerShell commands for Azure and AD FS *(continued)*

Command	Description
Enable-AdfsLocalClaimsProviderTrust	This command allows an administrator to enable a local claims provider trust.
Get-AdfsApplicationGroup	Administrators can use this command to view an application group.
Get-AdfsAttributeStore	This command allows an administrator to view the attribute stores of the Federation Service.
Get-AdfsAuthenticationProvider	Administrators can use this command to view a list of all authentication providers in AD FS.
Get-AdfsCertificate	This command allows an administrator to view the certificates from AD FS.
Get-AdfsCertificateAuthority	Administrators can use this command to view a certificate authority.
Get-AdfsClient	This command allows an administrator to view registration information for an OAuth 2.0 client.
Get-AdfsFarmInformation	Administrators can use this command to view AD FS behavior level and farm node information.
Initialize-ADDeviceRegistration	Admins can use this command to initialize the Device Registration Service configuration in the Active Directory forest.
New-AdfsApplicationGroup	This command creates a new application group.
New-AdfsClaimRuleSet	Administrators can use this command to create a set of claim rules.
New-AdfsOrganization	This command allows an administrator to create a new organization information object.
Register-AdfsAuthenticationProvider	Administrators can use this command to register an external authentication provider in AD FS.

Command	Description
Remove-AdfsApplicationGroup	This command allows an administrator to remove an application group.
Set-AdfsFarmInformation	This command allows an admin to remove a stale or offline farm node from the farm information table.
Set-AdfsProperties	Administrators can use this command to set the properties that control global behaviors in AD FS.
Set-AdfsServerApplication	This command allows an administrator to modify configuration settings for a server application role of an application in AD FS.
Set-AdfsWebConfig	Administrators can use this command to modify web customization configuration settings.

Summary

This chapter covered the basics of implementing an Active Directory within your organization. We looked at the different pieces of an Active Directory onsite (or Azure VM) setup.

We then examined the different components of Azure AD. I showed you all of the benefits and features of Azure AD in addition to the common questions and answers about Azure AD directly from Microsoft's website.

You were introduced to the Azure AD dashboard and many of its different sections. I showed you how to create an Azure AD users account and an Azure AD group. I then talked about the Azure AD Password Reset option and how to configure that feature.

This chapter also covered the benefits of using the Azure AD Identity Protection feature, and I showed you how to add that feature to your subscription. You learned how to configure Identity Protection and set up an email address so that you can receive alerts.

You saw how you can set up a hybrid network and the importance of setting up an onsite network along with your Azure AD network.

This chapter then covered the different authentication methods and what each method could do for you. I also explained Azure AD Connect and how it can link your onsite AD with Azure AD.

I explained the benefits of using Site-to-Site VPN gateway connections. I showed you the requirements and how to set up and configure the different components needed for Site-to-Site VPN gateway connections.

Finally, I explained Active Directory Federation Services, which provides Internet-based clients with a secure identity access solution that works on both Windows and non-Windows operating systems. You saw how to install and configure AD FS onto a Windows Server machine.

Exam Essentials

Know the prerequisites for promoting a server to a domain controller.   You should understand the tasks that you must complete before you attempt to upgrade a server to a domain controller. Also, you should have a good idea of the information you need in order to complete the domain controller promotion process.

Understand the steps of the Active Directory Installation Wizard.   When you run the Active Directory Installation Wizard, you'll be presented with many different choices. You should understand the effects of the various options provided in each step of the wizard.

Be familiar with the tools you will use to administer Active Directory.   Three main administrative tools are installed when you promote a Windows Server machine to a domain controller. Be sure that you know which tools to use for which types of tasks.

Understand the features of Azure AD.   Make sure you understand the features and benefits of using Azure AD. This is not only important for taking the Microsoft exams, but it is also important to determine if Azure AD is the correct choice for your organization.

Understand the Q&As of Azure AD.   This is very important for many reasons. First, and most obvious, for the Microsoft exam you need to understand what Azure AD can do and not do. Second, you need to make sure that Azure AD can handle all of the services your organization is trying to provide.

Know the Azure AD Dashboard.   You need to understand the Azure AD dashboard and where you set the different components for Azure AD. You also need to know how to access other dashboards (like the Azure AD Identity Protection dashboard) so that you can properly navigate Azure AD and its features.

Know how to set up and configure password resets.   You should understand what the process is for password resets and how to configure different authentication methods. Understand how to verify the users by using text messages or emails for verification.

Understand Azure AD Identity Protection.   Understand how to add Azure AD Identity Protection to your Azure subscription. Make sure you know how to configure the different policies and how to set alerts for an Azure administrator.

Know about hybrid networks.   It is important to understand why we use hybrid networks and the different authentication methods that can be used for setting up a hybrid network.

Understand Azure AD Connect.   Understand why we use Azure AD Connect. Azure AD Connect allows you to connect your onsite AD with Azure AD. This allows your user accounts and passwords to be replicated.

Know about Site-to-Site VPN Gateway Connections.   Know and understand what Site-to-Site VPN Gateways can do for your company. Site-to-Site VPN gateway connections allow you to connect both of your networks together over a secure IPsec/IKE VPN tunnel.

Understand Active Directory Federation Service.   Active Directory Federation Service gives users the ability to do a single sign-on and access applications on other networks without needing a secondary password. Organizations can set up trust relationships with other trusted organizations so that a user's digital identity and access rights can be accepted without a secondary password.

Know the Azure AD PowerShell commands.   Microsoft announced that all of their Microsoft exams would start asking questions about using PowerShell. This is going to be true for all chapters in this book, but make sure you understand the basic Azure AD PowerShell commands that can be used.

Review Questions

1. You are the system administrator of a large organization that has recently decided to add an Azure AD subscription. Your boss has asked you about Azure security and making sure that user logins are secure. What feature can you explain to your boss to ease their concerns?

    A. Azure AD User Security

    B. Azure AD Identity Protection

    C. Azure AD Security add-on

    D. Azure Identity Protection

2. You want to create a new Azure Active Directory policy for your users. What PowerShell command would you use to accomplish this task?

    A. `New-AzurePolicy`

    B. `New-AzureActiveDirectoryPolicy`

    C. `Set-AzurePolicy`

    D. `New-AzureADPolicy`

3. You want to look at an Azure Active Directory policy for your users. What PowerShell command would you use to accomplish this task?

    A. `Get-AzureADPolicy`

    B. `Get-AzureADPolicy`

    C. `View-AzurePolicy`

    D. `View-AzureADPolicy`

4. You are the administrator for a large organization that has subscribed to a new Azure AD subscription. You want your users to be able to reset passwords themselves. What Azure AD feature allows this to happen?

    A. User enabled password resets

    B. Azure password reset feature

    C. Self-service password reset

    D. Password reset service

5. You are the new Azure AD Global administrator for your organization. Your company wants to set up a way to integrate their on-site AD with Azure AD. What tool can you use to do this?

    A. Site-to-Site VPN Gateway Connectors.

    B. Azure AD Connect.

    C. Azure AD Replication.

    D. Active Directory Replicator.

6. You want to look at an Azure Active Directory application policy for your user's applications. What PowerShell command would you use to accomplish this task?

   A. `Add-AzureADPolicy`

   B. `Add-AzureADApplicationPolicy`

   C. `Create-AzurePolicy`

   D. `Install-AzureADPolicy`

7. You want to change an Azure Active Directory policy for your users. What PowerShell command would you use to accomplish this task?

   A. `New-AzureADPolicy`

   B. `Edit-AzureADPolicy`

   C. `New-AzurePolicy`

   D. `Set-AzureADPolicy`

8. You are the new Azure AD Global administrator for your organization. Your company has an Azure AD domain name of ContosoAzure.onmicrosoft.com. Your bosses want you to change the default domain name to Contoso.onmicrosoft.com. How can you change the initial domain name?

   A. Use the Custom Domain Names section of Azure AD and change the name.

   B. In Azure AD, go to default directories and change the domain name.

   C. Use PowerShell to change the default domain name.

   D. This can't be done.

9. You are the new Azure AD Global administrator for your organization. Your company has an Azure AD domain name of ContosoAzure.onmicrosoft.com. Your bosses want you to add a new domain name for Contoso.onmicrosoft.com. How can you add the new domain name to your existing domain?

   A. Use the Custom Domain Names section of Azure AD and change the name.

   B. In Azure AD, go to default directories and add the domain name.

   C. Use the Azure Administrative Center to add the new domain name.

   D. This can't be done.

10. You want to view your Azure AD directory settings for your Azure AD subscription. What PowerShell command would you use to accomplish this task?

   A. `View-AzureADDirectorySetting`

   B. `Get-AzureADDirectorySetting`

   C. `Add-AzureADDirectorySetting`

   D. `Set-AzureADDirectorySetting`

Chapter

3

Managing Devices

MICROSOFT EXAM OBJECTIVES COVERED IN THIS CHAPTER:

✓ **Implement conditional access and compliance policies for devices**

- Implement conditional access policies; manage conditional access policies; plan conditional access policies; implement device compliance policies; manage device compliance policies; plan device compliance policies

✓ **Configure device profiles**

- Implement device profiles; manage device profiles; plan device profiles.

✓ **Plan and implement co-management**

- Implement co-management precedence; migrate group policy to MDM policies; recommend a co-management strategy.

So now that you understand how to install Windows 10 and set up Active Directory, it's time to work with devices. In this chapter, I will show you how to set up and manage your Windows 10 devices both on site and using Intune and Azure AD.

When you install Windows 10, you designate the initial configuration for your disks. Through Windows 10's utilities and features, you can change that configuration and perform disk-management tasks.

For file-system configuration, it is recommended that you use NTFS, although you could also format the disk drive as FAT32. You can also convert a FAT32 partition to NTFS. This chapter covers the features of each file system and how to use the Convert utility to convert to NTFS.

Another factor in disk management is choosing the configuration for your physical drives. Windows 10 supports basic, dynamic, and GPT disks. Dynamic disks allow you to create simple volumes, spanned volumes, and striped volumes. If your system is configured as a Basic Disk, in order to utilize volumes, you must first convert the machine's basic disks to dynamic disks.

Once you decide how your disks should be configured, you implement the disk configurations through the Disk Management utility. This utility helps you view and manage your physical disks and volumes. In this chapter, you will learn how to manage multiple types of storage and how to convert from basic storage to dynamic storage.

Another item that needs to be discussed is Windows 10 configuration with Azure. One of the advantages to using Azure is the ability to connect to your Azure network using many different device styles (Microsoft, Apple, etc.). But that means that you have to set up Azure to accept these different device types.

Also, you have the ability to set up policies and rules for the devices that connect to your Azure network. This chapter is going to show you how to set up those policies.

Understanding File Systems

The Microsoft MD-101 exam primarily focuses on using Windows 10 with the cloud. But I am starting this chapter with basic Windows 10 configuration settings. The reason for this is twofold.

First, you will see test questions about Windows 10 and how a Windows 10 device is configured (nothing to do with the cloud). Second, and probably even more important, is that I not only want you to pass the exam but I want to make sure that you know how to do your day-to-day tasks at work. Part of this is properly setting up and configuring Windows 10 so that you can get it on the cloud. So let's take a look at setting up file systems.

A partition is a logical division of hard drive space. Each partition you create under Windows 10 must have a file system associated with it. Partitions allow a single physical hard drive to be represented in the operating system as multiple drive letters and to be used as if there were multiple hard drives installed in the machine.

When selecting a file system, you can select FAT32 or NTFS. You typically select a file system based on the features you want to use and whether you will need to access the file system using other operating systems. If you have a FAT32 partition and want to update it to NTFS, you can use the Convert utility. The features of each file system and the procedure for converting file systems are covered in the following sections.

File System Selection

Your file system is used to track the storage of files on your hard drive in a way that is easily understood by end users while still allowing the operating system the ability to retrieve the files as requested. One of the fundamental choices associated with file management is the choice of your file system's configuration. It is recommended that you use the NTFS file system with Windows 10 because doing so will allow you to take advantage of features such as local security, file compression, and file encryption. You should choose the FAT32 file system only if you want to dual-boot your computer with a version of Windows that does not support NTFS, since it is backward compatible with other operating systems.

Table 3.1 summarizes the capabilities of each file system, and they are described in more detail in the following sections. These volume size numbers are the current values at the time this book was written. Make sure you continue to check with Microsoft to see if the volume sizes have increased since this book's publication.

TABLE 3.1   File-system capabilities

Feature	FAT32	NTFS
Supporting operating systems	All Windows operating systems above Windows 95	Windows 7, 8, 10, Windows Server 2008 /2008 R2; Windows Server 2012/2012 R2, 2016, 2019 (Other previous versions of Windows supports NTFS but they are not mentioned since they are no longer supported.)
Long filename support	Yes	Yes
Efficient use of disk space	Yes	Yes

TABLE 3.1 File-system capabilities *(continued)*

Feature	FAT32	NTFS
Compression support	No	Yes
Encryption support	No before Windows 10 Yes after Windows 10	Yes
Support for local security	No	Yes
Support for network security	Yes	Yes
Maximum volume size	32 GB	16 TB with 4 KB clusters or 256 TB with 64 KB clusters

Windows 10 also supports Compact Disk File System (CDFS). However, CDFS cannot be managed. It is used only to mount and read CDs. Let's start looking at the supported disk file systems.

FAT32

FAT32 is an updated version of File Allocation Table (FAT). The FAT32 version was first shipped with Windows 95 OSR2 (Operating System Release 2) and can be used by every Windows operating system since.

One of the main advantages of FAT32 is its support for smaller cluster sizes, which results in more efficient space allocation than was possible with FAT16. Files stored on a FAT32 partition can use 20 to 30 percent less disk space than files stored on a FAT16 partition. FAT32 supports drive sizes from 512 MB up to 2 TB, although if you create and format a FAT32 partition through Windows 10, the FAT32 partition can only be up to 32 GB. Because of the smaller cluster sizes, FAT32 can also load programs up to 50 percent faster than FAT16 partitions can.

The main disadvantages of FAT32 compared to NTFS are that it does not provide as much support for larger hard drives and it does not provide very robust security options. It also doesn't offer native support for disk compression. Now that you understand FAT32, let's take a look at NTFS.

NTFS

NTFS, which was first used with the NT operating system, offers the highest level of service and features for Windows 10 computers. NTFS partitions can be up to 16 TB with 4 KB clusters or 256 TB with 64 KB clusters.

NTFS offers comprehensive folder-level and file-level security. This allows you to set an additional level of security for users who access the files and folders locally or through the network. For example, two users who share the same Windows 10 computer can be assigned different NTFS permissions so that one user has access to a folder but the other user is denied access to that folder. This is not possible on a FAT32 file system.

NTFS also offers disk-management features—such as compression and encryption capabilities—and data-recovery features.

You should also be aware that there are several different versions of NTFS. Every version of Windows 2000 uses NTFS 3.0. Windows 7/8/10, Windows Vista, Windows XP, Windows Server 2003, Windows Server 2008 / 2008 R2, and Windows Server 2012 / 2012 R2 use NTFS 3.1. NTFS versions 3.0 and 3.1 use similar disk formats, so Windows 2000 computers can access NTFS 3.1 volumes and Windows 10 computers can access NTFS 3.0 volumes. NTFS 3.1 includes the following features:

- When files are read or written to a disk, they can be automatically encrypted and decrypted.

- Reparse points are used with mount points to redirect data as it is written or read from a folder to another volume or physical disk.

- There is support for sparse files, which are used by programs that create large files but allocate disk space only as needed.

- Remote storage allows you to extend your disk space by making removable media (for example, external tapes) more accessible.

- You can use recovery logging on NTFS metadata, which is used for data recovery when a power failure or system problem occurs.

Now that you have seen the differences between FAT32 and NTFS, let's discuss how to convert a FAT32 drive to an NTFS drive.

File System Conversion

In Windows 10, you can convert FAT32 partitions to NTFS. File-system conversion is the process of converting one file system to another without the loss of data. If you format a drive, as opposed to converting it, all the data on that drive will be lost.

To convert a partition, you use the Convert command-line utility. The syntax for the Convert command is as follows:

```
Convert [drive:]/fs:ntfs
```

For example, if you wanted to convert your D: drive to NTFS, you would type the following from a command prompt:

```
Convert D:/fs:ntfs
```

When the conversion process begins, it will attempt to lock the partition. If the partition cannot be locked—perhaps because it contains the Windows 10 operating system files or the system's page file—the conversion will not take place until the computer is restarted.

In Exercise 3.1, you will convert your D: drive from FAT32 to NTFS. For this exercise, it is assumed that you have a D: drive that is formatted with the FAT32 file system. If you don't have a FAT32 drive, open Disk Management by right-clicking the Start button and choosing Disk Management. Click on your C: partition, right-click, and shrink the drive by only 5 to 10 GBs. Now create a simple volume and format it as FAT32 (follow the steps in Exercise 3.1 but choose FAT32).

Using the Convert Command

You can use the /v switch with the Convert command. This switch specifies that you want to use verbose mode, and all messages will be displayed during the conversion process. You can also use the /NoSecurity switch, which specifies that all converted files and folders will have no security applied by default so they can be accessed by anyone.

EXERCISE 3.1

Converting a FAT32 Partition to NTFS

1. Copy some folders to the D: drive.

2. Select Start, and then type **cmd** into the Search box to open a command prompt.

3. In the Command Prompt dialog box, type **Convert D:/fs:ntfs** and press Enter.

4. After the conversion process is complete, close the Command Prompt dialog box.

5. Verify that the folders you copied in step 1 still exist on the partition.

Stopping a Conversion

If you choose to convert a partition from FAT32 to NTFS and the conversion has not yet taken place because it is scheduled on next reboot, you can cancel the conversion by editing the registry with the REGEDIT or REGEDT32 command. The key that needs to be edited is

HKEY_LOCAL_MACHINE\System\CurrentControlSet\Control\SessionManager

The BootExecute value needs to be changed from autoconv\DosDevices\x:/FS:NTFS to autocheck autochk*.

Once you decide which file system you want to use, you need to decide what disk storage type you want to configure. Let's look at some of the disk storage options you have.

Be careful when converting your file system. Once you change a FAT32 file system to NTFS, you cannot change it back without formatting the disk and losing your data.

Configuring NTFS

As mentioned earlier, NTFS has many advantages over FAT32. The main advantages are NTFS Security, Compression, Encryption (EFS), and Quotas. Let's take a look at some of these advantages in greater detail.

NTFS Security   One of the biggest advantages of NTFS is security. NTFS Security (shown in Figure 3.1) is one of the most important aspects of an IT administrator's job. An advantage of NTFS security is that the security can be placed on individual files and folders. It does not matter whether you are local to the data (in front of the machine where the data is stored) or remote to the share (coming across the network to access the data); the security is always in place with NTFS. The default security permission is Users = Read on new folders or shares.

FIGURE 3.1   NTFS Security tab

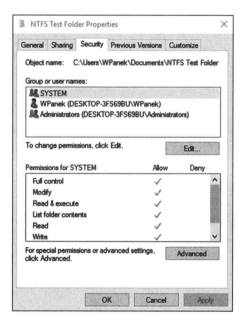

Compression   *Compression* helps compact files or folders to allow for more efficient use of hard drive space. For example, a file that usually takes up 20 MB of space might use only

13 MB after compression. To enable compression, just open the Advanced Attributes dialog box for a folder and check the Compress Contents To Save Disk Space box.

Encryption   *Encrypting File System (EFS)* allows a user or administrator to secure files or folders by using encryption. Encryption employs the user's security identification (SID) number to secure the file or folder. To implement encryption, open the Advanced Attributes dialog box for a folder and check the Encrypt Contents To Secure Data box (see Figure 3.2).

If files are encrypted using EFS and an administrator has to unencrypt the files, there are two ways to do this. First, you can log in using the user's account (the account that encrypted the files) and unencrypt the files. Second, you can become a recovery agent and manually unencrypt the files.

FIGURE 3.2   Setting up encryption on a folder

Quotas   Disk *quotas* give administrators the ability to limit how much storage space a user can have on a hard drive. You have a few options available to you when you set up disk quotas. You can set up disk quotas based on volume or on users.

Setting Quotas by Volume   One way to set up disk quotas is by setting the quota by volume, on a per-volume basis. This means that if you have a hard drive with C:, D:, and E: volumes, you would have to set up three individual quotas (one for each volume). This is your umbrella. This is where you set up an entire disk quota based on the volume for all users.

Setting Quotas by User   You have the ability to set up quotas on volumes by user. Here is where you would individually let users have independent quotas that exceed your umbrella quota.

Specifying Quota Entries   You use quota entries to configure the volume and user quotas. You do this on the Quotas tab of the volume's Properties dialog box. (See Exercise 3.2.)

Creating Quota Templates   Quota templates are predefined ways to set up quotas. Templates allow you to set up disk quotas without needing to create a disk quota from scratch. One advantage of using a template is that when you want to set up disk quotas on multiple volumes (C:, D:, and E:) on the same hard drive, you do not need to re-create the quota on each volume.

Exercise 3.2 will show you how to set up an umbrella quota for all users. This is the disk quota that all users will then follow for whichever drive you set this up on.

EXERCISE 3.2

Configuring Disk Quotas

1. Open Windows Explorer.

2. Right-click the local disk (C:), and choose Properties.

3. Click the Quotas tab.

4. Check the Enable Quota Management check box. Also check the Deny Disk Space To Users Exceeding Quota Limit box.

5. Click the Limit Disk Space To option, and enter **1000MB** in the box.

6. Enter **750MB** in the Set Warning Level To boxes.

7. Click the Apply button. If a warning box appears, click OK. This warning is just informing you that the disk may need to be rescanned for the quota.

8. Now that you have set up an umbrella quota to cover everyone, close the disk quota tool.

Configuring Disk Storage

Windows 10 supports three types of disk storage: basic, dynamic, and GUID Partition Table (GPT). Basic storage is backward compatible with other operating systems and can be configured to support up to four partitions. Dynamic storage is supported by Windows 2000, Windows XP, Windows Vista, Windows 7, Windows 8, Windows 10, and Windows Server 2003 (and above) and allows storage to be configured as volumes. GPT support begins with the Windows 2003 SP1 release and allows you to configure volume sizes larger than 2 TB and up to 128 primary partitions. The following sections describe the basic storage, dynamic storage, and GPT storage configurations.

Basic Storage

Basic storage consists of primary and extended partitions and logical drives that exist within the extended partition. The first partition that is created on a hard drive is called a primary partition and is usually represented as the C: drive. Primary partitions use all of the space that is allocated to the partition, and a single drive letter is used to represent the partition. Only a single extended partition is allowed on any basic disk. Each physical drive can have up to four partitions. You can set up four primary partitions, or you can have three primary partitions and one extended partition. With an extended partition, you can allocate the space however you like, and each suballocation of space (called a logical drive) is represented by a different drive letter. For example, a 500 MB extended partition could have a 250 MB D: partition and a 250 MB E: partition.

At the highest level of disk organization, you have a physical hard drive. You cannot use space on the physical drive until you have logically partitioned the physical drive.

One of the advantages of using multiple partitions on a single physical hard drive is that each partition can have a different file system. For example, the C: drive might be FAT32 and the D: drive might be NTFS. Multiple partitions also make it easier to manage security requirements.

Basic storage is the default, and this is the type that many users continue to use. But what if you want some additional functionality from your storage type? Let's look at some of the more advanced disk storage options.

Dynamic Storage

Dynamic storage is a Windows 10 feature that consists of a dynamic disk divided into dynamic volumes. Dynamic volumes cannot contain partitions or logical drives.

Dynamic storage supports three dynamic volume types: simple volumes, spanned volumes, and striped volumes. Dynamic storage also supports a Redundant Array of Independent Disks (RAID).

To set up dynamic storage, you convert or upgrade a basic disk to a dynamic disk. When converting a basic disk to dynamic, you do not lose any of your data. After the disk is converted, any partitions that existed on the basic disk are converted to dynamic simple volumes and you can then create any additional dynamic volumes required within the dynamic disk.

You create dynamic storage with the Windows 10 Disk Management utility, which is discussed in the section "Using the Disk Management Utility" later in this chapter. Let's take a closer look at the different types of dynamic volumes.

Simple Volumes

A *simple volume* contains space from a single dynamic drive. The space from the single drive can be contiguous or noncontiguous. Simple volumes are used when you have enough disk space on a single drive to hold your entire volume. Figure 3.3 illustrates two simple volumes on a physical disk.

FIGURE 3.3   Two simple volumes

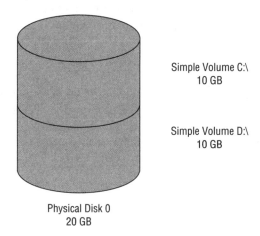

Simple Volume C:\
10 GB

Simple Volume D:\
10 GB

Physical Disk 0
20 GB

Spanned Volumes

A *spanned volume* consists of disk space on two or more dynamic drives; up to 32 dynamic drives can be used in a spanned volume configuration. Spanned volume sets are used to dynamically increase the size of a dynamic volume. When you create spanned volumes, the data is written sequentially, filling space on one physical drive before writing to space on the next physical drive in the spanned volume set. Typically, administrators use spanned volumes when they are running out of disk space on a volume and want to dynamically extend the volume with space from another hard drive.

You do not need to allocate the same amount of space to the volume set on each physical drive. This means you could combine 500 MB on one physical drive with two 750 MB volumes on other dynamic drives, as shown in Figure 3.4.

FIGURE 3.4   A spanned volume set

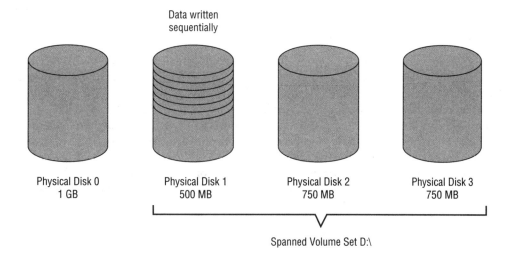

Data written
sequentially

Physical Disk 0
1 GB

Physical Disk 1
500 MB

Physical Disk 2
750 MB

Physical Disk 3
750 MB

Spanned Volume Set D:\

Because data is written sequentially, you do not see any performance enhancements with spanned volumes as you do with striped volumes (discussed next). The main disadvantage of spanned volumes is that if any drive in the spanned volume set fails, you lose access to all of the data in the spanned set.

Striped Volumes

A *striped volume* stores data in equal stripes between two or more (up to 32) dynamic drives, as illustrated in Figure 3.5. Since the data is written sequentially across the stripe, you can take advantage of multiple I/O performance and increase the speed at which data reads and writes take place. Typically, administrators use striped volumes when they want to combine the space of several physical drives into a single logical volume and increase disk performance.

FIGURE 3.5   A striped volume set

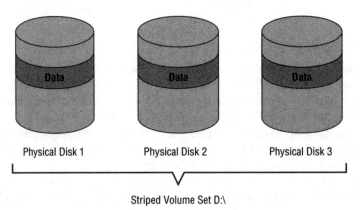

The main disadvantage of striped volumes is that if any drive in the striped volume set fails, you lose access to all of the data in the striped set.

GUID Partition Table

The *GUID Partition Table (GPT)* is available for Windows 10 and was first introduced as part of the Extensible Firmware Interface (EFI) initiative from Intel. Basic and dynamic disks use the Master Boot Record (MBR) partitioning scheme that all operating systems have been using for years. Basic and dynamic disks use Cylinder-Head-Sector (CHS) addressing with the MBR scheme. CHS allows computers to assign addresses to data on the computer's hard-disk drives. This has been an effective way to store data on a hard drive, but there is a newer, more effective way.

The GPT disk-partitioning system uses the GPT to configure the disk area. GPT uses an addressing scheme called Logical Block Addressing (LBA), which is a newer method of accessing hard-disk drives. LBA uses a unique sector number only instead of using the cylinder, head, and sector number. Another advantage is that the GPT header and partition table are written to both the front and the back ends of the disk, which provides for better redundancy.

The GPT disk-partitioning system gives you many benefits over using the MBR system:

- Allows a volume size larger than 2 TB

- Allows up to 128 primary partitions

- Used for both 32-bit and 64-bit Windows 10 editions

- Includes cyclic redundancy check (CRC) for greater reliability

However, there is one disadvantage to using the GPT drives. You can convert a GPT drive only if the disk is empty and unpartitioned. I will show you the steps to creating a GPT disk later in this chapter.

To convert any disk or format any volume or partition, you can use the Disk Management utility. I will show you how to manage your disks using the Disk Management utility in the section "Using the Disk Management Utility."

Cloud-Based Storage

One of the fastest growing parts of the IT world is cloud-based services. From cloud-based user storage to cloud-based corporate data storage, it seems like the cloud is all we hear about anymore.

Microsoft has cloud-based subscription services called Microsoft Azure and OneDrive.

Microsoft Azure

Microsoft Azure (`https://azure.microsoft.com/en-us/`) can be used by almost any operating system on the market (Windows, Linux, etc.), by most applications (Java, .Net, PHP, etc.), and by most device types (Windows, Android, and iOS).

Microsoft Azure is different than many other cloud-based systems because Microsoft Azure doesn't make you choose either your network or the cloud. Many cloud-based service providers want you to use their cloud to run all of your applications and/or storage from their location. Microsoft Azure allows you to extend your current network infrastructure into the cloud to take full advantage of both worlds.

This way you can still have a full IT server room with full-time IT employees but get the benefits of storing data both locally and also in a cloud environment which is then available from anywhere in the world.

One advantage to using Microsoft Azure is that you only pay for what you need. The more cloud-based storage you need, the more you pay for and the less you need means less money. Table 3.2 shows you the maximum amount of data that can be stored on Microsoft Azure.

TABLE 3.2   Microsoft Azure Data Size Availability

Operating System	Maximum Size of Data Source
Windows Server 2012 or above	54400 GB
Windows 8 or above	54400 GB
Windows Server 2008, Windows Server 2008 R2	1700 GB
Windows 7	1700 GB

If you decide that you want your company to use Microsoft Azure for some of its cloud-based storage or all of its cloud-based storage, please go to https://azure.microsoft.com/en-us/ to get the current subscription rates.

Microsoft OneDrive

Another Microsoft-based subscription is called OneDrive (used to be known as SkyDrive). Microsoft's OneDrive is built into Windows 10 by default (see Figure 3.6). OneDrive is a cloud-based storage subscription so home users can store their documents and then access those documents from anywhere in the world (provided that you have Internet access).

FIGURE 3.6   OneDrive Welcome Screen

OneDrive was designed for the average home user who is looking to store data in a safe, secure, cloud-based environment. OneDrive, when first released, was also a consideration for corporate environments, but with the release of Windows Azure, OneDrive is really intended for the home user or corporate user who wants to store some of their own personal documents in the cloud. Corporations would be more inclined to use Microsoft Azure and all of its corporate benefits.

If you or your company decides to purchase the Office 365 subscription, then OneDrive is included for cloud-based storage. If you didn't purchase Office 365, then you have to choose from one of the subscriptions shown in Table 3.3.

Please note that these are the current prices at the time this book was written and these prices may have changed. Be sure to check out Microsoft's
OneDrive web page for current prices (`https://onedrive.live.com/
options/Upgrade`).

TABLE 3.3   OneDrive Subscriptions

Amount of Storage	Subscription Monthly Fee
5 GB	Free
100 GB	$1.99
1000 GB	$6.99

Exercise 3.3 will show you how to set up a OneDrive account for your user account. To
do this access, you must have a Microsoft account. You get 5 GB for free from Microsoft
on the OneDrive cloud-based storage.

EXERCISE 3.3

Configuring OneDrive

1. Open OneDrive.

2. Log into OneDrive using your Microsoft Account as seen in Figure 3.7.

FIGURE 3.7   OneDrive sign-in screen

EXERCISE 3.3 *(continued)*

3. You will see a screen that will show you where your files will be located on your system, as seen in Figure 3.8. Click the Next button.

FIGURE 3.8   OneDrive File Location screen

4. At the Sync files screen, choose what folders that you want to sync with Microsoft and then click Next.

5. A screen will appear telling you that your OneDrive is set up and ready to go (see Figure 3.9).

FIGURE 3.9   OneDrive verification screen

6. Click the Open My OneDrive Folder button to open your folders and Microsoft's OneDrive.

7. Close OneDrive.

Using the Disk Management Utility

The Disk Management utility is a Microsoft Management Console (MMC) snap-in that gives administrators a graphical tool for managing disks and volumes within Windows 10. In the following sections, you will learn how to access the Disk Management utility and use it to perform basic tasks, including managing basic storage and dynamic storage. You will also learn about troubleshooting disks through disk status codes.

But before we dive into the Disk Management utility, let's explore the MMC. It is important to understand the MMC since Disk Management (like many other tools) is actually an MMC snap-in.

Using the Microsoft Management Console

The *Microsoft Management Console (MMC)* is the console framework for application management. The MMC provides a common environment for snap-ins. Snap-ins are administrative tools developed by Microsoft or third-party vendors. Some of the MMC snap-ins that you may use are Computer Management, Active Directory Users and Computers, Active Directory Sites and Services, Active Directory Domains and Trusts, and DNS Management. When you look at the administrative tools, you know that each one of these tools are running inside of an MMC (shown in Figure 3.10).

FIGURE 3.10   The Administrative Tools running in MMCs

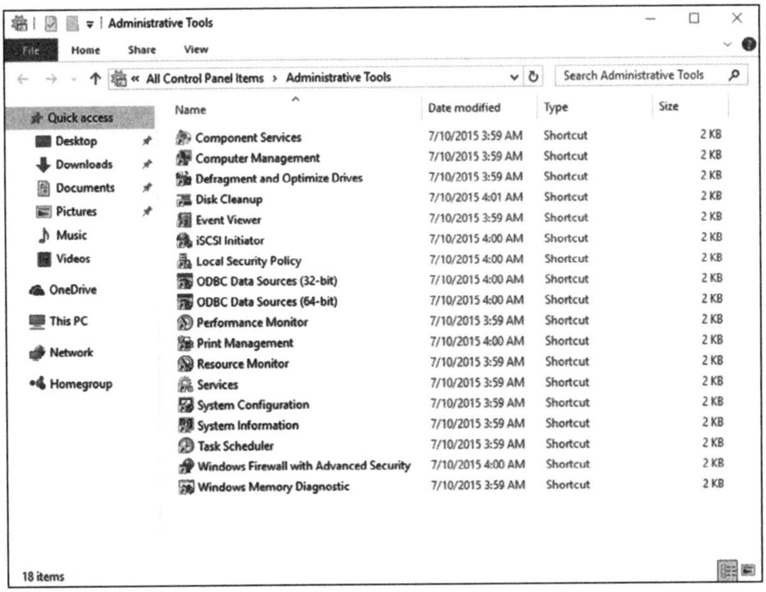

Knowing how to use and configure the MMC snap-ins will allow you to customize your work environment. For example, if you are in charge of Active Directory Users and

Computers and DNS, you can add both of these snap-ins into the same window. This would then allow you to open just one application to configure all your tasks. The MMC offers many other benefits:

- The MMC is highly customizable—you add only the snap-ins you need.

- Snap-ins use a standard, intuitive interface, so they are easier to use than previous versions of administrative utilities.

- You can save customized MMCs and share them with other administrators.

- You can configure permissions so that the MMC runs in authoring mode, which an administrator can manage, or in user mode, which limits what users can access.

- You can use most snap-ins for remote computer management.

As shown in Figure 3.11, by default, the MMC contains three panes: a console tree on the left, a details pane in the middle, and an optional Actions pane on the right. The console tree lists the hierarchical structure of all snap-ins that have been loaded into the console. The details pane contains a list of properties or other items that are part of the snap-in that is highlighted in the console tree. The Actions pane provides a list of actions that the user can access depending on the item selected in the details pane.

FIGURE 3.11   The MMC tree, details pane, and Actions pane

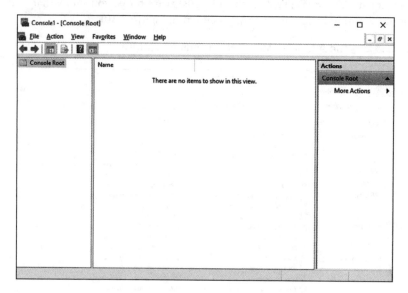

On a Windows 10 computer, to open the MMC, click the Start button and type **MMC** in the Search dialog box. When you first open the MMC, it contains only the Console Root folder, as shown in Figure 3.11. The MMC does not have any default administrative functionality. It is simply a framework used to organize administrative tools through the addition of snap-in utilities.

The first thing that you should decide when using the MMC is which of the different administrative mode types you will employ. You need to decide which mode type is best suited to use for your organization.

Configuring MMC Modes

You can configure the MMC to run in author mode for full access to the MMC functions or in one of three user modes, which have more limited access to the MMC functions. To set a console mode, while in the MMC editor, select File ➢ Options to open the Options dialog box. In this dialog box, you can select from the console modes listed in Table 3.4.

TABLE 3.4   MMC modes

Console Mode	Description
Author mode	Allows use of all the MMC functions.
User mode—full access	Gives users full access to window-management commands, but they cannot add or remove snap-ins or change console properties.
User mode—limited access, multiple window	Allows users to create new windows but not close any existing windows. Users can access only the areas of the console tree that were visible when the console was last saved.
User mode—limited access, single window	Allows users to access only the areas of the console tree that were visible when the console was last saved, and they cannot create new windows.

After you decide which administrative role you are going to run, it's time to start configuring your MMC snap-ins.

Adding Snap-Ins

The biggest advantage of using the MMC is to configure snap-ins the way your organization needs them. Adding snap-ins is a very simple and quick procedure. To add a snap-in to the MMC and save it, complete Exercise 3.4.

EXERCISE 3.4

Adding an MMC Snap-In

1. To start the MMC editor, click Start, type **MMC** into the search box, and press Enter.

2. From the main console window, select File ➢ Add/Remove Snap-In to open the Add Or Remove Snap-Ins dialog box.

3. Highlight the snap-in you want to add as seen in Figure 3.12, and click the Add button.

FIGURE 3.12   The MMC Add Or Remove Snap-ins screen

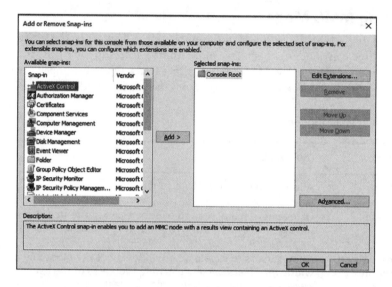

4. If prompted, specify whether the snap-in will be used to manage the local computer or a remote computer. After you choose the MMCs you want in your custom snap-in (shown in Figure 3.13), click the Finish button.

FIGURE 3.13   The MMC Console screen

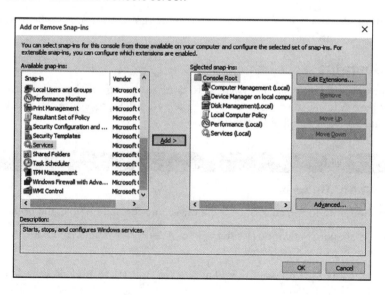

5. When you have finished adding snap-ins, click OK.

6. After you have added snap-ins to create a console, you can save it by selecting File ≻ Save As and entering a name for your console. Place the console on the Desktop as shown in Figure 3.14.

FIGURE 3.14   The MMC Console on the Desktop

You can save the console to a variety of locations, including a program group or the Desktop. By default, custom consoles have a `.msc` filename extension.

Many applications that are MMC snap-ins, including Disk Management, are already configured for you under the Administrative Tools section of Windows 10. Next, let's look at the Disk Management utility.

Understanding the Disk Management Utility

The Disk Management utility, located under the Computer Management snap-in by default, is a one-stop shop for configuring your disk options.

First of all, to have full permissions to use the Disk Management utility, you must be logged on with local Administrative privileges. You can access the Disk Management utility a few different ways. You can right-click Computer from the Start menu and select Manage, and then in Computer Management, select Disk Management. You could also use Control Panel ≻ Administrative Tools ≻ Computer Management.

Once you have launched Computer Management, you must expand the storage section of the console in order to access the Disk Management toolset. The Disk Management utility's opening window, shown in Figure 3.15, displays the following information:

- The volumes that are recognized by the computer

- The type of disk, either basic or dynamic

- The type of file system used by each partition

- The status of the partition and whether the partition contains the system or boot partition

- The capacity (amount of space) allocated to the partition

- The amount of free space remaining on the partition
- The amount of overhead associated with the partition

FIGURE 3.15   The Disk Management window

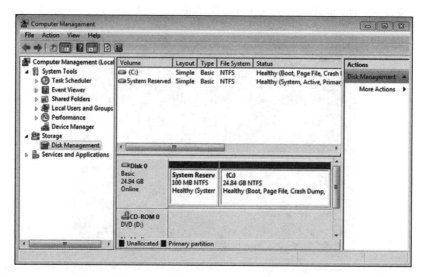

Windows 10 also includes a command-line utility called diskpart, which can be used as a command-line alternative to the Disk Management utility. You can view all of the options associated with the diskpart utility by typing **diskpart** (as seen in Figure 3.16) at a command prompt and then typing **?** at the diskpart prompt.

FIGURE 3.16   The diskpart window

The Disk Management utility allows you to configure and manage your disks. Let's take a look at some of the tasks that you can perform in disk administration.

Managing Administrative Hard-Disk Tasks

The Disk Management utility allows you to perform a variety of hard drive administrative tasks:

- View disk properties.
- View volume and local disk properties.
- Add a new disk.
- Create partitions and volumes.
- Upgrade a basic disk to a dynamic or GPT disk.
- Change a drive letter and path.
- Delete partitions and volumes.

These tasks are discussed in the sections that follow.

Viewing Disk Properties

To view the properties of a disk, right-click the disk number in the lower panel of the Disk Management main window and choose Properties from the context menu. This brings up the disk's Properties dialog box. Click the Volumes tab to see the volumes associated with the disk, as shown in Figure 3.17, which contains the following disk properties:

- The disk number
- The type of disk (basic, dynamic, CD-ROM, removable, DVD, or unknown)
- The status of the disk (online or offline)
- The partition style
- The capacity of the disk
- The amount of unallocated space on the disk
- The amount of space reserved on the disk
- The logical volumes that have been defined on the physical drive

If you click the General tab of a disk's Properties dialog box, the hardware device type, the hardware vendor that produced the drive, the physical location of the drive, and the device status are displayed.

FIGURE 3.17   The Volumes tab of a disk's Properties dialog box

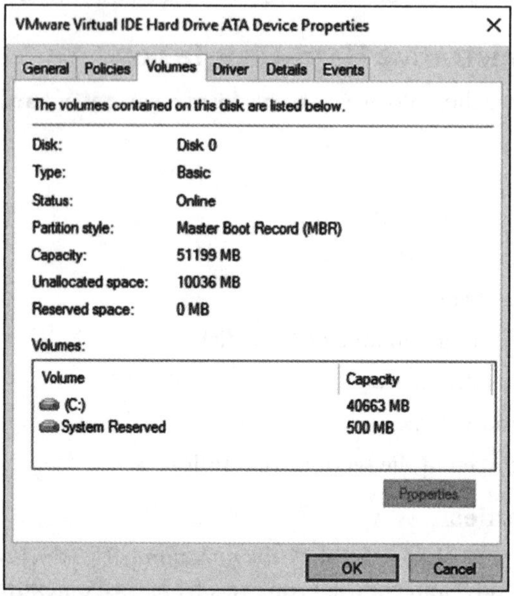

Viewing Volume and Local Disk Properties

On a dynamic disk, you manage volume properties. On a basic disk, you manage partition properties. Volumes and partitions perform the same function, and the options discussed in the following sections apply to both. (The examples here are based on a dynamic disk using a simple volume. If you are using basic storage, you will view the partition properties rather than the volume properties.)

To see the properties of a volume, right-click the volume in the upper panel of the Disk Management main window and choose Properties. This brings up the volume's Properties dialog box. Volume properties are organized on seven tabs: General, Tools, Hardware, Sharing, Security, Previous Versions, and Quota. The Security tab and Quota tab appear only for NTFS volumes. All these tabs are covered in detail in the following items.

General   The information on the General tab of the volume's Properties dialog box, as shown in Figure 3.18, gives you a general idea of how the volume is configured. This dialog box shows the Label, Type, File system, Used and Free space, and Capacity of the volume. The label is shown in an editable text box, and you can change it if desired. The space allocated to the volume is shown in a graphical representation as well as in text form.

The label on a volume or local disk is for informational purposes only. For example, depending on its use, you might give a volume a label such as APPS or ACCTDB.

The Disk Cleanup button starts the Disk Cleanup utility, which you can use to delete unnecessary files, thereby freeing disk space.

FIGURE 3.18   General properties for a volume

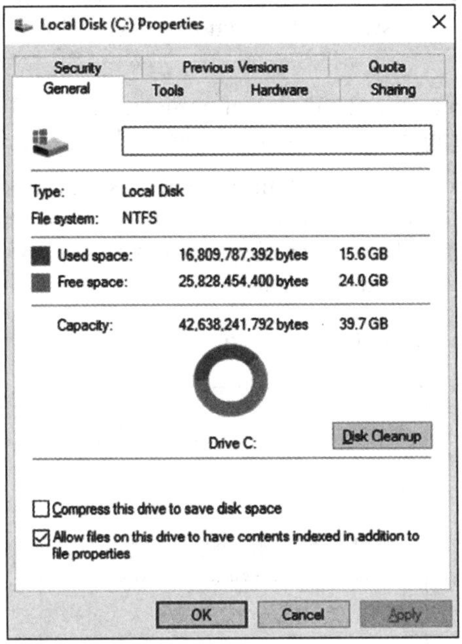

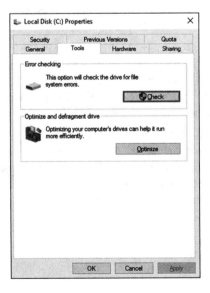

This tab also allows you to configure compression for the volume and to indicate whether the volume should be indexed.

Tools   The Tools tab of the volume's Properties dialog box, shown in Figure 3.19, provides access to two tools.

FIGURE 3.19   The Tools tab of the volume's Properties dialog box

Click the Check button to run the Error-Checking utility to check the volume for errors. You may do this if you were experiencing problems accessing the volume or if the volume had been open during a system restart that did not go through a proper shutdown sequence.

Click the Optimize button to run the Disk Defragmenter utility. This utility defragments files on the volume by storing the files contiguously on the hard drive.

Hardware   The Hardware tab of the volume's Properties dialog box, shown in Figure 3.20, lists the hardware associated with the disk drives that are recognized by the Windows 10 operating system. The bottom half of the dialog box shows the properties of the device that is highlighted in the top half of the dialog box.

FIGURE 3.20   The Hardware tab of the volume's Properties dialog box

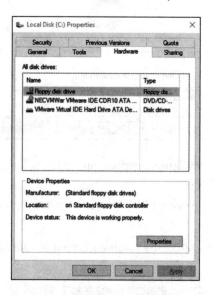

For more details about a hardware item, highlight it and click the Properties button in the lower-right corner of the dialog box. This brings up a Properties dialog box for the item. Your Device Status field should report, "This device is working properly." If that's not the case, you can click the Troubleshoot button (it will appear if the device is not working properly) to get a troubleshooting wizard that will help you discover the problem.

Sharing   On the Sharing tab of the volume's Properties dialog box, shown in Figure 3.21, you can specify whether or not the volume is shared on the network. Volumes are not shared by default. Clicking the Advanced Sharing button will allow you to specify whether the volume is shared and, if so, what the name of the share should be. You will also be able to specify who will have access to the shared volume.

FIGURE 3.21   The Sharing tab of the volume's Properties dialog box

Security   The Security tab of the volume's Properties dialog box, shown in Figure 3.22, appears only for NTFS volumes. The Security tab is used to set the NTFS permissions for the volume.

FIGURE 3.22   The Security tab of the volume's Properties dialog box

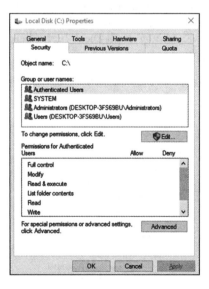

Previous Versions   The Previous Versions tab displays shadow copies of the files that are created by System Restore, as shown in Figure 3.23. Shadow copies of files are backup

copies created by Windows in the background to allow you to restore the system to a previous state. On the Previous Versions tab, you can select a copy of the volume and either view the contents of the shadow copy or copy the shadow copy to another location. If System Restore is not enabled, then shadow copies of a volume will not be created.

FIGURE 3.23   The Previous Versions tab of the volume's Properties dialog box

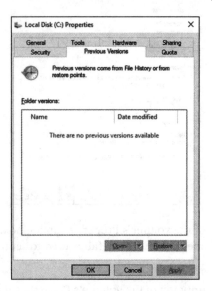

Quota   Quotas give you the ability to limit the amount of hard-disk space that a user can have on a volume or partition (see Figure 3.24). By default, quotas are disabled. To enable quotas, check the Enable Quota Management check box. There are a few options that can be configured when enabling quotas.

FIGURE 3.24   The Quota tab of the volume's Properties dialog box

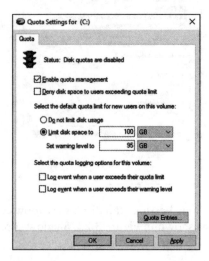

The Deny Disk Space To Users Exceeding Quota Limit check box is another option. When this box is enabled, any user who exceeds their quota limit will be denied disk storage. You can choose not to enable this option, which allows you to just monitor the quotas. You also have the ability to set the quota limit and warning size and to log all quota events as they happen.

Adding a New Disk

New hard disks can be added to a system to increase the amount of disk storage you have. This is a fairly common task that you will need to perform as your application programs and files grow larger.

How you add a disk depends on whether your computer supports hot swapping of drives. Hot swapping is the process of adding a new hard drive while the computer is turned on. Most desktop computers do not support this capability. Remember, your user account must be a member of the Administrators group to install a new drive. The following list specifies configuration options:

Computer Doesn't Support Hot Swapping If your computer does not support hot swapping, you must shut down the computer before you add a new disk. Then add the drive according to the manufacturer's directions. When you've finished, restart the computer. You should find the new drive listed in the Disk Management utility.

Computer Supports Hot Swapping If your computer does support hot swapping, you don't need to turn off your computer first. Just add the drive according to the manufacturer's directions. Then open the Disk Management utility and select Action ➢ Rescan Disks. You should find the new drive listed in the Disk Management utility.

Creating Partitions and Volumes Once you add a new disk, the next step is to create a partition (on a basic disk) or a volume (on a dynamic disk). Partitions and volumes fill similar roles in the storage of data on disks, and the processes for creating them are the same.

Creating a Volume or a Partition

Creating a volume or partition is a fairly easy process. To create the new volume or partition, right-click the unformatted free space and start the wizard.

Exercise 3.5 walks you through the New Volume Wizard for creating a new volume.

EXERCISE 3.5

Creating a New Volume

1. In the Disk Management utility, right-click an area of free storage space and choose the type of volume to create. If only one drive is installed, you will be able to create only a simple volume. You can click New Simple Volume to create a new simple volume.

2. The Welcome To The New Simple Volume Wizard appears. Click the Next button to continue.

3. The Select Volume Size screen appears. Select the size of volume to create, and then click Next to continue.

4. You should see the Assign Drive Letter Or Path screen. You can specify a drive letter, mount the volume as an empty folder, or choose not to assign a drive letter or drive path. If you choose to mount the volume into an empty folder, you can have a virtually unlimited number of volumes, negating the drive-letter limitation. If you choose not to assign a drive letter or path, users will not be able to access the volume. Make your selections, and click Next to continue (shown in Figure 3.25).

FIGURE 3.25   Assign Drive Letter Or Path screen

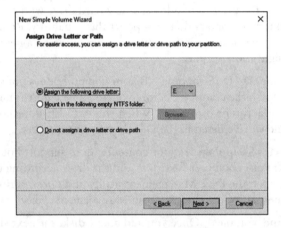

5. The Format Partition screen appears (see Figure 3.26). This screen allows you to choose whether you will format the volume. If you choose to format the volume, you can format it as FAT32 or NTFS. You can also select the allocation unit size, enter a volume label (for information only), specify whether or not you would like to perform a quick format, and choose whether or not to enable file and folder compression. After you've made your choices, click Next.

FIGURE 3.26   Format Partition screen

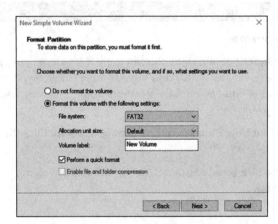

6. The Completing The New Volume Wizard screen appears. Verify your selections. If you need to change any of them, click the Back button to reach the appropriate screen. When everything is correctly set, click the Finish button.

Now that you know how to create a new volume or partition, let's see how to convert a basic disk to dynamic or GPT.

Upgrading a Basic Disk to a Dynamic or GPT Disk

When you perform a fresh installation of Windows 10, your drives are configured as basic disks. To take advantage of the features offered by Windows 10 dynamic or GPT disks, you must upgrade your basic disks to either of those disk configurations.

WARNING   Upgrading basic disks to dynamic disks is a one-way process as far as preserving data is concerned and is a potentially dangerous operation. Before you perform this upgrade (or make any major change to your drives or volumes), create a new backup of the drive or volume and verify that you can successfully restore the backup before proceeding with the change.

Any basic disk can be converted to a dynamic disk, but only a disk with all unformatted free space can be converted to a GPT disk. Exercise 3.6 walks you through converting an MBR based disk to a GPT disk.

EXERCISE 3.6

Converting a Basic Disk to a GPT Disk

1. If the disk that you want to convert has partitions or volumes defined, first delete the partition or volume.

2. Open the Disk Management utility by clicking the Start button, right-clicking Computers, and choosing Manage.

3. Click Disk Management in the lower-left section.

4. Right-click the disk and choose Convert To GPT Disk (shown in Figure 3.27).

EXERCISE 3.6 *(continued)*

FIGURE 3.27 Convert to GPT option

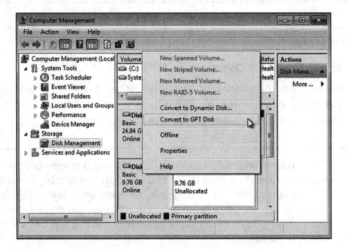

5. After the disk converts, you can right-click the disk and see that the Convert To MBR Disk option is now available.

There are a few other methods for converting an MBR based disk to a GPT disk. You can use the diskpart utility and type in the `Convert GPT` command. You can also create a GPT disk when you first install a new hard drive. After you install the new hard drive, during the initialization phase, you can choose GPT Disk.

Another type of conversion that you may need to perform is that from a basic disk to a dynamic disk. Complete Exercise 3.7 to convert a basic disk to a dynamic disk.

EXERCISE 3.7

Converting a Basic Disk to a Dynamic Disk

1. In the Disk Management utility, right-click the disk you want to convert and select the Convert To Dynamic Disk option.

2. In the Convert To Dynamic Disk dialog box, check the disk that you want to convert and click OK.

3. In the Disks To Convert dialog box, click the Convert button.

4. A confirmation dialog box warns you that you will no longer be able to boot previous versions of Windows from this disk. Click the Yes button to continue to convert the disk.

As you are configuring the volumes or partitions on the hard drive, other things that you may need to configure are the drive letters and paths.

Changing the Drive Letters and Paths

There may be times when you need to change drive letters and paths when you add new equipment. Let's suppose you have a hard drive with two partitions: drive C: assigned as your first partition and drive D: assigned as your second partition. Your DVD drive is assigned the drive letter E:. You add a new hard drive and partition it as a new volume. By default, the new partition is assigned as drive F:. If you want your logical drives to be listed before the DVD drive, you can use the Disk Management utility's Change Drive Letter And Paths option to reassign your drive letters.

When you need to reassign drive letters, right-click the volume for which you want to change the drive letter and choose Change Drive Letter And Paths. This brings up the dialog box shown in Figure 3.28. Click the Change button to access the Change Drive Letter Or Path dialog box. Use the drop-down list next to the Assign The Following Drive Letter option to select the drive letter you want to assign to the volume.

FIGURE 3.28   The dialog box for changing a drive letter or path

In Exercise 3.8, you will edit the drive letter of the partition you created.

EXERCISE 3.8

Editing a Drive Letter

1. Right-click Start ➢ Computer Management; then expand Storage ➢ Disk Management.

2. Right-click a drive that you have created and select Change Drive Letter And Paths.

3. In the Change Drive Letter And Paths dialog box, click the Change button.

4. In the Change Drive Letter Or Path dialog box, select a new drive letter and click OK.

5. In the dialog box that appears, click the Yes button to confirm that you want to change the drive letter.

Another activity that you may need to perform is deleting a partition or volume that you have created. The next section looks at these activities.

Deleting Partitions and Volumes

When configuring your hard disks, there may be a time that you want to reconfigure your drive by deleting the partitions or volumes on the hard drive. You may also want to delete a volume so that you can extend another volume. These are tasks that can be configured in Disk Management.

When deleting a volume or partition, you will see a warning that all the data on the partition or volume will be lost. You have to click Yes to confirm that you want to delete the volume or partition. This confirmation is important because once you delete a partition or volume, it's gone for good along with any data content that was contained within it.

 The system volume, the boot volume, or any volume that contains the active paging (swap) file can't be deleted through the Disk Management utility. If you are trying to remove these partitions because you want to delete Windows 10, you can use a third-party disk-management utility.

In Exercise 3.9, you will delete a partition that you have created. Make sure that if you delete a partition or volume, it is empty; otherwise, back up all the data that you would like to retain before the deletion.

EXERCISE 3.9

Deleting a Partition

1. In the Disk Management utility, right-click the volume or partition that you want to remove and choose Delete Volume.

2. A warning box appears, stating that once this volume is deleted, all data will be lost. Click Yes.

3. The volume will be removed and the area will be returned as unformatted free space.

You may be worried about your users removing devices from their Windows 10 machines. Microsoft has helped you in this situation. You can use removable-device policies to help restrict your users from removing their hardware. Removable-device policies can be created through the use of a Group Policy Object (GPO) on the server. GPOs are policies that are set on a computer or user and allow you to manipulate the Windows 10 environment.

Now that we have explored some of the basic administrative tasks of Disk Management, let's look at how to manage storage.

Managing Storage

The Disk Management utility offers support for managing storage. You can create, delete, and format partitions or volumes on your hard drives. You can also extend or shrink volumes on dynamic disks. Additionally, you can delete volume sets and striped sets.

Managing Dynamic Storage

As noted earlier in this chapter, a dynamic disk can contain simple, spanned, or striped volumes. Through the Disk Management utility, you can create volumes of each type. You can also create an extended volume, which is the process of adding disk space to a single simple volume. The following sections describe these disk-management tasks.

Creating Simple, Spanned, and Striped Volumes

As explained earlier, you use the New Volume Wizard to create a new volume. To start the New Volume Wizard, in the Disk Management utility right-click an area of free space where you want to create the volume. Then, you can choose the type of volume you want to create: simple, spanned, or striped.

When you choose to create a spanned volume, you are creating a new volume from scratch that includes space from two or more physical drives, up to a maximum of 32 drives.

When you choose to create a striped volume, you are creating a new volume that combines free space from 2 to 32 drives into a single logical partition. The free space on all drives must be equal in size in a striped volume. Data in the striped volume is written across all drives in 64 KB stripes. (Data in spanned and extended volumes is written sequentially.) Striped volumes offer you better performance and are normally used for temporary files or folders. The problem with a striped volume is if you lose one of the drives in the volume, the entire striped volume is lost.

Another option that you have with volumes is to extend the volumes to create a larger storage area. In the next section, we will look at that process.

Creating Extended Volumes

When you create an extended volume, you are taking a single, simple volume (maybe one that is almost out of disk space) and adding more disk space to it, using free space that exists on the same physical hard drive. When the volume is extended, it is seen as a single drive letter. To extend a volume, the simple volume must be formatted as NTFS. You cannot extend a system or boot partition.

An extended volume is created when you are using only one physical drive. A spanned volume is created when you are using two or more physical drives. Exercise 3.10 shows you how to create an extended volume.

EXERCISE 3.10

Creating an Extended Volume

1. In the Disk Management utility, right-click the volume you want to extend and choose Extend Volume.

2. The Extend Volume Wizard starts. Click Next.

3. The Select Disks screen appears (see Figure 3.29). You can specify the maximum size of the extended volume. The maximum size you can specify is determined by the amount of free space that exists in all of the dynamic drives on your computer. Click Next to continue.

FIGURE 3.29   The Select Disks screen

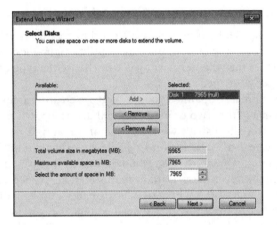

4. The Completing The Extend Volume Wizard screen appears. Click the Finish button. You will see the new volume.

Once a volume is extended, no portion of the volume can be deleted without losing data on the entire set. However, if there is unneeded space on a volume, you can shrink that volume without losing data by using the Shrink Volume option in Disk Management.

 Real World Scenario

You're Running Out of Disk Space

Crystal, a user on your network, is running out of disk space. The situation needs to be corrected so she can be brought back up and running as quickly as possible. Crystal has a 250 GB drive (C:) that runs a very large customer database. She needs additional space added to the C: drive so the database will recognize the data because it must be stored on a single drive letter. Crystal's computer has a single IDE drive with nothing attached to the second IDE channel.

You have two basic options for managing space in this circumstance. One is to upgrade the disk to a larger disk, but this will necessitate reinstalling the OS and the applications and restoring the user's data. The other choice is to add a temporary second drive and extend the volume. This will at least allow Crystal to be up and running—but it should not be considered a permanent solution. If you do choose to extend the volume and then either drive within the volume set fails, the user will lose access to both drives. When Crystal's workload allows time for maintenance, you can replace the volume set with a single drive.

One issue you may run into with hard drives is that they go bad from time to time. If you have ever heard a hard drive fail, you know the sound: it is a distinct clicking. Once you have experienced it, you will never forget it.

Windows 10 Devices in Azure

So now that we have looked at configuring the actual Windows 10 device, it's time to look at how we can use Azure to help set up and manage our Windows 10 devices.

The Devices section in Azure allows an Azure AD administrator to set up which devices can access Azure AD. Administrators can also configure device settings and device roaming settings (Enterprise State Roaming). Azure AD administrators can perform auditing and troubleshooting from the Devices section.

But to make sure that your users and devices can access Azure, you need to make sure that you purchase Azure licenses. The Licenses section in Azure AD allows you to view purchased licensing for additional Azure AD components. If you purchase additional Azure AD components (for example, Azure Active Directory Premium P2 or Enterprise Mobility + Security E5), those additional components will show up in this Licenses section. You can also see if there are any licensing issues in this section.

The Licenses section also allows you to view additional components that are available and what those components do. Azure AD administrators can also view auditing and get troubleshooting from this section.

So after you purchase your licenses and you are ready to go, you can then configure Azure AD with Compliance Policies. These policies allow you to setup and configure how Windows 10 devices will work within the Azure network.

Before we dive in to policies and profiles for your devices, let's take a look at Microsoft Intune. Intune will be discussed in detail in Chapter 4, "Planning and Managing Microsoft Intune," but I want to just explain a bit of what Intune can do for you. It's important to understand a little about Intune because even though these policies and profiles are added to devices and users, you create them in Intune.

Microsoft Intune is a device management system. Microsoft Intune allows administrators to manage mobile devices, mobile applications, and PC management capabilities all from the cloud.

Administrators using Intune can provide their users with access to corporate applications, data, and resources from almost anywhere and on almost any device while also keeping your corporate information secure.

Microsoft Intune also helps you save money because Intune allows you to license users instead of licensing devices. So, if you have a user that works from multiple devices (laptop, tablet, and Windows phone), you only pay once for the user license instead of multiple times for all of the user's devices.

Administrators can use Microsoft Intune to support and manage Windows 10. Administrators can use Intune on a Windows 10 device for the following:

- Enrollment
- Organization resource access
- Application management
- Policies
- Inventory
- Reporting
- Remote wipe

Microsoft Intune is an add-on to your Azure subscription, but if you want to deploy software using the cloud or set up rules for how your devices and users will function, Intune is a subscription that you should add to your cloud-based utilities. Let's now take a look at how you can set up policies and profiles for your devices and users.

Compliance Policies

One of the advantages to using Azure is the ability to protect the corporate data by ensuring that users and devices meet certain requirements. When using Intune, this is referred to as compliance policies. Compliance policies are rules and settings that your users and their devices must follow in order to connect and access Intune.

Compliance policies, along with Conditional Access, ensures that administrators can stop users and devices that don't follow the rules that your organization has determined as necessary for access. For example, the Intune administrator can require some of the following:

- Corporate users must enter a password on their mobile devices to access data.
- Ensures that the device hasn't been cracked, rooted, or jail broken. Administrators can ensure that devices are under a minimum threat level.
- Ensure that devices have a minimum operating system along with updates.

Azure Active Directory, along with Conditional Access, allows Intune to enforce the compliances that your organizations want to use. When devices enroll in Intune, the enrollment registration begins with Azure AD and the device information gets placed into

Azure AD. As part of this registration process is the device's compliance status. This device compliance status is then used by the policies in Conditional Access and based on that, corporate resources are either blocked or allowed.

One advantage that you get using compliance policies is that an administrator can assign the policy to either a user (using a user group) or a device (using a device group). If a policy is assigned to a user, all the user's devices are also checked for policy compliance.

Microsoft recommends that if you are using Windows 10 version 1803 or higher, the policy should be deployed to the device group if the user doesn't enroll the device. By using device groups, Azure administrators can use compliancy reporting to ensure that the devices meet complexity.

Conditional Access

The Conditional Access section (see Figure 3.30) allows an Azure AD administrator to set security policies. When it comes to Azure, one of the biggest concerns for organizations is cloud-based security. Azure allows users to access their networks from anywhere in the world and from almost any device. Because of this, just securing resource access is not enough. This is where Conditional Access Policies comes in to play.

FIGURE 3.30   Conditional Access Policies section

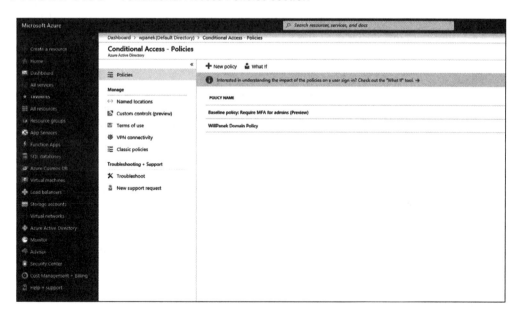

Conditional Access policies allow an organization to set how resources are accessed using access control decisions (who has access to resources) through Azure AD. Setting up Conditional Access policies allows an organization to have automated access control decisions based on the policies that your organization sets. Some of the situations that Conditional Access policies can help with are sign-in risk, network location risk, device management, and client applications.

With Conditional Access

If a device complies to the policy rules that you have configured, that device can get access to data, email, and other company resources. If the device does not meet the minimum policies that you have set up, then that device will not have access to any of the company's resources. This is how conditional access works when it is set up and enabled.

Without Conditional Access

If you decide that you do not want to use conditional access, you can still use compliance policies. If you decide to use compliance policies without conditional access, you can access reports showing the device compliance status. Administrators can evaluate this information and decide if conditional access is then needed or if you can continue to use Azure without any conditional access policies.

Azure Classic Portal vs. Azure Portal

In January 2018, Microsoft discontinued the Azure classic portal. When it comes to using device compliance policies, the version of the Azure portal that you used would help determine how you could set up your policies. The difference between the two portals is how compliances function.

- If an administrator uses the classic Azure portal, only one device compliance policy is used for all of your different devices.
- In the new Azure portal, compliances can be created for each different type of device platform that connects to an Azure subscription.

When an administrator created a device compliance policy using the classic Azure portal, the policy would not have shown up in the current Azure portal. The policy would still be in effect and the policy would have had to be managed using the classic Azure portal.

If a Device Compliance Policy was created in the classic Azure portal and then one is created in the current Azure portal, the current Azure portal policy will take precedence over the policy created in the classic portal. If an Azure administrator wants their devices to use all of the new compliance policy features, the administrator must create the policy in the current Azure portal.

Creating a Compliance Policy

To create a compliance policy, the Azure administrator needs to ensure that a few requirements and steps are completed before creating the policies. The following requirements are needed to set up compliance policies:

- Subscriptions
- Microsoft Intune
- To use Conditional Access, your organization needs an Azure Active Directory (AD) Premium edition. If using Microsoft Intune compliance only, your organization doesn't require an Azure AD subscription.

- Supported platforms
  - Android
  - Android Enterprise
  - iOS
  - MacOS
  - Windows 10
  - Windows 8.1
  - Windows Phone 8.1

The administrator must also enroll devices in Intune (required to see the compliance status). It is also necessary to enroll the devices to one user or enroll the device without a primary user assigned. Enrolling devices to multiple users is not supported.

Once you have ensured that your organization has met the minimum requirements to set up compliance policies, then the next step is to actually create the policy. The following steps will walk you through the process of creating a policy:

1. Sign in to the Intune portal.

2. Select Device Compliance. Administrators can choose from the following options:

   - **Overview:** This will show you a summary of devices along with the number of devices that are compliant or not evaluated. This screen will also show the list of policies and individual settings in those policies.

   - **Manage:** This screen allows an administrator to create new device policies, send notifications to non-compliant devices, and it will also allow an administrator to enable network fencing. Network fencing allows an administrator to create a compliance policy based on a network location.

   - **Monitor:** This section allows an administrator to check the compliance status of their devices along with checking the status at the setting and policy levels.

   - **Setup:** This option allows an administrator to use built-in compliance policies, use Jamf Pro software to manage your end-users' Macs, add a mobile threat defense connector, and enable Microsoft Defender advanced threat protection (ATP).

3. Select Policies ➢ Create Policy. To create a policy, the administrator needs to fill in the following properties:

   - **Name:** Administrators need to enter a name for the new policy.

   - **Description:** Administrators should enter a description for the policy so that the policy is easy to recognize and maintain in the future. This setting is optional, but highly recommended.

   - **Platform:** Here is where the administrator can choose the platform of their devices. Administrators have the following options to choose from:
     - Android
     - Android Enterprise
     - iOS

- MacOS

- Windows Phone 8.1

- Windows 8.1 and later

- Windows 10 and later

- **Settings:** This section allows the administrator to choose which policy settings that they want to implement.

4. Once you have completed filling in all the sections, select OK and then choose **Create** to save your changes.

The policy is now created and the policy will now show up in the policy list. The next step is to assign the policy to your user groups. To assign user groups to your policy, complete the following steps:

1. Choose the policy that you want to assign to a user group. Policies are shown in **Device Compliance ≻ Policies.**

2. Select the policy and then choose **Assignments.** Administrators have the ability to include or exclude Azure Active Directory (AD) security groups.

3. To see your Azure AD security groups, choose the **Selected Groups** option. Select the user groups that you want this policy to apply to and then choose **Save** to deploy the policy to the users.

Migrating Policies to MDM

Once an organization decides to move to Microsoft Azure, one of the tasks that an administrator will need to consider is moving on-site Group Policy Object settings (GPOs) to MDM. The first thing that the administrator needs to do before migrating their GPOs to MDM is to analyze their current GPOs and figure out what needs to be moved to the MDM management tool in Azure.

Microsoft understands that GPO analysis needs to be done and that's why they developed the MDM Migration Analysis Tool (MMAT) to help administrators complete this task.

MMAT looks at your organization's GPOs to see which ones have been created for a user or computer. MMAT then generates a report that an administrator can use to see which equivalent MDM policies will need to be set. The report that MMAT will generate can be in both XML and HTML formats.

To ensure that your administrators get all of the current features of MMAT, make sure that you download the current version. If you would like to get more information about the MDM Migration Analysis tool or download the most current version of the tool, please visit https://github.com/ WindowsDeviceManagement/MMAT.

If your Azure administrator decides that they want to use the MMAT, they will need to complete the following steps:

1. Install the Remote Server Administration Tools.

2. Install the zipped folder for MMAT to your computer and unzip the folder.

3. Open Windows PowerShell as an administrator.

4. In PowerShell, change the directory location to where you installed the MMAT files (these files include PowerShell scripts).

5. Run the following PowerShell script:

```
Set-ExecutionPolicy -ExecutionPolicy Unrestricted -Scope Process
$VerbosePreference="Continue" ./Invoke-MdmMigrationAnalysisTool.ps1
-collectGPOReports -runAnalysisTool
```

After the `Invoke-MdmMigrationAnalysisTool.ps1`script is completed, the Azure administrator will have three reports that they can look at:

MDMMigrationAnalysis.xml   This file is the XML version of the MMAT report and it contains information about the policies that are set for the targeted user and computer. It will also show you how these policies map to MDM.

MDMMigrationAnalysis.html   This file is the HTML version of the same XML report.

MdmMigrationAnalysisTool.log   This file is a log file that will give Azure administrators more information about how the MMAT tool ran.

Device Configuration Profiles

Another way to set up Intune rules as an administrator is a Device Configuration Profile. Profiles work like policies since they are also another way to put rules onto your Intune devices.

Microsoft Intune, along with device configuration profiles, allows an administrator to configure settings and features that can be enabled or disabled on the different devices that your users will connect with.

Device Configuration Profile Options

Device configuration profile settings and features are added to your configuration profiles. Administrators can build these profiles for devices and platforms, including iOS, Android, and Windows. After these profiles are built, then an Intune administrator can apply or assign these profiles to their devices. These device configuration settings and features can include some of the following:

Administrative Templates   Administrative templates have hundreds of Windows 10 (and above) settings that an administrator can set for programs and features including Internet Explorer, OneDrive, Office, and other programs. These settings are very similar to setting up GPOs but they are all cloud based settings.

Certificates   Certificate settings allow an Intune administrator to configure certificates for applications like WiFi, VPN, and email profiles. These settings can be configured for many different devices including Android and Android Enterprise, iOS and MacOS, Windows Phone 8.1, Windows 8.1, and Windows 10 and later.

Custom Profile   Custom profile settings allow an Intune Administrator to configure options that are not automatically included with Intune. For example, an administrator can set a custom profile that allows you to create ADMX-backed policy or even enable self-service password resets. Custom profile allows you to set options for Android and Android Enterprise, iOS and MacOS, and Windows Phone 8.1 devices.

Delivery Optimization   Delivery optimization allows Intune administrators to set up and configure updates to Windows 10 (and above) devices that connect to the cloud.

Device Features   Device features make it easy for administrators to configure iOS and MacOS devices. These settings allow administrators to configure things like AirPrint, notifications, and lock screen messages. Administrators can set these configurations on iOS and MacOS devices.

Device Restrictions   Device restrictions allow an Intune administrator to configure settings for things like hardware, data, and security settings on your devices. Device restrictions can be created to prevent iOS device users from using their device's camera. Device restrictions can be used on Android and Android Enterprise, iOS and MacOS, Windows 10 Team, and Windows 10 and later devices.

Edition Upgrade   Edition upgrade allows you to upgrade Windows 10 (and later) devices to a newer version of Windows.

Email   Email options allow you to create, monitor, and assign Email Exchange ActiveSync email settings for your devices. For example, email profiles allow your users to have access to your organization's email while using their own personal devices. Email options can be set for Android and Android Enterprise, iOS, Windows Phone 8.1, and Windows 10 and later devices.

Endpoint Protection   Endpoint protection allows you to set Windows 10 (and above) options for BitLocker and Windows Defender settings. For example, you can set Windows Defender for a threat score setting. If a user with a high threat score rating attempts to access cloud-based resources, you can stop this device from accessing your resources.

Identity Protection   Identity protection allows an Intune administrator to control the Windows Hello for Business experience on Windows 10 and Windows 10 Mobile devices. Identity protection settings allow you to configure options for devices such as PINs and gestures for Windows Hello for Business.

Kiosk   Kiosk settings allow an administrator to configure a Windows 10 (and later) device to run a single application or run many applications. Kiosk systems are normally designed for use in a location where many people can use the same device and that device will only run limited applications. Administrators have the ability to also customize other features, including a start menu and a web browser. Kiosk settings are also available for Android and Android Enterprise and iOS devices, but you need to configure these devices as device restrictions. So it can still function as a Kiosk device but it's configured differently.

Shared Multi-User Device   Shared multi-user devices are devices where multiple users will use the device to do day to day activities. This is different than a Kiosk based machine. Kiosk based machines are machines used by many users but they run limited programs. Shared multi-user devices are devices that users use to do their job while at work but other users will use the same device. These devices normally run all of the organization's software so people can do their jobs. For example, if you are in an environment where you have shift workers. You may have multiple shifts and different people will use a machine when they are working during their shift.

Shared multi-user device settings allow an administrator to control many of the device features and manage these shared devices through Intune.

 To see a complete or updated list of device configuration profile settings, please visit Microsoft's website at https://docs.microsoft.com/en-us/intune/device-profiles.

Building Device Configuration Profiles

One nice advantage that you will notice is that building device configuration profiles work a lot like building device compliances. Many of the same settings are available as you build the device configuration profile. To build a device configuration profile, you would complete the following steps:

1. Sign in to the Intune portal.

2. Select **Device Configuration**. Administrators can choose from the following options:

   - **Overview:** This will show you the status of your profiles and it also provides additional details on the different profiles that you have assigned to your users and devices.

   - **Manage:** This screen allows an administrator to create device profiles, upload PowerShell scripts that can run within the profile, and add data plans to eSIM devices.

   - **Monitor:** This section allows an administrator to view the status of a device configuration profile and see if that profile was a success or failure. This screen also allows you to view logs about your profiles.

   - **Setup:** This option allows an administrator to add a certificate authority or enable Telecom Expense Management in the profile.

3. Select **Profiles ➤ Create Profile** to create a profile. The Intune administrator needs to fill in the following properties:

   - **Name:** Administrators need to enter a name for the new profile.

   - **Description:** Administrators should enter a description for the profile so that the profile is easy to recognize and maintain in the future. This setting is optional, but highly recommended.

- **Platform**: Here is where the administrator can choose the platform of their devices. Administrators have the following options to choose from:
  - Android
  - Android Enterprise
  - iOS
  - MacOS
  - Windows Phone 8.1
  - Windows 8.1 and later
  - Windows 10 and later
- **Profile type**: Select the type of settings you want to create. The list that will be shown will depend on the platform you choose.
- **Settings**: This section allows the administrator to choose which profile settings that they want to implement.

4. Once you have completed filling in all the sections, select **OK** and then choose **Create** to save your changes.

Once you have completed building the device configuration profile, the next step would be to add a scope tag to the profile. Scope tags allow an administrator to assign and filter policies to a specific group (for example HR or Sales) of employees. To add a scope tag, complete the following steps.

1. Select **Scope (Tags)**.
2. Select **Add** to create a new scope tag. Or, select an existing scope tag from the list.
3. Select **OK** to save your changes.

Summary

There are two different ways that you can format your hard disk in a Windows 10 operating system: FAT32 and NTFS. NTFS has many advantages over FAT32, including security, disk quotas, and compression, just to name a few. If you format a FAT32 partition using Windows 10, then encryption will be available. But on any older Windows clients, FAT32 will not include encryption.

In addition to the way you format your hard disk, you can configure your hard disk as a basic disk or a dynamic disk and must choose to either leave your disk partition system as the default MBR or choose to convert it to a GPT disk. You can use the Disk Management MMC snap-in to configure your hard disks and file system.

In this chapter, I explained how compliance polices, along with Conditional Access, ensures that administrators can stop users and devices that don't follow the rules that your organization has determined as necessary for access.

I also talked about converting onsite GPOs to MDM using the MMAT tool. The MMAT tool allows an administrator to analyze GPOs and determine which MDM policies will be the equivalent setting.

Finally, you learned about using device configuration profiles. Device configuration profiles work like GPO policies but they are policies that are designed strictly for cloud-based rules.

Exam Essentials

Understand the different hard-disk storage types.   Windows 10 supports three types of disk storage: basic, dynamic, and GUID partition table (GPT). Basic storage is backward compatible with other operating systems and can be configured to support up to four partitions. Dynamic storage is supported by all Windows operating systems above Windows 2000 and allows storage to be configured as volumes. GPT storage allows you to configure volume sizes larger than 2 TB and up to 128 primary partitions.

Know Compliance Policies   Make sure you understand how compliance policies, along with Conditional Access, ensures that administrators can stop users and devices that don't follow the rules that your organization has determined as necessary for access.

Understand the MMAT Tool   Understand that GPO analysis needs to be done and how the MDM Migration Analysis Tool (MMAT) helps administrators complete this task.

Know Device Configuration Profiles   Device configuration profile settings and features are added to your configuration profiles. Administrators can build these profiles for devices and platforms, including iOS, Android, and Windows and these settings are for cloud based Intune devices.

Review Questions

1. You are the administrator for an organization that has 100 devices that run Windows 10 Pro. The devices are joined to Azure AD and enrolled in Microsoft Intune. You need to upgrade the computers to Windows 10 Enterprise. What should you configure in Intune?

   A. A device enrollment policy

   B. A device cleanup rule

   C. A device compliance policy

   D. A device configuration profile

2. You are creating a device configuration profile in Microsoft Intune. You need to implement an ADMX-backed policy. Which profile type should you use?

   A. Identity protection

   B. Custom

   C. Device restrictions

   D. Device restrictions (Windows 10 Team)

3. You are the network administrator for a large training organization. Your organization plans to deploy Windows 10 tablets to 50 meeting rooms. These tablets will be managed by using Microsoft Intune. The tablets have an application named Storm1 that many users will use. You need to configure the Windows 10 tablets so that any user can use Storm1 without having to sign in. Users must not be able to use other applications on the tablets. Which device configuration profile type should you use?

   A. Kiosk

   B. Endpoint protection

   C. Identity protection

   D. Device restrictions

4. You have 175 computers that run Windows 10. The computers are joined to Microsoft Azure Active Directory (AD) and enrolled in Microsoft Intune. You have been asked to enable self-service password reset on the sign-in screen. Which settings should you configure in Microsoft Intune?

   A. Device configuration

   B. Device compliance

   C. Device enrollment

   D. Conditional access

5. Will has installed Windows 10 on his Windows XP computer. The machine is now a dual-boot computer. He has FAT32 for Windows XP and NTFS for Windows 10. In addition, he boots his computer to Windows XP Professional for testing an application's compatibility with both operating systems. Which of the following file systems will be seen by both operating systems?

   A. Only the FAT32 partition will be seen by both operating systems.

   B. Only the NTFS partition will be seen by both operating systems.

   C. Neither the FAT32 partition nor the NTFS partition will be seen by both operating systems.

   D. Both the FAT32 partition and the NTFS partition will be seen by both operating systems.

6. Paige is considering upgrading her basic disk to a dynamic disk on her Windows 10 computer. She asks you to help her understand the function of dynamic disks. Which of the following statements is true of dynamic disks in Windows 10?

   A. Dynamic disks can be recognized by older operating systems such as Windows NT 4 in addition to new operating systems such as Windows 10.

   B. Dynamic disks are supported only by Windows 2000 Server and Windows Server 2003.

   C. Dynamic disks support features such as simple partitions, extended partitions, spanned partitions, and striped partitions.

   D. Dynamic disks support features such as simple volumes, extended volumes, spanned volumes, mirrored volumes, and striped volumes.

7. Bruce frequently works with a large number of files. He is noticing that the larger the files get, the longer it takes to access them. He suspects that the problem is related to the files being spread over the disk. What utility can be used to store the files contiguously on the disk?

   A. Disk Defragmenter

   B. Disk Manager

   C. Disk Administrator

   D. Disk Cleanup

8. You have a Microsoft 365 subscription. All computers are enrolled in Microsoft Intune. You have business requirements for securing your Windows 10 devices. You need to lock any device that has a high Windows Defender Advanced Threat Protection (Windows Defender ATP) risk score. Which device configuration profile type should you use?

   A. Kiosk

   B. Endpoint protection

   C. Identity protection

   D. Device restrictions

9. You have been asked by your boss to set up a device configuration profile in Intune to allow your users to be able to reset their own passwords. Which device configuration profile option should you configure in Microsoft Intune?

   A. Kiosk

   B. Endpoint protection

   C. Identity protection

   D. Custom

10. Your company uses Microsoft Intune to manage all devices. The company uses conditional access to restrict access to Microsoft 365 services for devices that do not comply with the company's security policies. You want to view which devices will be prevented from accessing Microsoft 365 services. What should you use?

    A. The Device Health solution in Windows Analytics

    B. The Windows Defender Security Center

    C. Device compliance in the Intune admin center

    D. The Conditional access blade in the Azure Active Directory admin center

Chapter
4

Planning and Managing Microsoft Intune

MICROSOFT EXAM OBJECTIVES COVERED IN THIS CHAPTER:

✓ **Manage Intune device enrollment and inventory**

  ▪ Configure enrollment settings; configure Intune automatic enrollment; enable device enrollment; enroll non-Windows devices; enroll Windows devices; generate custom device inventory reports; review device inventory

✓ **Deploy and update applications**

  ▪ Assign apps to groups; Deploy apps by using Intune; deploy apps by using Microsoft Store for Business; deploy O365 ProPlus; enable sideloading of apps into images; gather Office readiness data; configure IE Enterprise mode; configure and implement assigned access or public devices

✓ **Implement Mobile Application Management (MAM)**

  ▪ Implement MAM policies; manage MAM policies; plan MAM; configure Windows Information Protection; implement Azure Information Protection templates; securing data by using Intune

In this chapter, I am going to talk about Microsoft Intune and how you can use it to manage devices and software. I will show you how to set up and configure an Intune subscription and how you can use that subscription to help your network users get the most out of the network resources and software.

I will start the chapter by talking about managing devices using Intune. I will show you how to provision user accounts and enroll devices. I will also discuss how to manage and configure devices using the Microsoft Intune subscription.

I will continue the discussion by showing you how to deploy and configure updates using Intune. I will show you how to use the in-Console monitoring tools and how to approve and decline updates.

I will then talk about working with mobile devices, including Windows tablets, broadband metering and tethering, and how to wipe mobile devices for employees who leave the company.

Finally I will show you how to use Intune to help deploy and maintain your company's software packages. I will also talk to you about SideLoading applications into your users' devices. We will then talk about the different type of reports that you can run to check on the different hardware and software in your environment.

So let's get started with the ability to use Microsoft Intune to help manage and maintain your corporate devices.

It looks like Microsoft is rebranding Microsoft Intune. The new name seems to be Intune Microsoft Enterprise Mobility + Security. This issue is that the exam objectives still are showing the name as Intune. Since the exam objectives still use the name Intune, I will refer to it that way in this chapter. But even if the name does change, the information is still the same.

Managing Devices with Microsoft Intune

I think that the first thing we need to discuss in this chapter is exactly what Microsoft Intune is. Microsoft Intune is a device management system (see Figure 4.1). Microsoft Intune allows administrators to manage mobile devices, mobile applications, and PC management capabilities all from the cloud.

FIGURE 4.1   Microsoft Intune Dashboard

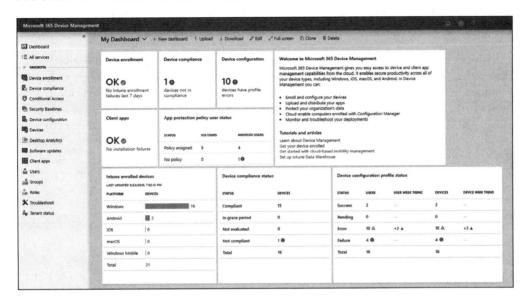

Administrators using Intune can provide their users with access to corporate applications, data, and resources from almost anywhere and on almost any device while also keeping your corporate information secure.

Microsoft Intune also helps you save money because Intune allows you to license users instead of licensing devices. So if you have a user that works from multiple devices (laptop, tablet, and Windows phone) you only pay once for the user license instead of multiple times for all of the user's devices.

Administrators can use Microsoft Intune to support and manage Windows 10. Administrators can use Intune on a Windows 10 device for the following tasks:

- Enrollment
- Organization resource access
- Application management
- Policies
- Inventory
- Reporting
- Remote wipe

Microsoft Intune is built on Microsoft Azure Active Directory and System Center. Active Directory is a Directory Services database created by Microsoft. Directory Services was originally designed by Novell and starting in Windows Server 2000, Microsoft's version, Active Directory, was introduced to the world. To put this in an easy way to think about, Active Directory is just a database that allows administrators to control access to the network.

Microsoft has now taken Active Directory to a new level with cloud based Active Directory or Azure Active Directory. Now instead of requiring your organization to buy Windows Server and the required hardware, you can just use a cloud based version of Active Directory.

Microsoft System Center Configuration Manager (SCCM) allows administrators to have a wide-ranging solution for change and configuration management. Configuration Manager allows an administrator to perform some of the following tasks:

- Deploy corporate operating systems, applications, and updates.

- Monitor and fix computers for compliance requirements.

- Monitor hardware and software inventory.

- Remotely administer devices.

Understanding Microsoft Intune Benefits

Microsoft Intune provides many different benefits to help an IT department be more productive and keep systems running all on the same software. Intune allows an IT department the ability to keep corporate data secure while allowing users to access the same company software from any device that they want to work from. Let's take a look at some other Intune benefits:

- Multiple device enrollments for users. Licenses are per user and not per device. So users can work from multiple devices.

- Corporate data security for users and applications like Microsoft Exchange, Outlook, and Office.

- The ability to use Office 365 from any approved device.

- Since Microsoft Intune is a cloud based system, the IT department is not required to build an infrastructure. This saves the additional cost of buying and maintaining hardware and software.

- Microsoft Intune extends your System Center Configuration Manager through both the cloud and on premise versions by connecting the two systems together through the use of an application connector.

- Microsoft 24/7 support is available through worldwide phone support or online support. Also administrators have access to Microsoft.com for Intune FAQs and knowledge base.

- Corporations have multiple licensing options available to them to choose from. Intune is also part of the Enterprise Mobility Suite by default.

Configuring Intune Subscriptions

When you are considering using Microsoft Intune, you must think about the subscription type you want. You can start with a free 30-day trial or move directly into a full paid subscription. Either choice allows you to start managing mobile devices and corporate computers immediately.

One of the nice advantages of Intune subscriptions is available if you decide to add at least 150 user licenses. If you reach 150 licenses, you get to use Microsoft's FastTrack Benefits Center. This benefit also allows a Microsoft specialist to work with your organization as part of the FastTrack benefits. The Microsoft specialist then helps you get the most out of using Intune and all of its benefits.

The process to start using Microsoft Intune is very easy and free. You go to Microsoft's website and sign up for a free 30-day trial of Intune. Then you start adding your users, groups, and devices. If you decide that Microsoft Intune is right for your organization, you can then sign up for one of the monthly rates.

Once you have decided to take that next step, you need to start redesigning your company's infrastructure to include the cloud-based subscription. This can be as easy as setting up your DNS servers to include the cloud-based services or as complex as adding all of your devices to the cloud and phasing out many of the infrastructure servers that you currently have running in house.

Whatever you decide, one of the most important phases of moving to a cloud-based system is planning. Once you have made the decision to move to the cloud, that's when the real work and planning comes into play:

- Will you be moving all users to Azure Active Directory?

- Will you be using the cloud just for device and software deployment?

- Will you be phasing out in-house equipment?

- Will you allow users to use their own devices (Bring Your Own Device [BYOD])?

- If users use their personal devices, will you supply them with corporate software applications?

- Will you be using Office 2019 or Office 365?

When you sign up for a Microsoft Intune account, you will choose a domain for your Intune subscription. After you sign up for your Intune subscription, Microsoft will send you an email that will contain your Intune information. Figure 4.2 shows you an example of the information contained within the Microsoft Intune email.

FIGURE 4.2   Microsoft Intune email

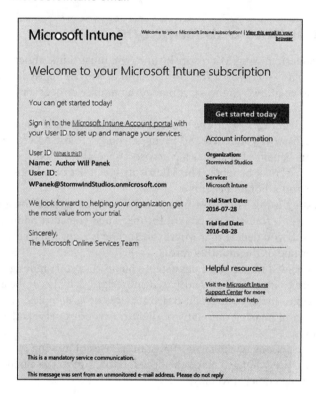

In Exercise 4.1, I will show you how to set up a free Microsoft Intune 30-day trial account. You will need to complete this exercise to do some of the other exercises during this chapter.

EXERCISE 4.1

Setting Up a Microsoft Intune Account

1. Go to the Microsoft Intune website (`https://www.microsoft.com/en-us/ microsoft-365/enterprise-mobility-security/compare-plans-and-pricing`).

2. Click the Try Now button.

3. At the Welcome to Microsoft Intune page, fill out the required information (Country, First Name, Last Name, etc.) and then click Next (shown in Figure 4.3).

FIGURE 4.3   Microsoft Intune Signup

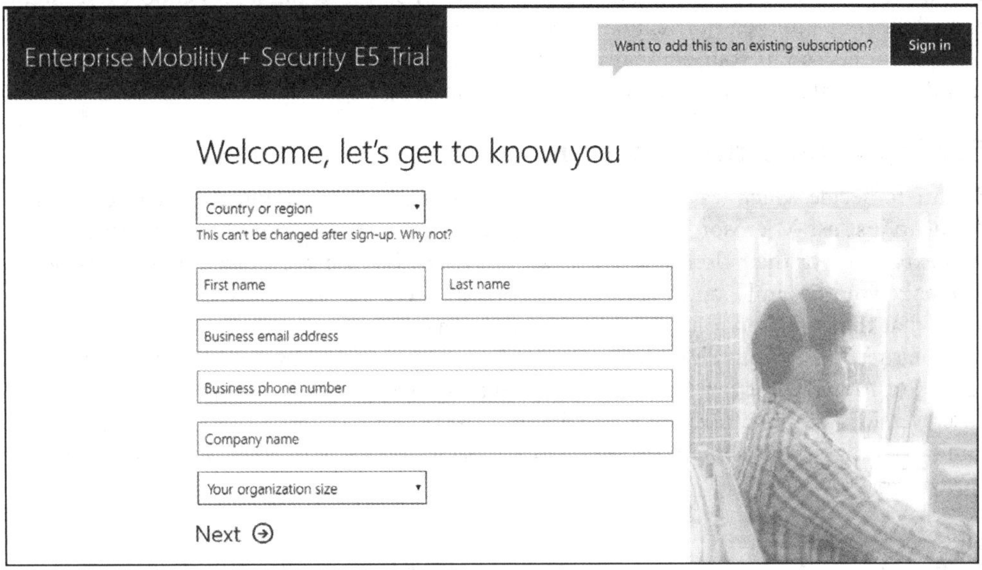

4. At the Create Username screen, create a username and password. Click Next.

5. You will need to prove you're not an Internet robot by verifying your account. Enter in a cell phone number so that a verification code can be texted to you. Enter the code and click Verify. Then click the Create My Account link.

6. You will see a screen showing you a link to your portal and your username. Print this page out for later use.

7. Type the portal link into your web browser and put in your username and password.

8. In the lower-left corner of the Menu window, click the Intune link to bring up the Intune Enterprise Mobility + Security dashboard.

Provisioning User Accounts

Once you have decided to sign up for the Microsoft Intune subscription, you next need to start assigning your corporate users and groups to Intune. By assigning users and groups, you are choosing which individuals get to access the cloud based services of Intune and the IT Departments get to start using all of the Intune benefits.

As stated previously, once you sign up for the Microsoft Intune subscription, you will receive an email with your user information along with a link to the Microsoft Intune Enterprise Mobility + Security Portal. Click on that link and then sign in. Once you sign in, you will automatically be redirected to the Intune Enterprise Mobility + Security Dashboard. This is where you can start creating your users and groups.

During the Microsoft Intune subscription process, you create a domain name and that domain is added to a Microsoft extension by default. So for example, if I choose a domain named Stormwind, then the default Microsoft subscription will look like; Stormwind .onmicrosoft.com. If your company already owns its own domain name, then you can use that domain instead of the default Microsoft option.

Setting Administrator Accounts

Be sure to decide which way you want to set up your cloud based domain because if you decide to just use Microsoft's default, all of your users will end up with an onmicrosoft. com extension for their User Principal Names (UPN). Using a pre-owned domain name can make your life in IT much easier because your users will log in using the same domain name that they are used to using now on a daily basis.

When setting up your cloud based Azure Active Directory, you can have the cloud based version of Active Directory (Azure Active Directory) work with the on-premise server based version of Active Directory by using the Azure Active Directory (AD) Connect tool (formerly known as the Directory Synchronization tool, Directory Sync tool, or the DirSync.exe tool).

 You can download the Azure Active Directory (AD) Connect tool on Microsoft's Azure website. After logging into your Azure dashboard, choose Azure AD and then choose the Azure AD Connect link.

The Azure Active Directory (AD) Connect tool is a server-based application that can be installed onto a server that is currently joined to your local domain. The connect tool allows your corporate on-site users to synchronize to your cloud based services.

When you decide to connect your cloud based Azure Active Directory to your on-site server based Active Directory, user administration becomes much easier for your IT department members. It allows your users to use a single sign-on to access both the local resources and the cloud based resources. When users have to log in using different accounts, it puts mores stress on an IT Department and / or help desk.

The first users that you should add to Microsoft Intune are your administrators. By adding the administrators first, then they can start to help also build other user accounts. When you are choosing administrative privileges, you can choose from three choices; Tenant Administrator, Service Administrator, or Device Enrollment Manager. So let's go ahead and take a look at each of the following administrator's permissions.

Tenant Administrator

Organizations have the ability to set an administrator up as Tenant Administrators. Tenant Administrators are used for very specific tasks. Normally, Tenant Administrators are assigned only one administrator role. This one administrative role determines the administrative scope for the user and the tasks they can manage. Tenant Administrators can be any of the following roles:

Billing Administrator   The Billing Administrator is allowed to make purchases, handle company subscriptions, manage support items, and handle service health issues.

Global Administrator   The Global Administrator has the ability to access all administrative features. By default, the administrator who signs up for the Intune subscription is the Global Administrator for your organization.

- Global Administrators are the only administrators that can assign other administrators their rights.
- Organizations have the ability to have more than one Global Administrator within your organization.

Password Administrator   Password Administrators have the ability to deal with user password issues like resetting passwords, managing requests, and monitors service health. Password Administrators are allowed to reset passwords for users and other Password Administrators.

Service Support Administrator   The Service Support Administrators can manage service requests and they can handle service health requests.

User Management Administrator   User Management Administrators can deal with user issues like resetting passwords, handling service health requests, and managing user accounts and groups.

Service Administrator

This is a tough role to truly understand because Intune really doesn't assign a Service Administrator role. Actually the Service Administrator role is just a Tenant Administrator role with the Global Administrator permission assigned to the individual who signed up for the Microsoft Intune subscription. Service Administrators use the administrative console to handle the daily tasks for Intune.

Device Enrollment Manager

One of the great benefits of using Microsoft Intune is the ability of users to enroll multiple devices. By default, each user can enroll five devices if they want. If you want a user to help other users enroll devices, then you can also make a user a Device Enrollment Manager. This role allows an administrator or user the ability to enroll devices for other users. This is also useful for companies that have Kiosk type machines. Your Device Enrollment Manager can enroll these types of systems.

Creating a User in Intune

Once you have decided to use Microsoft Intune, you must start setting up user accounts within Intune so that your users can start accessing the benefits of using Intune.

For users to access Intune, they must have a valid license. When a user has a valid user license, they can then enroll up to five of their devices. This way they can use different devices to do different tasks from both work and home.

When adding users into the Intune portal, you can do it either one user at a time or by bulk import from a CSV file. When adding users, you must assign licenses to each of these users. No matter how you add a user, adding a license to that user is not needed at the time that the user is created. But a license must be associated to that user before that user can access Intune.

If you decide to import your users from your on-site Active Directory to the cloud, the users will NOT have a license. You will be required to assign licenses to your users after the Active Directory merger to Intune.

So let's take a look at how easy it is to create a new user. In Exercise 4.2, I will walk you through the process of creating a new user in the Intune Management Console.

EXERCISE 4.2

Adding Users into Microsoft Intune

1. Open the Microsoft Intune Portal by clicking the link in the email that you received from creating your subscription in Exercise 4.1.

2. Once in the Intune Dashboard, under Management, click the Users link.

3. In the center console under Users, you will see a New with a down arrow. Click on New and choose User (shown in Figure 4.4).

FIGURE 4.4   Intune New User

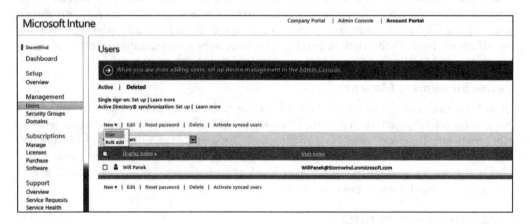

4. If you are asked to log back in, put in your Intune username and password.

5. At the New User Details screen, enter the User's Name and Username in the form of a user principal name (UPN) (see Figure 4.5).

FIGURE 4.5   Intune New User Details

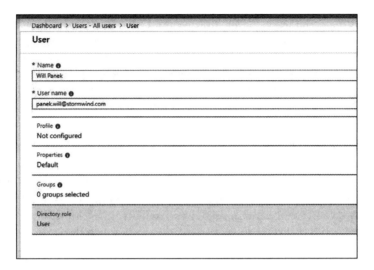

6.   At the Assign Role field, you must decide if this new user should have administrative rights and which type.

7.   At the Group field, don't choose any groups. We will add users to a group in another exercise.

8.   At the Send Results In An Email screen, make sure there is an email address for this user and click Create.

9.   At the Results screen, print out the user's temporary password (see Figure 4.6). Click Finish.

FIGURE 4.6   Intune New User Results Page

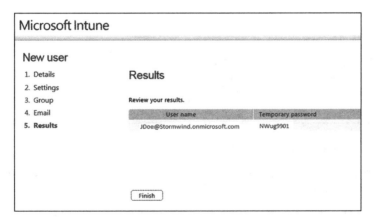

10. Close the Portal.

Now that we have looked at creating a user in the Intune Management Console, let's take a look at how to create groups.

To manage devices and users, Intune uses Azure Active Directory (Azure AD) groups. An administrator can utilize groups to fit an organization's needs. Creating groups in Intune helps administrators have more flexibility when it comes to Intune management. Administrators can setup groups based on devices, users, geographic locations, departments, or even hardware types. Creating the groups are done in about the same way, but deciding which groups to create is where the planning and decision making takes place.

Administrators can add these group types:

- Assigned groups: Manually add users or devices into a static group.

- Dynamic groups: Automatically add users or devices to user groups or device groups based upon a created expression. Dynamic groups require Azure AD Premium.

Any users and groups that are created can also be seen in the Microsoft 365 admin center, the Azure Active Directory admin center, and in Microsoft Intune in the Azure portal. Microsoft recommends that if an administrator's primary role is device management, that they utilize the Microsoft Endpoint Manager Admin Center. In Exercise 4.3, I will show you how to create a new group.

EXERCISE 4.3

Create a New Group

1. Open the Microsoft Endpoint Manager Admin Center and sign in.

2. Select Groups ➤ New Group as shown in Figure 4.7.

FIGURE 4.7   Choosing the New Group Link

3. In the Group type, choose one of the following options:

- Security: Security groups are used to define who has access to resources. Security groups are recommended for groups in Intune.

- Office 365: These groups are intended to control access and to share Office 365 resources.

4. Enter a specific Group name and Group description for the new group so others will know what the group is used for.

5. Enter the Membership type. There are several options available for Membership types as shown in Figure 4.8. These include:

   - Assigned: an administrator manually assigns users or devices to this group, and can remove users or devices.

   - Dynamic User: an administrator creates membership rules to add and remove members automatically.

   - Dynamic Device: an administrator creates dynamic group rules to add and remove devices automatically.

FIGURE 4.8   Choosing the Membership Type

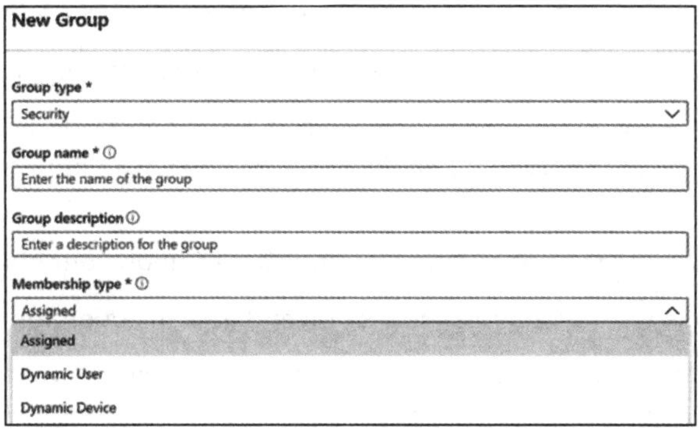

6. To add the new group, select Create. The new group is now shown in the list.

After you create the new group, you can manage that group from the administrative console. Administrators have the ability to change the group membership at any time. Managing and maintaining groups is easily accomplished from the administrative console.

Now that we have seen how to create users and groups, let's take a look at how to set up Intune Policies.

Creating Intune Policies

Administrators have the ability to place rules on security settings, firewall settings, and Endpoint Protection settings on your Intune mobile devices and applications. Think of Intune Policies as network Group Policies. These are rules that you can put on devices or users.

Once you decide to move to Microsoft Intune for your devices, it's important to use Intune policies to help manage the devices on your network and setup Endpoint protection. Microsoft Intune helps your IT staff deploy devices and applications and Intune policies allow the IT team to manage the settings on these deployments. When you build a policy, you can deploy that policy to the user groups that you setup in the previous section. Then when the users log into Intune, the policy then becomes their baseline policy.

You can create policies for the different types of devices available for Microsoft Intune. You can create policies for Androids, iOS, Mac OS X, Windows, Software, Computer Manager, and Common Mobile Device Settings.

In Exercise 4.4, I will walk you through the steps required to setup a Microsoft Intune policy. Administrators have the option to change the policy at any time.

EXERCISE 4.4

Creating an Intune Policy

1. Open the Intune administration portal.

2. In the left pane, click Device Compliance.

3. In the Manage section on the Device Compliance page, click the Policies link.

4. When the result page opens, click Create Policy on the top of the results pane.

5. In the Create Policy window, type in a policy name and description. Then choose the platform for the policy. Depending on the platform chosen, configuration settings will populate.

6. You can now change the Configuration settings based upon your platform choice.

7. Select the Actions for Noncompliance section and add an action for noncompliance.

8. Once you have completed the field and are satisfied, you can click Create.

Now that we have looked at how to setup Intune, users and groups, and policies, it's time to look at how an administrator enrolls devices in Intune.

Enrolling Devices Using Intune

To take advantage of using Intune, you must enroll devices into the Intune system. To enroll clients into this system, you must download the Intune client software onto the devices that need to be enrolled.

Now for some of the different devices on the market today, you may need to take additional steps in order for them to work with your Intune network. For example, to use the Apple iOS, an Apple Push Notification service (APNs) certificate must be imported from Apple so that you can manage iOS devices. This certificate allows Intune administrators to manage iOS.

When an administrator goes to enroll the many different devices on the Intune network, as stated, some of the different devices require different installation options.

Apple iOS   Administrators need to import an Apple Push Notification service (APNs) certificate from Apple so that you can manage iOS devices. Administrators need to open the Microsoft Intune administration portal and then go to Administration ➤ Mobile Device Management ➤ iOS and Mac OS X ➤ Download the APNs Certificate Requests (see Figure 4.9). Administrators then must save the certificate signing request (.csr) file locally. The .csr file is then used to request a trust relationship certificate from the Apple Push Certificates Portal. The administrator then needs to click the Upload the APNs certificate.

FIGURE 4.9   Upload an APNs Certificate Screen

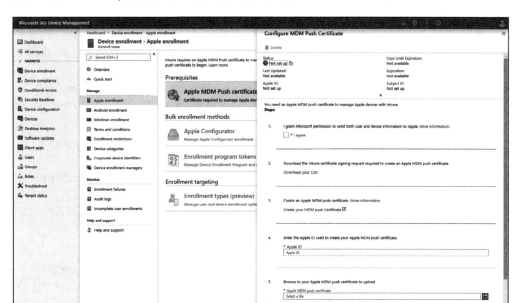

Android Devices   No additional configurations in the Intune console are needed to enable Android mobile device enrollment.

Windows Phone   Administrators must set up some management requirements before Windows Phones will work with your Intune network. DNS Administrators need to create CNAME records in order for users to connect to the Intune network resources. Windows Phones also require a certificate to establish encrypted communications between the client device and the Intune cloud based system.

Windows Devices   Windows devices get connected basically the same way as Windows Phones. The DNS Administrators have to create a CNAME record and then applications can be SideLoaded into the Windows computer. Users can also connect to Intune by using the Intune Management portal.

> Sideloading applications using Intune will be explained in greater detail later in this chapter. Sideloading basically means loading pre-bought or company applications using the Windows Store, Intune, or images.

Administrators can use the Mobile Device Management (MDM) tools to help your company users enroll different devices and manage their Intune accounts. MDM has some of the following benefits:

- MDM gives users the capabilities of enrolling their own devices through the use of the self-service Company Portal. After users enroll their devices, the users can install corporate applications.

- Once a device is enrolled, MDM helps deploy certificates, WiFi, VPN, and email profiles automatically. This allows users to have access to corporate resources with the necessary security configuration options.

- MTM allows administrators to use broad management tools for managing mobile devices, passcode resets, device lockouts, data encryption, and the ability to fully wipe a stolen device to help protect against corporate data loss.

- MTM helps simplify the enrollment of corporate devices using bulk enrollment tools like the Apple Configurator.

- MTM allows administrators to easily enroll Apple iOS devices with the Device Enrollment Program (DEP).

- MTM allows administrators to enforce a much stricter lock down policy for iOS, Android, and Windows Phone devices.

To enroll clients into the Intune network, you can install the software in a variety of ways. The company administrator can provide an installation package to allow users to enroll their systems. Administrators can setup a Group Policy that can be used to enroll the computer into Intune or users can self-enroll using the Intune portal.

If you decide to use MDM, you must first set up the mobile device management authority. This enables management of device platforms, and allows your devices to be enrolled with the company portal app.

Before enrolling your Windows 10 Desktop, you must confirm which version of Windows that you have installed. In Exercise 4.5, I will walk through how to verify which version of Windows you have.

EXERCISE 4.5

Confirm the Version of Windows

1. To display Windows Settings options, right-click the Windows Start icon and select Settings (see Figure 4.10).

FIGURE 4.10 Windows Settings Screen

2. Select System ➤ About (see Figure 4.11).

FIGURE 4.11 Windows About Screen

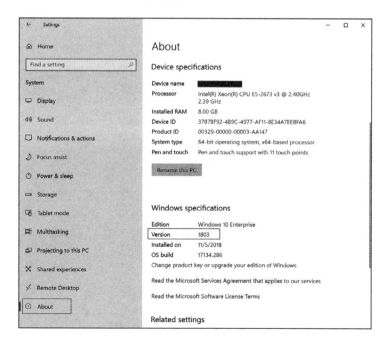

EXERCISE 4.5 *(continued)*

3. In the Settings window you will see a list of Windows specifications for your computer. Within this list, locate the version.

4. Confirm that the Windows 10 version is 1607 or higher.

The steps presented in this book are for Windows 10 version 1607 or higher; if the version you are using is 1511 or lower, follow the steps located on Microsoft's website: https://docs.microsoft.com/en-us/intune-user-help/enroll-windows-10-device#enroll-windows-10-version-1511-and-earlier-device. In Exercise 4.6, I will show you how to enroll a Windows 10 desktop version 1607 or higher device.

EXERCISE 4.6

Enroll Windows 10 Desktop Version 1607 or Higher

1. Return to Windows Settings and select Accounts (see Figure 4.12).

FIGURE 4.12   Windows Settings Screen

2. Select Access work or school ➢ Connect (see Figure 4.13).

FIGURE 4.13   Access Work or School Screen

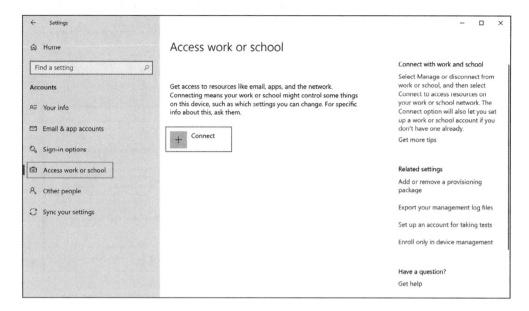

3.   Sign in to Intune with your work or school account (see Figure 4.14) and then select Next.

FIGURE 4.14   Setup a Work or School Account Screen

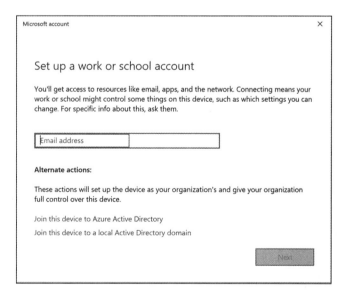

You will see a message showing that the device is registering with your company or school.

4.   When you see the "You're all set!" screen, select Done.

EXERCISE 4.6 *(continued)*

5. You will now see the added account as part of the Access work or school settings on your Windows Desktop (see Figure 4.15).

FIGURE 4.15   Added Account Screen

6. Now you need to confirm that the device is enrolled in Intune by signing into the Microsoft Endpoint Manager Admin Center as a Global Administrator or an Intune Service Administrator.

7. To view the enrolled devices in Intune, select Devices ➤ All devices.

8. Verify that the device is enrolled within Intune as shown in Figure 4.16.

FIGURE 4.16   Intune Enrolled Devices Screen

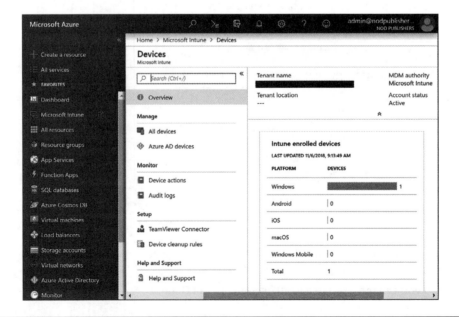

Configuring the Intune Connector Site

To understand how connectors work, we must first understand what a connector does and why we use them in the computer industry. Connectors allow different types of devices to communicate with each other. So for example, let's say we had a Microsoft Exchange server and a UNIX based mail server. You would add a connector in to the Exchange server so that it could communicate and understand the UNIX mail server. That's how Intune Connectors work also.

Intune connectors allow Microsoft Intune to communicate and understand other types of devices and software. So if we decide to use Azure Active Directory and Azure Exchange, we can install a connector so that the Azure Exchange can work with the corporate Exchange mail server.

Exchange devices have the ability to be managed through both the on premise Exchange servers and the hosted Exchange Servers in the cloud. The Exchange connector connects your users with your Exchange deployments and the connector lets you manage your mobile devices through the Intune console.

Administrators who have been using System Center Configuration Manager to manage their computers, Macs, and UNIX based devices can add the Intune connector so that they can manage all of these devices from one console.

To configure connectors, in the Intune Management Console, click on the Admin link. Then expand the Mobile Device Management section. You would then click on the device or software package and then setup the connector.

Configuring Intune Alerts

One of the nice advantages of using Intune is the ability to monitor and see alerts within Intune. When looking at these Intune alerts, there are different levels of severity within the alerts. Table 4.1 shows you the different alert types and what each type means.

TABLE 4.1   Intune Alert Types

Alert	Description
Critical	This alert shows you that you have a serious issue that needs to be investigated and fixed.
Warning	This alert shows you that there may be an issue but that issue is not very serious at this time. These alerts need to be investigated to make sure that they do not become a problem in the future.
Informational	This alert shows you that there is some information about a product but it's not a problem. For example, an informational alert may tell you that there is an upgrade to a connector that you have installed.

When dealing with Intune monitoring and alerts, there are a few settings that you can setup to help configure how alerts work. For example, under the Alerts section in the Azure portal, you can setup recipients who will receive emails when alerts happen.

So if you get a critical error, an email can be sent to an administrator so that the IT department can work on resolving the issue as fast as possible. If you don't setup email alerts, someone will need to monitor the Intune system daily to watch for issues. Intune Administrators have the ability to set different email recipients for different alert types. So Critical alerts can go to one IT person and warnings can go to another.

Administrators also have the ability to enable or disable certain alert types. So if you are getting a warning that you know is not going to affect your Intune system, you can disable the warning to remove it completely. This way it's not a message your Intune Administrators need to see on a daily basis.

To configure your Alerts and Notifications, in the Intune Management Console, click on the Admin link. Then expand Alerts and Notifications. You can then create new alert rules and notifications.

Supporting Applications

Microsoft Intune gives an organization the ability to deploy and maintain software from the cloud. The advantage to this is that the software issued through Intune is licensed to the user and not the hardware. So what this means is that you can deploy a copy of Office to a user using multiple devices and when that user works on corporate data, that data is secure. That's the real advantage to Intune. This allows your users to work securely from their iPhone, Windows laptops, or tablet.

Microsoft Intune also allows an organization to use their current business apps by using the Intune App Wrapping tool. The Intune App Wrapping tool is a command line application that builds a package around the in-house application. Then the business application can be managed by the Intune mobile application management policies.

The Intune App Wrapping tool also gives you secure data viewing through the Intune Managed Browser, AV Player, Image viewer, and the PDF viewer. Administrators also have the ability to deny specific applications or web addresses from being accessed from specific types of mobile devices. Finally, when dealing with corporate data and security, Administrators have the ability to wipe out a device in the event that the device is stolen, lost, or the employee leaves the company.

Deploying Applications Using Intune

The way that we do business in the corporate world continues to change on a daily basis. Today, many of our users bring in their own devices (BYOD: Bring Your Own Device). Because of BYOD, it is getting harder for IT departments to deploy software.

As stated earlier in this chapter, Microsoft Intune (Figure 4.17) is a cloud-based desktop and mobile device management tool. Intune helps IT departments provide their users with access to company applications, data, and resources. The users have the ability to access these resources from any type of device (i.e., Apple, Android, or Windows devices).

FIGURE 4.17   Microsoft Intune

One of the issues that we face as IT administrators is that we have multiple copies of software throughout a company and multiple version types (Apple versions of Office compared to Windows versions). Let's take a look at Office as our example. Many times we have older versions of Office (Office 2010/2016) and newer versions of Office (Office 2019 / Office 365).

This is where Microsoft Intune can help out an IT department. You can upload software packages to Intune and your users can get current copies of the software from the web. Also, Intune helps your organization protect its software by giving you extra security and features. Intune also allows you to setup application management policies that allow an IT department to manage applications on different devices.

As long as a device is compatible with Microsoft Intune, you can deploy the applications to that device. Depending on the device and the application, deployment options may vary. Administrators have the ability to upload their applications to Microsoft Intune or link a Windows Store application to Microsoft Intune storage.

To deploy applications using Intune, you must use the proper software installation type based on the different devices that your users may be using. Microsoft gives you a trial subscription of 2 GB of cloud storage. You can purchase more storage depending on how much money you want to spend.

Intune Software Publisher

To make an application available for your users to deploy, you must upload the installation package and then publish the package. As soon as you add or modify an application in Microsoft Intune, the Microsoft Intune Software Publisher starts. Then from the publisher, you can choose and configure the software installation type.

To use the Microsoft Intune Software Publisher, you must have Microsoft .NET 4.0 installed onto the Windows system. After you install .NET, restart the system and you should be able to use the Microsoft Intune Software Publisher.

Sideload Apps by Using Microsoft Intune

Sideloading an application means that you are loading an application that you already own or one that your company created into a delivery system (i.e. Intune, Microsoft Store, or images).

You may be familiar with Sideloading apps into the Windows Store. This is the process of building or buying your own application and then adding it to the Windows Store so that all of your users can download and use that app. Sideloading an application into Microsoft Intune means the same thing. We are taking an application that we built or bought and adding it into Microsoft Intune for user downloads.

Think about how you deploy software today. You buy a package and either manually install the software to your users or use some type of deployment package like System Center Configuration Manager. The only difference now is that the application gets loaded into the cloud and can be deployed to any device that is compatible with the application.

On Windows 10 devices, Intune supports many different app types and deployment scenarios. After an administrator has added an app to Intune, they can then then assign that app to users and devices.

The app types supported on Windows 10 devices are Line-of-business (LOB) apps and Microsoft Store for Business apps.

An LOB app is one that is added from an app installation file. The following steps will help you to add a Windows LOB app to Microsoft Intune.

Adding a Windows LOB App to Microsoft Intune

Step 1: Specify the software setup file:

1. Sign in to the Microsoft Endpoint Manager Admin Center.

2. Select Apps ➢ All Apps ➢ Add.

3. Select Line-of-Business app as the App type in the Add App pane.

Step 2: Configure the app package file:

1. Select App Package File in the Add App pane.

2. Select the Browse button in the App Package File pane. Then select a Windows installation file with the extension `.msi`, `.appx`, or `.appxbundle`.

3. Select OK when done.

Step 3: Configure app information:

1. Select App Information in the Add App pane.

2. In the App Information pane, configure the information such as name, description, publisher, etc.

3. Select OK when done.

Step 4: Finish up:

1. Verify that the app information is correct in the Add App pane.

2. To upload the app to Intune, select Add.

Step 5: Update a line-of-business app:

1. Sign in to the Azure portal.

2. Select All Services ➤ Intune. Intune is in the Monitoring + Management section.

3. Select Client Apps ➤ Apps.

4. Find and select the desired app in the list of apps.

5. In the Overview blade, select Properties.

6. Select App package file.

7. Select the folder icon and browse to the location of the updated app file. Select Open. The app information is updated with the package information.

8. Confirm that the App version reflects the updated app package.

An administrator can install apps on a Windows 10 device in one of two ways depending on the app type. The app types are:

- User Context: The app is installed for that user on the device when the user signs in to the device.

- Device Context: The app is installed directly to the device by Intune.

After an app is added to Intune, the app can then be assigned to users and devices. An administrator can assign an app to a device whether or not the device is managed by Intune.

Once an application has been uploaded to Intune you'll want to deploy the app to your users. To do this, you'll need to assign the app to an Intune group. You need to click on the Apps link and then choose the app for deployment in the Windows Intune portal. The following steps show how to assign an app:

1. Sign in to the Microsoft Endpoint Manager Admin Center.

2. Select Apps ➤ All Apps.

3. Select the app you want to assign in the Apps pane.

4. Select Assignments in the Manage section of the menu.

5. Select Add Group to open the Add Group pane.

6. Next, you will want to select the assignment type. There are several options available:

    - Available for enrolled devices: Assigns the app to groups of users who can install the app from the Company Portal app or website.

    - Available with or without enrollment: Assigns the app to groups of users whose devices are not enrolled with Intune.

- ▪ Required: The app is installed on devices in the selected groups.
- ▪ Uninstall: The app is uninstalled from devices in the selected groups.

7. Select Included Groups to select the groups of users.

8. After you have selected one or more groups, select Select.

9. Select OK in the Assign pane.

10. Select Exclude Groups if you want to exclude any groups.

11. Select Select if you have chosen to exclude any groups.

12. Click OK in the Add Group pane.

13. Select Save in the app Assignments pane.

To monitor the properties of apps, you can:

1. Sign in to the Microsoft Endpoint Manager Admin Center.

2. Select Apps ➢ All Apps.

3. Select an app to monitor in the list of the apps. This will open the app pane, which shows an overview of the device status and the user status.

Deep-Link Applications by Using Microsoft Intune

One of the nice advantages of using Windows 10 is that you can purchase Windows Store applications. After you purchase the applications, you can deploy the Windows Store application (deep-link) to all of your users.

Supporting Broadband Connectivity

Administrators have a few weapons in their broadband arsenal. Two different options that we can setup as Administrators is the ability to see how much network or software bandwidth is being used (metering) and how we can setup our Windows 10 devices to use your cellular Internet connections (tethering).

Understanding Metering

Administrators have the ability to limit and monitor network usage by configuring the network as a metered network. Network metering allows network downloading to be watched or metered and then administrators can charge users or departments for the network usage.

This is becoming something that many IT departments have started doing due to budgeting. Many IT departments are non-revenue-generating departments and because of this, it can be difficult for an IT administrator to get a budget passed. But with network metering, you can charge other departments for the amount of bandwidth and network that is being used.

When setting up your company's Internet connection, your ISP has the ability to charge by the amount of data used. That's called a metered Internet connection. If you have a metered Internet connection, setting your network connection to metered in Windows can help you reduce the amount of data you send and receive. To set this up in Windows, you would take the following steps;

1. Click Start ➢ Settings, and then tap Network & Internet.

2. Tap or click on the Wi-Fi link and then, under Metered Connection, turn Set As A Metered Connection on or off.

Administrators also have the ability to limit how much bandwidth a user or department gets to use when downloading applications. This is referred to as Software metering.

To setup software metering, an Administrator must use a combination of Microsoft Windows Intune and System Center Configuration Monitor.

Understanding Broadband Tethering

Tethering allows a user to use their Windows 10 mobile device through their cellular phone. If you have a Windows 10 mobile device and want it to access the Internet, you can go through your cell coverage to get online.

Tethering can also be connecting one mobile device to another mobile device for Internet access. So let's say I have an iPad with a cellular Internet connection. I can connect another Windows 10 tablet to that iPad to gain Internet access. So tethering is the ability to connect one device to another for Internet access. Before you set up tethering, there are a few things that you should know:

- There may be extra charges when connecting your data connection with another device.

- Applications and updates may not be downloaded over a metered connection and by default, tethered and mobile broadband connections are metered.

- Many cellular carriers require that you pay an extra fee for allowing your phone to be a hotspot for tethering. To enable tethering on most devices, you setup your mobile device as an Internet hotspot.

Understanding Data Synchronization

Data Synchronization allows you to synchronize your devices with your servers. These servers can be network based or cloud based. Administrators have the ability to synchronize work folders and they can also use the Sync Center to use one application for all of their synchronization needs.

To enable synchronization on the Windows 10 device, click on the Start button and choose Settings. When you are in the Settings window, click on the Accounts link to setup your user accounts and synchronization (see Figure 4.18).

FIGURE 4.18   Data Synchronization

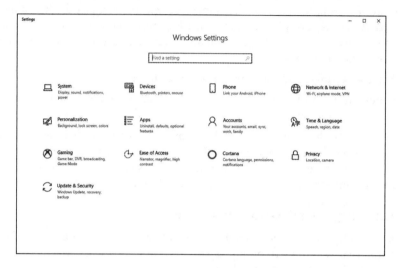

Once you enter into the Account link, you can choose the bottom option (Sync your settings) to setup all of your synchronization settings (see Figure 4.19).

FIGURE 4.19   Sync your settings

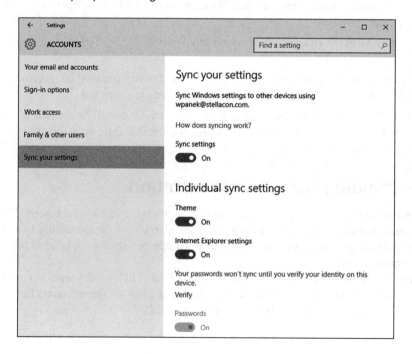

One of the final things that you want to look at in the Accounts link is the Work access link. The Work access link allows you to connect your device to your work or school, sign into Azure, and enroll in to device management (see Figure 4.20).

FIGURE 4.20 Sync your settings

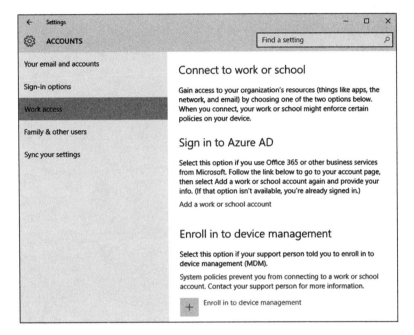

Using Mobile Application Management

One of the advantages to using Intune is the ability to download applications to many different platforms. One concern that IT departments may have is that their users will download corporate applications on personal devices. Since many companies now allow BYOD, there needs to be tools that allow a company to control company data on personal devices. This is where *Mobile Application Management (MAM)* can help your organization.

Mobile application management is part of Intune and it is a suite of administrator management tools that allow you to manage, configure, publish, update, and monitor applications for your mobile devices.

The advantage to using MAM is that an administrator has the ability to manage and protect the company's data from within the application that the user is using. For example, an administrator can manage a work related application that has confidential information on it and that application can be on almost any type of device (including personal devices).

Mobile application management will work with many of the Microsoft productivity applications including:

- Microsoft Azure Information Protection Viewer
- Microsoft Bookings
- Microsoft Cortana
- Microsoft Dynamics CRM
- Microsoft Edge
- Microsoft Excel
- Microsoft Flow
- Microsoft Intune Managed Browser
- Microsoft Invoicing
- Microsoft Kaizala
- Microsoft Launcher
- Microsoft OneDrive for Business
- Microsoft OneNote
- Microsoft Outlook
- Microsoft Planner
- Microsoft PowerApps
- Microsoft Power BI
- Microsoft PowerPoint
- Microsoft SharePoint
- Microsoft To-Do
- Microsoft Skype for Business
- Microsoft StaffHub
- Microsoft Stream
- Microsoft Teams
- Microsoft Visio Viewer
- Microsoft Word

 For a complete list of applications that Intune and MAM will support, please visit Microsoft's website https://docs.microsoft.com/en-us/ intune/apps-supported-intune-apps.

There are two configurations that are supported by Intune MAM. These are:

- Intune MDM + MAM
- MAM without device enrollment (MAM-WE)

With Intune MDM + MAM, administrators can manage apps only by using MAM and using app protection policies only on devices that are enrolled with Intune MDM. To manage, you need to log into the Azure portal at `https://portal.azure.com` and use the Intune console.

With MAM-WE, administrators can manage apps using MAM and using app protection policies on devices that are not enrolled with Intune MDM. Apps can be managed by using Intune on devices that are registered with third-party Enterprise Mobility Management (EMM) providers. To do so, you can to log into the Azure portal at `https://portal.azure.com` and use the Intune console or use Intune on devices that are registered with the third-party providers or on devices that are not enrolled with MDM at all.

Windows Information Protection

Since corporations are allowing personnel to bring their own devices into the corporate network, there is an ever-mounting risk of possible data leaks from users using apps and services that are not controlled by the corporate network.

To help protect against the possible data leaks, Microsoft created, Windows Information Protection (WIP), which was formerly known as Enterprise Data Protection (EDP). WIP is a built-in Windows 10 feature that allows an administrator to maintain and monitor company data separate from any personal data that is on a user's device.

WIP aids in protecting against possible data leaks and protects enterprise apps and data on both enterprise-owned and personal devices without interfering with the user's experience while on the corporate network. Users do not need to open any special apps or enter into any specific modes in order for WIP to work. Users just use apps that they are used to and WIP will provide the data protection.

Besides separating corporate and personal data, WIP can also determine which users and apps have access to particular data and can determine what users are allowed to do with that corporate data. For example, an administrator has the ability to stop a user from copying corporate data from an approved app and pasting that data into another unapproved app.

The WIP Intune policy maintains a list of protected apps, corporate network locations, the levels of protection granted and the encryption settings.

WIP provides the following:

- Allows an administrator to track issues and find corrective actions by using audit reports.

- Integrates with existing management systems to deploy, configure and manage WIPs. Management systems can include Microsoft Intune, System Center Configuration Manager (SCCM), or an MDM.

- Provides added protection for present line-of-business apps without needing to update any apps.

- Provides the capability to remove corporate data from Intune MDM enrolled devices while, at the same time, not touching the personal data on a device.

- Separates personal data from corporate data, without the need for the user to change apps or settings.

An administrator can set a WIP policy with a different level of protection and management modes. There are four protection and management modes. They are as follows (see Figure 4.21):

- Block: Prevents users from engaging in unauthorized actions, such as copying and pasting corporate data. WIP searches for unacceptable data sharing and will stop the user from performing any further.

- Allow Overrides: Alerts users whenever they try to execute an unauthorized action. The user can ignore the warning and proceed with the unauthorized action; however, WIP will log the event in its audit log where an administrator can review it later.

- Silent: Will run in the background, tracking the user's actions with no indicator of an unauthorized action and logging any inappropriate data sharing. However, if an action is blocked, the action will be prevented as usual.

- Off: WIP is disabled and provides no protection or auditing.

FIGURE 4.21   Configure Windows Information Protection Settings

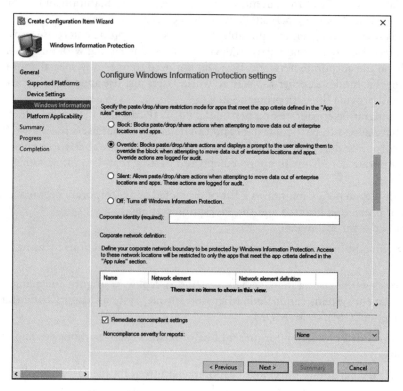

It's not recommended, but an administrator can turn off WIP. This can be done without data loss to the devices that were managed by WIP. WIP can be turned back on, but the previously applied decryption and policy information will not be automatically reapplied.

WIP uses System Center Configuration Manager (SCCM) to design and implement WIP policies. Once an administrator has set up SCCM they must create a configuration item for WIP; this is the WIP policy.

Creating a Configuration Item for WIP

To create a configuration item for WIP, follow the following steps:

1. Open the SCCM console, click the Assets And Compliance node, expand the Overview node, expand the Compliance Settings node, and then expand the Configuration Items node (see Figure 4.22).

FIGURE 4.22   System Center Configuration Manager console

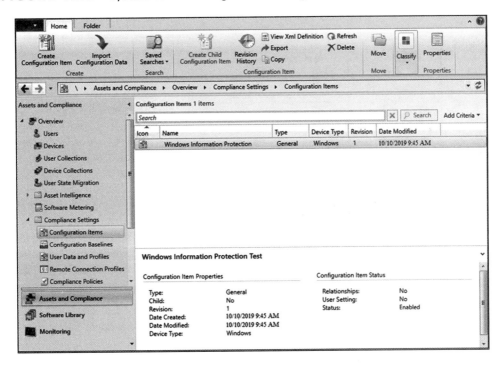

2. Click the Create Configuration Item button. The Create Configuration Item Wizard will start (see Figure 4.23).

FIGURE 4.23 Create Configuration Item Wizard

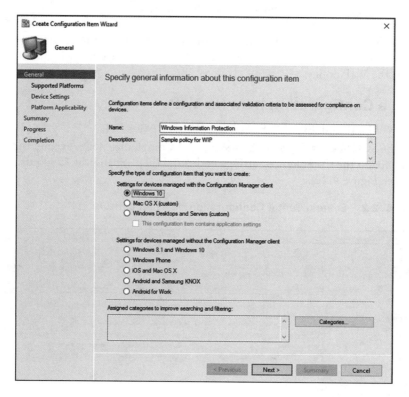

3. On the General Information screen, type a name (required) and a description (optional) for the policy into the Name and Description boxes.

4. In the Specify The Type Of Configuration Item That You Want To Create area, pick the option that represents whether you'd like to use SCCM for device management, and then click Next. The options are as follows:

   ▪ Settings For Devices Managed With The Configuration Manager Client: Windows 10

   ▪ Settings For Devices Managed Without The Configuration Manager Client: Windows 8.1 and Windows 10

5. On the Supported Platforms screen (see Figure 4.24), click the Windows 10 box, and then click Next.

FIGURE 4.24   Create Configuration Item Wizard - Supported Platforms

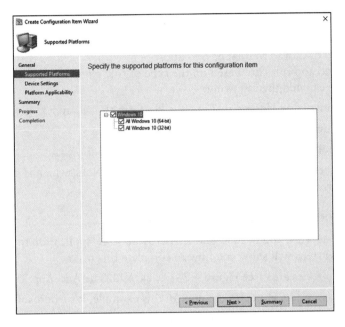

6.   On the Device Settings screen (see Figure 4.25), click Windows Information Protection, and then click Next.

FIGURE 4.25   Create Configuration Item Wizard - Device Settings

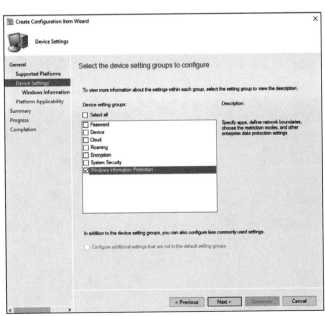

The Configure Windows Information Protection settings page appears, where an administrator can configure a policy for the company.

When an administrator creates a process in SCCM, they can choose the apps that will be granted access to corporate data via WIP. Apps on the list can protect and restrict data from being copied or moved to unapproved apps.

The steps to add app rules are based on the type of rule template that is being applied. An administrator can add the following:

- Store app (known as a Universal Windows Platform (UWP) app
- Signed Windows desktop app
- AppLocker policy file

In the follow sections, we will be adding Microsoft OneNote, which is a store app, to the App Rules list.

Adding a Microsoft Store Application

There may be times when you need to add a Microsoft Store application to the App Rules list. The following steps will show you how to complete this task:

1. From the App Rules area (see Figure 4.26), click Add. The Add App Rule box appears.

2. In the Title box, add a name for the app. In this example, it's Microsoft OneNote.

3. In the Windows Information Protection Mode drop-down list, click Allow. Clicking Allow turns WIP on to help protect that app's company data.

4. Pick Store App from the Rule Template drop-down list. The box will change to show the store app rule options.

5. Type the name of the app and the name of its publisher, and then click OK. For this UWP app example, the Publisher is CN=Microsoft Corporation, O=Microsoft Corporation, L=Redmond, S=Washington, C=US and the Product name is Microsoft .Office.OneNote.

FIGURE 4.26   Create Configuration Item Wizard - Add App Rule

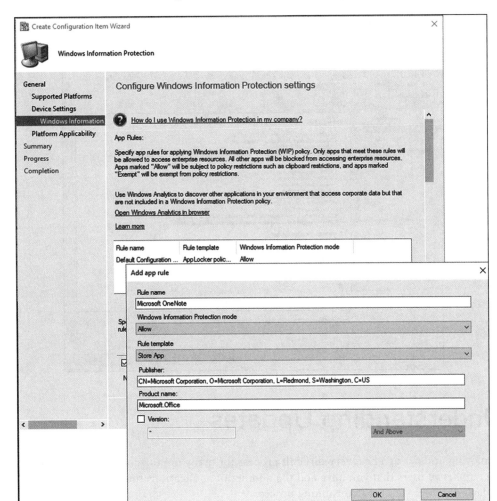

After configuring the policy, an administrator can review all of the settings by looking at the Summary screen. Click on Summary to review the policy choices (see Figure 4.27) and then click Next to finish and save the policy.

FIGURE 4.27   Create Configuration Item Wizard - Summary Screen

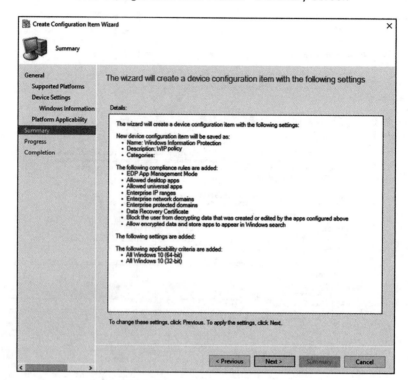

Understanding Updates

Deploying updates can be a very difficult process for many organizations. Depending on the number of users that you have and the number of applications that each user uses, updates can be a very time consuming process.

Many organizations install a Microsoft server called a Windows Server Update Services (WSUS). WSUS servers allow administrators to deploy Microsoft product updates to computers that are running the Windows operating system. Administrators can manage all of their organization's Microsoft updates from one application.

The downside to WSUS is that it is used for Microsoft updates. So you can deploy updates to all of your applications, Microsoft and Non-Microsoft, by using the Intune management portal.

Deploying Software Updates Using Intune

When you decide to use Intune to deploy your updates, you get a lot of options that you get to consider and setup. For example, do you want to approve all of your updates or do you want the updates to automatically deploy? Many administrators like to approve all of their updates so that they have a chance to test them first before deploying.

Intune stores only the update policy assignments, not the actual updates. The devices still need to access Windows Update to obtain the updates.

Intune provides the following policy types to manage updates:

- Windows 10 update ring—a collection of settings that configures when Windows 10 updates get installed.

- Windows 10 feature updates (public preview)—brings devices to the Windows version that you specify and freezes the feature set on those devices until you choose to update them. Figure 4.28 shows the Windows 10 update ring.

FIGURE 4.28   Overview of Update Types

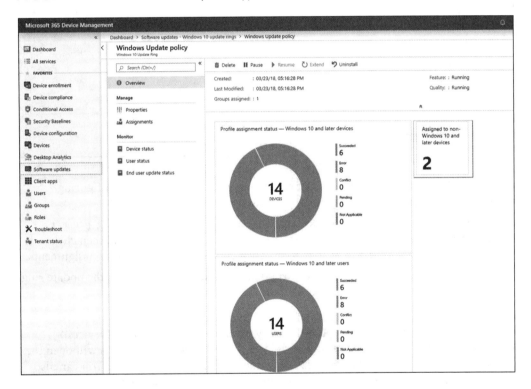

To create and assign update rings follow these steps:

1. Sign in to the Microsoft Endpoint Manager Admin Center.

2. Select Devices ➤ Windows ➤ Windows 10 Update Rings ➤ Create.

3. Under Basics, specify a name, a description (optional), and then select Next (as shown in Figure 4.29).

FIGURE 4.29   Create Windows 10 Update Ring

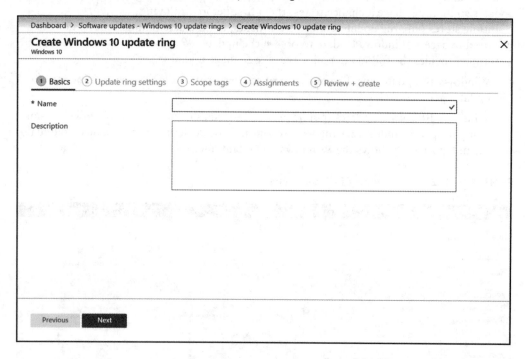

4. Under Update Ring Settings, configure your required settings. After configuring update and user experience settings, click Next.

5. If you want to apply scope tags, you can do that under Scope Tags. Select + Select Scope Tags to open the Select Tags pane. Choose one or more tags, and then click Select and return to the Scope Tags page. Then click Next to continue to Assignments.

6. Under Assignments, choose + Select Groups To Include and then assign the update ring to one or more groups. Click Next to continue.

7. Under Review + Create, review the settings and then click Create.

To manage your Windows 10 update rings, go to the portal, navigate to Devices ➤ Windows ➤ Windows 10 Update Rings and select the policy to manage. This will open the policy Overview page. From here you can view the rings' assignment status. You can also delete, pause, resume, extend, and uninstall the update ring by selecting the actions from the top of the Overview pane (see Figure 4.30).

FIGURE 4.30   Overview Pane Actions

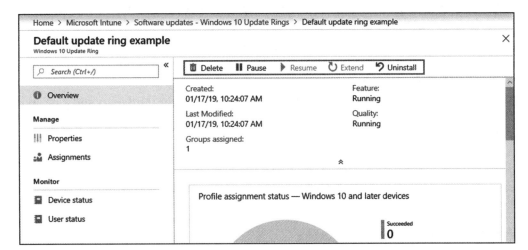

Identifying Required Updates

When you decide to use Intune for updates, you need to decide which type of updates that you want to install. Administrators have the ability to choose what type of updates they want to install.

All Updates   All updates section means just that, all updates. Every possible update that can be deployed will be shown under the All updates Section.

Critical Updates   Critical updates are updates that are released to fix a specific issue that is for a critical bug that is not security related.

Security Updates   Security updates are updates that need to be applied to fix a security issue. These security issues are used by hackers to either hack into a device or software.

Definition Updates   Definition updates are normally software updates that contain additions to a product's definition database. Definition databases get used to identify objects that have very specific attributes. These attributes look for malicious code, phishing websites, or junk mail.

Service Packs   Service packs are a collective set of all current hotfixes, security updates, critical updates, and updates. Normally service packs also contain additional fixes for known issues that are found since the release of the product. Service packs may also contain customer requested design changes or features.

Update Rollups   Update rollups are current hotfixes, security updates, critical updates, and updates that are bundled together for easy deployment. Update rollups are normally used to target a specific component or software package.

Mandatory Updates   Mandatory updates are updates that are released to either fix or replace a software or hardware issue. Mandatory updates are required to run or the device or Windows system may stop functioning properly.

Non-Microsoft Updates   Non-Microsoft updates are updates for third party software and hardware devices. These are updates that other vendors release for solving problems or improving their product.

When you configure settings for Windows 10 update rings in Intune, the administrator is also configuring the Windows Update settings. If a Windows update setting has a Windows 10 version dependency, the version dependency is noted in the settings details.

Windows 10 Feature Updates

With Windows 10 feature updates, the administrator selects the Windows feature version that they want devices to stay at. When a device receives a Windows 10 feature updates policy, the device will update to the version of Windows specified. If a device already runs a later version of Windows, then it will remain at its current version.

Until you modify or remove the Windows 10 feature updates policy, devices won't install a new Windows version. If the policy is edited to specify a newer version, devices can then install the features from that Windows version.

To create and assign Windows 10 feature updates, follow these steps:

1.   Sign in to the Microsoft Endpoint Manager Admin Center.

2.   Select Devices ➤ Windows ➤ Windows 10 Feature updates ➤ Create.

3.   Under Basics, specify a name, a description (optional), and for Feature Update To Deploy, select which version of Windows you want, and then select Next.

4.   Under Assignments, choose + Select Groups and then assign the update ring to one or more groups. Click Next.

5.   Under Review + Create, review the settings and click Create to save.

To manage the Windows 10 feature updates, follow these steps:

1.   In the admin center, go to Devices ➤ Windows ➤ Windows 10 Feature Updates and select the policy to manage. The policy opens to its Overview pane.

2.   From the Overview pane, the administrator can configure the following options:

     ▪   Select Delete to delete the policy from Intune and remove it from devices.

     ▪   Select Properties to modify the deployment. On the Properties pane, select Edit to open the deployment settings or assignments to modify the deployment.

     ▪   Select End User Update Status to view information about the policy.

Using Intune Compliance Reports

An administrator can use Intune to deploy Windows updates to Windows 10 devices. The administrator will want to review a policy report on the deployment status for the configured Windows 10 update rings. To do so, follow these steps:

1. Sign in to the Microsoft Endpoint Manager Admin Center.

2. Select Devices ➤ Overview ➤ Software Update Status.

3. To view additional details, select Monitor. Then below Software Updates, select Per Update Ring Deployment State and choose the deployment ring to review.

In the Monitor section, the administrator can choose one of the following reports to view more detailed information about the update ring:

- Device status: Shows the device configuration status.

- User status: Shows the username, status, and last report date.

- End user update status: Shows the Windows device update state.

Using Intune Reports

One of the best tools that Microsoft Intune offers is the ability to obtain all of the different types of reports. The Intune Reports help an Administrator monitor the status of your enrolled devices and see if there are any issues that need to be addressed. The reports also allow an Administrator to examine both the hardware and software inventory.

Microsoft Intune reports allow an administrator to monitor the health and activity of endpoints, and provides other reporting data across Intune. Examples include being able to see report regarding device compliance, device health, and device trends. An administrator is also able to build custom reports.

Intune reports are categorized into the following areas of focus:

- Operational: Provides targeted data that helps an administrator focus and take action.

- Organizational: Provides a wider summary of an overall view, such as device management state.

- Historical: Provides patterns and trends over a period of time.

- Specialist: Allows an administrator to use raw data to create their own custom reports.

Using Intune reports allows an administrator to search and sort, perform data paging, review performance, and export data.

- Search and sort: Search and sort across every column.

- Data paging: Scan data based on paging, either page by page or by jumping to a specific page.

- Performance: Quickly generate and view reports created from large tenants.

- Export: Export reporting data generated from large tenants.

PowerShell Commands

Table 4.2 is a list of just some of the PowerShell commands that administrators can use to manage, configure, and view applications in Azure.

TABLE 4.2   PowerShell commands

Command	Description
Add-AzureADApplicationOwner	This command is used to add an owner to an application.
Add-AzureADApplicationPolicy	Administrators can use this command to add a policy to an application.
Get-AzureADApplication	This command allows an administrator to view an application.
Get-AzureADApplicationExtensionProperty	This command allows you to view the extension properties of an application.
Get-AzureADApplicationOwner	This command allows an administrator to view who is the owner of an application.
Get-AzureADApplicationPasswordCredential	Administrators can use this command to view an application password.
Get-AzureADApplicationPolicy	This command allows an administrator to view an application policy.
New-AzureADApplication	This command allows an administrator to create a new application in Azure.
New-AzureADApplicationExtensionProperty	Administrators can use this command to create extension properties of an application.
New-AzureADApplicationPasswordCredential	This command creates password credentials for an application.
Remove-AzureADApplication	Administrators can use this command to delete an application.

Command	Description
`Remove-AzureADApplicationExtensionProperty`	This command allows an administrator to remove an extension property of an application.
`Remove-AzureADApplicationOwner`	Administrators can use this command to remove an owner from an application.
`Remove-AzureADApplicationPasswordCredential`	This command allows an administrator to remove the password credentials from an application.
`Set-AzureADApplication`	Administrators can use this command to update an application.

Summary

In this chapter, we talked about the cloud and Microsoft Intune. I showed you how Microsoft Intune can help you manage devices and software. I showed you how to set up and configure an Intune subscription and how you can use that subscription to help your network users get the most out of their network resources and software.

I also talked about managing devices using Intune. I showed you how to provision user accounts and enroll devices. I also discussed how to manage and configure devices using the Microsoft Intune subscription.

I then continued the chapter by discussing how to deploy and configure software and updates using Intune.

I then talked about how to work with mobile devices including Windows tablets, broadband metering and tethering and I also showed you how to wipe mobile devices for employees who leave the company. I spoke about using MAM and WIP and how you can set policies to help control how applications are deployed to your users. I then showed you how to use Intune to help deploy and maintain your company's software packages and updates.

I showed you the different types of reports that an Administrator can run using Intune. These reports can help an Administrator see what devices still need updates and also what hardware may need to be installed or replaced.

Exam Essentials

Understand Microsoft Intune. Understand what Microsoft Intune can do to help your network. Make sure you understand how users and devices get connected to Intune.

Know how to configure a Microsoft Intune Subscription.   Understand how to setup and manage a Microsoft Intune Subscription. Understand how to configure a device to use Microsoft Intune.

Understand the Microsoft Intune Benefits.   Understand what Microsoft Intune benefits can be used in a corporate environment. Understand how these benefits, like remote wipe, can help you protect corporate data.

Understand Intune Connectors.   Understand Microsoft Intune Connectors allow Microsoft Intune to work with software within a network. The connector allows the cloud based software to communicate properly with the infrastructure based software.

Know how to setup Intune Alerts.   Understand each type of Intune alerts and which alerts are important to fix immediately or which alerts just are giving you information. Understand how to setup notifications for each alert type.

Understand Intune MAM and WIP.   Understand Microsoft Intune Mobile Application Management (MAM) and Windows Information Protection (WIP) and how these tools can help you manage and protect applications.

Know how to work with Intune Reports.   Understand that the different Reports help an administrator monitor the status of Intune managed devices. These Reports give you information on the status of software updates, software installed, and certificate compliance. Understand how reports also let you examine the inventory of your network's hardware and software.

Review Questions

1. You are the network administrator for your organization. Your users use both desktops and tablets to access the network. Your tablet users use a 4G mobile broadband Wi-Fi connection. You need to watch how much data your users are using on this connection. How do you do that?

    A. Configure the broadband connection as a metered network.

    B. Turn on network resource monitoring.

    C. Enable performance monitoring.

    D. Enable tablet metering in the tablets settings.

2. You manage 1,000 Windows 10 computers. All of the computers are enrolled in Microsoft Intune. You manage the servicing channel settings by using Intune. What should you do if you want to review the servicing status of a computer?

    A. From Device configuration-Profiles, view the device status.

    B. From Device compliance, view the device compliance.

    C. From Software updates, view the audit logs.

    D. From Software updates, view the Per update ring deployment state.

3. You are the IT Manager of a large manufacturing company. Sales personnel are allowed to bring their own personal Windows 10 devices to the office. The company allows the sales people to install company software and use their devices to retrieve company mail by using the management infrastructure agent. One of your sales people reports that their Windows 10 laptop was stolen while at the airport. You need to make sure that no one can steal any of the corporate data or access any corporate emails. Which two actions should you perform? Each correct answer presents part of the solution. (Choose two.)

    A. Prevent the computer from connecting to the corporate wireless network.

    B. Remove the computer from the management infrastructure.

    C. Reset the user's password.

    D. Do a remote wipe on the user's laptop.

4. You are the IT Director for a large school system. The school has decided that students can bring in their own devices to do school work with. Your organization uses Microsoft Azure Active Directory and Intune for all of the student's applications and network authentication. You need to be sure that students that are using iPads as well as Windows 10 devices have full access. What do you need to do to be sure that all iOS devices can get access?

    A. Add a Student Portal app from the Apple App Store.

    B. Create a device enrollment manager account.

    C. Configure an Intune Service Connector for Exchange.

    D. Import an Apple Push Notification service (APNs) certificate.

5. You have 200 Windows 10 computers that are joined to Microsoft Azure Active Directory (AD) and enrolled in Microsoft Intune. You want to enable self-service password reset on the sign-in screen. Which settings should you configure from the Microsoft Intune blade?

   A. Device configuration

   B. Device compliance

   C. Device enrollment

   D. Conditional access

6. You are the IT Manager for WillPanek.com. The company has an Active Directory domain and a cloud based Azure Active Directory. The two are synchronized together by using the Azure Active Directory Synchronization Tool. The company also uses System Center Configuration Manager. You need to use Configuration Manager to manage devices registered with Intune. What do you need to do to accomplish this? (Choose two.)

   A. Create a new device enrollment manager account in Microsoft Intune.

   B. In Microsoft Intune, configure an Active Directory Connector.

   C. Configure the Microsoft Intune Connector role in Configuration Manager.

   D. Create the Microsoft Intune subscription in Configuration Manager.

7. Your company has a Microsoft Azure subscription. All the users in the marketing department use their own personal devices that run either iOS or Android based systems. All the devices are enrolled in Microsoft Intune. The company has developed a new mobile application named App1 for the Marketing department. You need to ensure that only the Marketing department users can download App1. What should you do first?

   A. Add App1 to Intune.

   B. Add App1 to a local server for users to use.

   C. Add App1 to Microsoft Store.

   D. Configure the iOS and Android systems to use the new application.

8. You are the IT director for a large company that has decided to move to the cloud. The company wants to use Azure Active Directory and Microsoft Intune. The company has been looking into this because users have been using multiple devices to get their job done. When your users get added to Intune and get licensed, how many devices can each user add by default?

   A. 4

   B. 10

   C. 15

   D. None. Device Administrators are the only person who can add devices to Intune.

9. You are the administrator of a company that builds its own applications. You have decided that you want to install a company application to all employees by using the Windows Store. Which term is used to refer to installing corporate apps through the Windows Store?

   A. WS Installations

   B. BranchCache

   C. Image Installation

   D. Sideloading

10. You are the IT Director for Stormwind training studios. Your company has decided to start using Microsoft Intune for all of their software deployments. You want to set up a notification system so that you see all alerts and your IT Manager only gets notified for Critical alerts. How do you accomplish this? Choose all that apply.

   A. Setup all event notifications for the IT Manager in Intune.

   B. Setup all event notifications for the IT Director in Intune.

   C. Setup Critical event notifications for the IT Manager in Intune.

   D. Setup Critical event notifications for the IT Director in Intune.

Chapter

5

Managing Security

MICROSOFT EXAM OBJECTIVES COVERED IN THIS CHAPTER:

✓ **Manage Windows Defender**

- Implement and manage Windows Defender Application Guard; implement and manage Windows Defender Credential Guard; implement and manage Windows Defender Exploit Guard; implement Windows Defender Advanced Threat Protection; integrate Windows Defender Application Control; manage Windows Defender Antivirus, Deploy and update applications

In this chapter, I am going to talk about defending your Windows 10 system directly by using the built-in security features of Windows Defender Security Center. I will show you the different ways that you can protect your system using the Defender Security Center options.

I will show you how to protect your Windows 10 devices by using the Windows 10 Firewall. The Windows 10 Firewall can help protect your client systems from being illegally breached, but when you're building a network, your Windows Firewall should NOT be your only firewall. Your network connection to the Internet should also be protected by some type of firewall, but that is an entirely different course (depending on your firewall type).

I am also going to dive into protecting Windows 10 and also using Azure to help protect your network. Windows 10 offers protection like Windows Firewall and Azure offers organizations multiple ways to protect devices and data by using Azure tools like Windows Defender Application Guard, Windows Defender Advanced Threat Protection, and Windows Defender Antivirus.

So let's get started by looking at protecting your Windows 10 devices by using Windows Firewall.

Managing Windows Security

Windows 10 includes built-in Windows Security (see Figure 5.1), which includes antivirus protection. Windows 10 devices are automatically protected from the very moment that your users start using Windows 10. Windows 10 Security is always scanning the system for viruses, malware (malicious software), and security dangers. Not only does Windows 10 provide real-time protection, Microsoft continually does updates to make sure that your corporate devices stay safe and that the devices are protected from any new threats.

FIGURE 5.1   Windows 10 Security dialog box

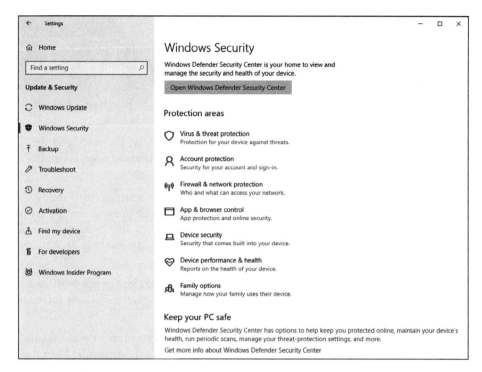

Windows Defender Security Center

Windows 10 includes the Windows Defender Security Center (see Figure 5.2). The Windows Defender Security Center is a built-in Windows 10 application that protects your system from viruses and spyware. It is included free with the operating system, and once you turn your operating system on, Windows Defender starts automatically protecting your system.

FIGURE 5.2   Windows Defender Security Center

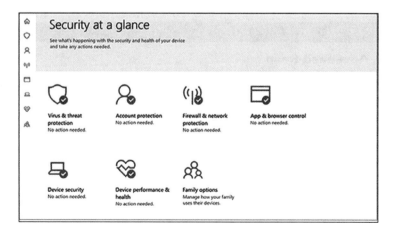

The Windows Defender Security Center has multiple options that you can set to help protect your system. So let's take a look at some of these options.

Virus and Threat Protection   Windows 10 will automatically monitor for threats that can impact your device, run scans on your system, and get updates to help protect against any new threats. Windows 10 has an antivirus built in and it will get automatic updates when your Windows 10 systems get updated.

Account Protection   Administrators can configure the user's sign-in options and account settings. These settings include using Windows Hello and dynamic lock.

Firewall & Network Protection   Windows 10 includes a Windows Firewall, and the Windows Firewall allows administrators to help prevent unauthorized users or malicious software from accessing their computer.

App & Browser Control   Administrators can configure update settings for Windows Defender SmartScreen and this helps protect your Windows 10 devices against potentially dangerous applications, downloads, files, and websites. This gives administrators the ability to control exploit protection and customize settings that will help protect your Windows 10 devices.

Device Security   Windows 10 Device Security allows administrators to use built-in security options to defend your organization's Windows 10 devices from malicious software attacks.

Device Performance & Health   Windows 10 allows administrators to view the status information about the device's performance health. This helps administrators keep their organization's devices clean and up-to-date with the latest version of Windows 10.

Family Options   The Family Options feature in Windows Security is not a feature that most administrators will configure in a corporate environment. These options provide tools to help manage children's computer access. Parents can use Family Options to help keep their children's devices clean and up-to-date with the latest version of Windows 10 and to protect their children when they are on the Internet.

In Exercise 5.1, I will show you how to run an advanced virus and threat scan on your Windows 10 device.

EXERCISE 5.1

Running an Advanced Scan

1. Click Start ➤ Settings ➤ Update & Security ➤ Windows Security and then choose Virus & Threat Protection.

2. Choose the link Run A New Advanced Scan (see Figure 5.3).

FIGURE 5.3   Run A New Advanced Scan link

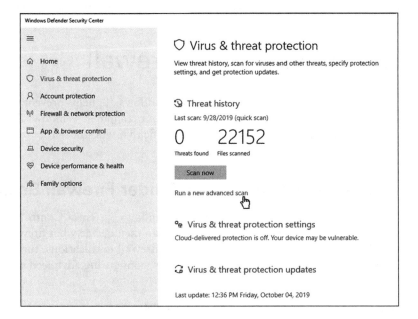

3.   Make sure the radio button is on Full Scan and click the Scan Now button (see Figure 5.4).

FIGURE 5.4   Advanced scan options

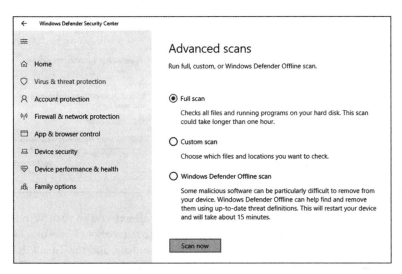

4.   The scan will take a while. After the scan finishes, close the Defender Security Center.

Now that you understand how to work with the Windows 10 Security Center, let's take a closer look at how to configure your Windows 10 firewall within that Security Center.

Configuring Windows Firewall

Windows Defender Firewall, which is included with Windows 10, helps prevent unauthorized users and malicious software from accessing your computer. Windows Defender Firewall does not allow unsolicited traffic, which is traffic that was not sent in response to a request, to pass through the firewall.

Understanding the Windows Defender Firewall Basics

You configure Windows Firewall by clicking Start ➤ Windows System ➤ Control Panel ➤ Large Icons View ➤ Windows Defender Firewall. You can then decide what firewall options you want to set (as shown in Figure 5.5), like changing firewall notifications, turning the Windows Defender Firewall on or off, restoring defaults, configuring advanced settings, and troubleshooting.

FIGURE 5.5   Windows Defender Firewall settings dialog box

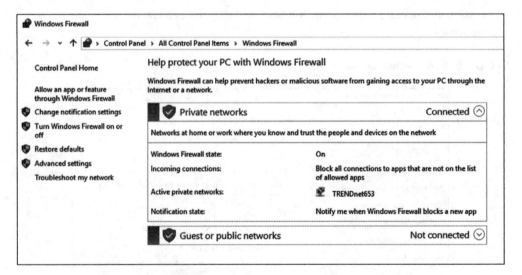

The Windows Defender Firewall settings dialog box allows you to turn Windows Defender Firewall on or off for both private and public networks. The Turn On Windows Defender Firewall setting will block incoming sources, and the Turn Off Windows Defender Firewall setting will allow incoming sources to connect.

There is also a check box for Block All Incoming Connections, Including Those In The List Of Allowed Apps. This feature allows you to connect to networks that are not secure. When Block All Incoming Connections is enabled, all incoming connections (even ones allowed in the allowed apps list) will be blocked by Windows Defender Firewall.

Windows Firewall with Advanced Security

You can configure more-advanced settings by configuring Windows Defender Firewall with Advanced Security. To do so, right-click Start and choose Windows System ➤ Control Panel ➤ Large Icons View ➤ Windows Defender Firewall ➤ Advanced Settings. The Windows Defender Firewall With Advanced Security dialog box appears, as shown in Figure 5.6.

FIGURE 5.6   Windows Defender Firewall With Advanced Security

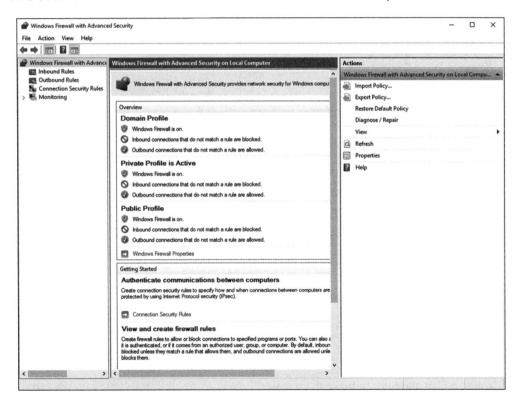

The scope pane to the left shows that you can set up specific inbound and outbound rules, connection security rules, and monitoring rules. The central area shows an overview of the firewall's status when no rule is selected in the left pane. When a rule is selected, the

central area shows the rule's settings. The right pane shows the same actions as the Action menu on the top. These are just shortcuts to the different actions that can be performed in Windows Firewall. Let's take a more detailed look at some of the elements in Windows Defender Firewall.

Inbound and Outbound Rules

Inbound and outbound rules consist of many preconfigured rules that can be enabled or disabled. Obviously, inbound rules (see Figure 5.7) monitor inbound traffic and outbound rules monitor outbound traffic. By default, many are disabled. Double-clicking a rule will bring up its Properties dialog box (Figure 5.8).

FIGURE 5.7   Inbound rules

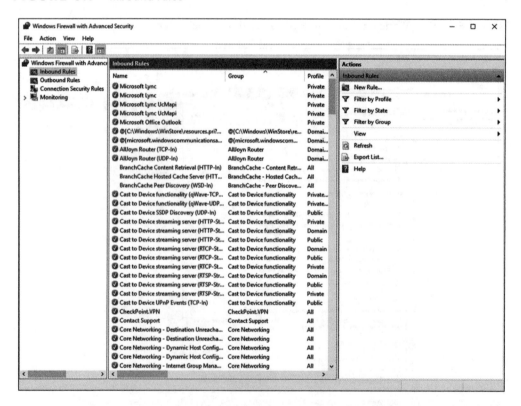

You can filter the rules to make them easier to view. Filtering can be based on the profile the rule affects, on whether the rule is enabled or disabled, or on the rule group. You can filter a rule by clicking which filter type you want to use in the right pane or by clicking the Actions menu on the top of the screen.

FIGURE 5.8   An inbound rule's Properties dialog box

If you can't find a rule that is appropriate for your needs, you can create a new rule by right-clicking Inbound Rules or Outbound Rules in the scope pane and then selecting New Rule. The New Inbound (or Outbound) Rule Wizard will launch, and you will be asked whether you want to create a rule based on a particular program, protocol or port, predefined category, or custom settings.

As you are setting up the firewall rules, you have the ability to configure authenticated exceptions. No matter how well your system security is set up, there are almost always times when computers on your network can't use IPsec. This is when you set up authenticated exceptions. It's important to understand that when you set up these authenticated exceptions, you are reducing the security of the network because it allows computers to send unprotected IPsec network traffic. So make sure that the computers that are added to the authenticated exceptions list are managed and trusted computers only. Table 5.1 shows you some of the most common port numbers and what those port numbers are used for.

TABLE 5.1   Common Port Numbers

Port Number	Associated Application or Service
20	FTP Data
21	FTP Control

TABLE 5.1 Common Port Numbers *(continued)*

Port Number	Associated Application or Service
22	Secure Shell (SSH)
23	Telnet
25	SMTP
53	DNS
67/68	DHCP/BOOTP
80	HTTP
102	Microsoft Exchange Server
110	POP3
443	HHTPS (HTTP with SSL)

Complete Exercise 5.2 to create a new inbound rule that will allow only encrypted TCP traffic.

EXERCISE 5.2

Creating a New Inbound Rule

1. Right-click Start ➤ Windows System ➤ Control Panel ➤ Large Icon View ➤ Windows Defender Firewall.

2. Click Advanced Settings on the left side.

3. Right-click Inbound Rules and select New Rule.

4. Choose a rule type. For this exercise, choose Custom so you can see all the options available to you. Then click Next.

5. At the Program screen, choose All Programs. Then click Next.

6. Choose the protocol type as well as the local and remote port numbers that are affected by this rule. For this exercise, choose TCP, and ensure that All Ports is selected for both Local Port and Remote Port. Click Next to continue.

7. At the Scope screen, choose Any IP Address for both local and remote. Then click Next.

8. At the Action screen, choose Allow The Connection Only If It Is Secure. Click Next.

9. At the Users screen, you can experiment with these options if you want by entering users to both sections. Once you click one of the check boxes, the Add and Remove buttons become available. Click Next to continue.

10. At the Computers screen, you can choose what computers you will authorize or allow through this rule (exceptions). Again, you can experiment with these options if you want. Click Next to continue.

11. At the Profiles screen, choose which profiles will be affected by this rule. Select one or more profiles and click Next.

12. Give your profile a name and description, and then click Finish. Your custom rule will appear in the list of inbound rules, and the rule will be enabled.

13. Double-click your newly created rule. Notice that you can change the options that you previously configured.

14. Delete the rule by right-clicking the new rule and choosing Delete. A dialog box will appear asking you if you are sure. Click Yes.

15. Close the Windows Defender Firewall.

Connection Security Rules

Connection security rules are used to configure how and when authentication occurs. These rules do not specifically allow connections; that's the job of inbound and outbound rules. You can configure the following connection security rules:

- Isolation: To restrict a connection based on authentication criteria
- Authentication Exemption: To specify computers that are exempt from authentication requirements
- Server-to-Server: To authenticate connections between computers
- Tunnel: To authenticate connections between gateway computers
- Custom

Monitoring

The Monitoring section shows detailed information about the firewall configurations for the Domain Profile, Private Profile, and Public Profile settings. These network location profiles determine what settings are enforced for private networks, public networks, and networks connected to a domain.

Real World Scenario

Use More Than Just Windows Defender Firewall

When doing consulting, it always makes me laugh when I see small to midsize companies using Microsoft Windows Defender Firewall and no other protection. Microsoft Windows Defender Firewall should be your *last* line of defense. You need to make sure that you have good hardware firewalls that separate your network from the world.

Also watch Windows Defender Firewall when it comes to printing. I have run into many situations where a printer that needs to communicate with the operating system has issues when Windows Defender Firewall is enabled. If this happens, make sure that the printer is allowed in the Allowed Programs section of the Windows Defender Firewall.

Datacenter Firewall

Firewalls allow an administrator to set up policies on who or what can be allowed past the firewall. For example, if you want to allow DNS traffic to pass through the firewall, you would enable port 53. If you want the traffic to leave the firewall, you would configure port 53 outbound. If you want to have the traffic enter into the company, you would configure inbound.

Datacenter Firewalls were introduced with Windows Server 2016 network layer, Stateful, multitenant firewalls. Network administrators that work with virtual network tenants can install and then configure firewall policies. These firewall policies can help protect their virtual networks from unwanted traffic from Internet and intranet networks.

The Datacenter Firewall allows you to set up granular access control lists (ACLs) and this allows you to apply firewall policies at the VM interface level or at the subnet level. To create ACLs on the Datacenter Firewall, an administrator can use Windows PowerShell.

The following is an example of the PowerShell command that is used to assign the ACL to the AccessControlList property of the network interface.

```
$nic.properties.ipconfigurations[0].properties.AccessControlList = $acl
```

Windows Server 2016/2019 Datacenter Firewall gives you the following tenant benefits.

- Administrators have the ability to define firewall rules that help protect Internet-facing workloads on virtual networks.

- Administrators have the ability to define firewall rules to protect data between virtual machines on the same Layer 2 or different Layer 2 virtual subnets.

- Administrators have the ability to define firewall rules to protect and isolate network traffic between tenants on a virtual network from a service provider.

So now that we have taken a look at Windows Defender Firewall, let's now look at protecting your Windows 10 devices by using Azure.

Managing Security

Another way that you can help defend your corporate devices is by using Microsoft Azure. Azure has many different tools that allow an administrator to control and protect the company's Windows 10 devices.

Earlier in the chapter, I talked about using the Windows Defender Security Center. Now we are going to look at using Windows Defender in Azure.

Implementing Azure Windows Defender Advanced Threat Protection

When talking about Windows Defender, it can be a little confusing to people. The reason for this is that Windows 10 has come with Windows Defender and Azure also now comes with Windows Defender. So when IT people are discussing Defender, it's important that they specify which version they are talking about. I am going to talk about Azure's version of Windows Defender and the benefits that it provides to organizations.

Your organization's IT department can have even better threat protection when they combine Azure Windows Defender Advanced Threat Protection (Windows Defender ATP) with Azure Advanced Threat Protection (Azure ATP), as shown in Figure 5.9. Figure 5.9 was taken directly from Microsoft's website and it shows all of the different ways Azure ATP and Windows Defender ATP can work together.

FIGURE 5.9   Inbound rules

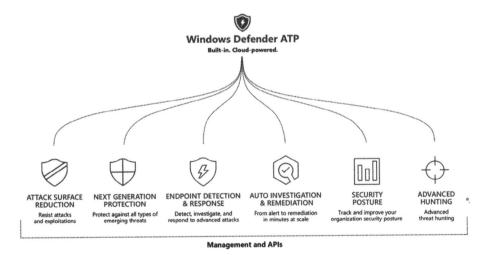

Azure ATP allows organizations to monitor domain controller traffic while Windows Defender ATP allows organizations to monitor endpoints (for example, user's devices).

Organizations can use both of these defenses together for the best possible protection and both of can be managed by using a single Azure interface.

When deciding to integrate Azure ATP and Windows Defender ATP together, you get the benefits of both systems working together. Some of these benefits include:

Endpoint Behavioral Sensors   Endpoint behavioral sensors are sensors that are built into the Windows 10 operating system and these sensors gather and process behavioral data for things like the registry, files, processors, and communications. This data is then sent to the Windows Defender ATP.

Azure ATP Sensors and Stand-Alone Sensors   These sensors can be placed directly onto your domain controllers or they can be set up to port mirror directly from your domain controller to Azure ATP. These sensors have the ability to collect and parse traffic for multiple protocols that work with authentication, or authorization or just for informational gathering.

Threat Intelligence   Threat intelligence is comprised of multiple Microsoft tools, security groups, and third party threat defending partners. Threat intelligence allows Windows Defender ATP to properly recognize tools and activities that hackers use and then report alerts when those tools or activities are observed.

Cloud Security Analytics   Cloud security analytics uses multiple detection signals and Microsoft insights to detect and recommend protection against advanced threats.

Azure ATP uses multiple technologies to detect suspicious behavior during all phases of a cyber based attack. These phases include:

The Investigation Phase (Reconnaissance)   This is the phase where hackers gather information on a target organization. This phase can include information gathering by using Internet investigation, dumpster diving, etc.

Scanning Phase   This phase is when an attacker tries to scan for vulnerabilities. These can be port scanners (looking for open ports to access), vulnerability scanning (looking for known vulnerabilities), and network scanning (looking at network components like routers and firewalls).

Access Phase   This is the phase when hackers try to gain access to your network based on the investigation phase and scanning phase.

Maintaining Access Phase   This is the phase when hackers try to put back doors or software in place so that the hackers can continue to gain access to your network.

Clearing Their Tracks Phase   Hackers that are any good will try to clear their tracks so that no one knows that they were there. This is when hackers will try to delete logs and any evidence that the hack even took place.

Windows Defender ATP uses Microsoft technologies and expertise to help detect and stop the different phases of a hacker. By using their experience, Microsoft has put in advanced methods to detect hacking before the hacks take place.

Understanding Windows Defender Application Guard

One of the biggest issues that we have in IT is the Internet. It's a world game changer and a company game changer. But that also means it's an IT game changer. We in IT have to rethink how we protect our networks and that's because of the Internet.

Years ago, hackers had to use phone lines, and that helped prevent a lot of hacker wannabes. Phone lines were easy to track, and it could be expensive for a young hacker to spend a lot of money on phone calls. Especially, if they were unsuccessful with their hacks.

Today, anyone can hack from anywhere because of the World Wide Web and they pay only a monthly fee for Internet access. So we must rethink how we protect our data and our companies. This is where Application Guard can help us.

Application Guard was specifically designed for Windows 10 and Microsoft Internet browsers (Edge & Internet Explorer). Application Guard works with Windows Edge to isolate untrusted web sites, thus protecting your organizations network and data while users are working on the Internet.

As an Enterprise Administrator, you can pick and choose which websites are defined as trusted sites. These sites can be internal websites, external websites, company websites, and cloud based organizations. If a site is not on the trusted list, it is then considered untrusted and automatically isolated when a user visits the site.

When a user accesses a website (using Edge or IE) that is not on the trusted list, Microsoft Edge will be automatically opened in an isolated Hyper-V enabled container. This container will be a separate environment from the host operating system and this will help protect untrusted websites from causing damage to the Windows 10 system. Also since the website will be isolated, any type of attack will not affect the corporate network or its data.

Windows Defender Application Guard is disabled by default. Windows Defender Application Guard works in two modes: Standalone or Enterprise. Standalone mode allows a non-corporate user to use Windows Defender Application Guard without any administrator configured policies. Enterprise mode is used in an enterprise environment and can be configured automatically by the Enterprise Administrator.

Windows Defender Application Guard Standalone Mode

If a user wants to use Standalone mode, they need to be using either Windows 10 Enterprise edition (version 1709 or higher) or Windows 10 Pro edition (version 1803). The user must install Application Guard manually on their Windows 10 device and then they need to manually start Microsoft Edge in Application Guard while they are browsing untrusted sites.

Exercise 5.3 will show you how to install Windows Defender Application Guard using the Windows 10 Control Panel.

EXERCISE 5.3

Installing Windows Defender Application Guard

1. Right-click Start ➤ Windows System ➤ Control Panel ➤ Large Icon View ➤ Programs And Features.

2. Click the link Turn Windows Features On Or Off.

3. Scroll down and check the box for Windows Defender Application Guard (shown in Figure 5.10) and then click the OK button.

FIGURE 5.10   Installing Windows Defender Application Guard

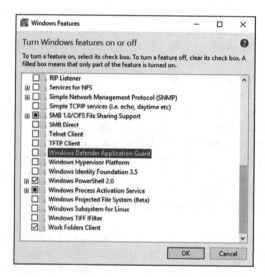

4. After Windows Defender Application Guard installs, close Control Panel.

Users can also install Windows Defender Application Guard by using PowerShell. To do this, you need to right-click on PowerShell and choose the top option, Run As Administrator (see Figure 5.11).

FIGURE 5.11   Opening PowerShell as an administrator

Once you are in the PowerShell window, you want to run the following PowerShell command and then you need to restart the Windows 10 device:

```
Enable-WindowsOptionalFeature -online -FeatureName Windows-Defender-
ApplicationGuard
```

In Exercise 5.4, I will show you how to use Windows Defender Application Guard in Standalone mode. I will be using Windows 10 and Microsoft Edge for this exercise. To complete this exercise, you must complete Exercise 5.3 and install Windows Defender Application Guard on your Windows 10 device.

EXERCISE 5.4

Using Windows Defender Application Guard

1. Open Microsoft Edge.

2. From the options menu, choose New Application Guard Window (see Figure 5.12).

FIGURE 5.12   New Application Guard Window option

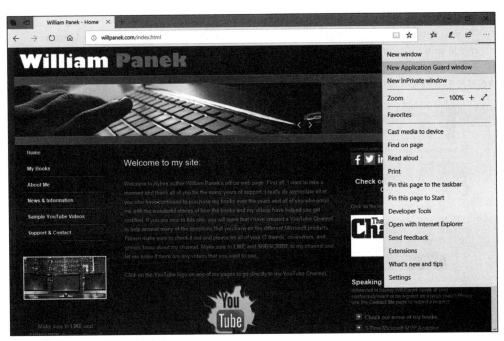

3. You will need to wait for Application Guard to set up the isolated environment (see Figure 5.13). This may take a few moments.

FIGURE 5.13   Application Guard starting screen

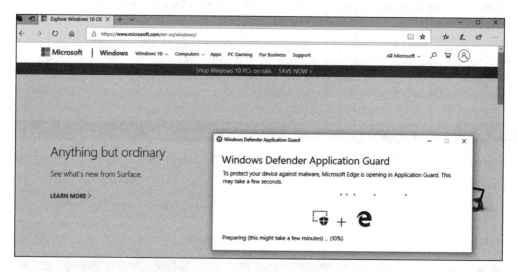

4.   As you can see in Figure 5.14, I opened Microsoft's website in Application Guard mode and you can see that in the upper left hand corner of the window. Close Edge.

FIGURE 5.14   Microsoft's website in Application Guard mode

Windows Defender Application Guard Enterprise Mode

Windows Defender Application Guard in the enterprise environment is not much different for the user as in Standalone mode. The main difference is that the Enterprise Administrator configures the Windows Defender Application Guard application. The Enterprise Administrator sets up and configures the application. When a user accesses an untrusted website, Windows Defender Application Guard automatically starts.

So let's take a look at some of the enterprise based systems will benefit from Windows Defender Application Guard:

Enterprise Desktops and Laptops   Enterprise desktops are machines that are joined to your domain and they are managed by your company's administrators. Enterprise Administrators can configure Windows Defender Application Guard through System Center Configuration Manager or Microsoft Intune with Enterprise Mobility + Security (EMS).

Microsoft Intune is now called Microsoft Intune with Enterprise Mobility + Security (EMS). For the rest of the chapter, I will refer to it as just Intune. There is no reason to add the "with Enterprise Mobility + Security (EMS)" every time we mention Intune.

Bring Your Own Device (BYOD) Laptops   Normally organizations that allow users to use their own devices for company business need to follow company rules. So these devices are normally managed by the Enterprise Administrators through Intune. If a user wants to use a personal device but they don't want to follow corporate rules, most companies won't allow the use of the personal device.

In Exercise 5.5, I will show you how to use Windows Defender Application Guard in Enterprise mode. Before your organization can use Application Guard in Enterprise mode, administrators must install Windows 10 Enterprise edition (version 1709 or higher) on their corporate network or the needed functionality will not work.

EXERCISE 5.5

Windows Defender Application Guard Enterprise

1. Install Application Guard using either a Group Policy Object, System Center, or Mobile Device Management (MDM).

2. In a Group Policy, set the Network Isolation settings that you want followed (see Figure 5.15). To set this option, in your GPO editor go to Administrative Templates\Network\Network Isolation\Enterprise Resource Domains Hosted In The Cloud setting.

FIGURE 5.15 Network Isolation GPO

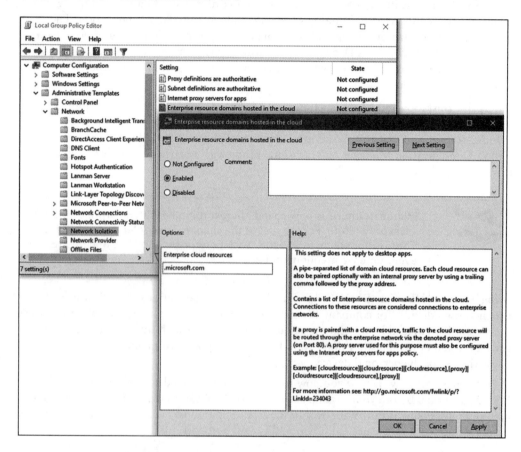

3. Next, go to Administrative Templates\Network\Network Isolation\Domains Categorized As Both Work And Personal setting. Enter in the websites that you trust.

4. Next, go to Computer Configuration\Administrative Templates\Windows Components\Windows Defender Application Guard\Turn On Windows Defender Application Guard In Enterprise Mode setting.

5. Click the Enabled radio button, choose Option 1 (see Figure 5.16), and click OK.

FIGURE 5.16   Turn On Windows Defender Application Guard In Enterprise Mode setting

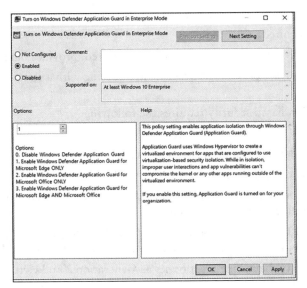

6. Close the GPO editor.

Understanding Windows Defender Credential Guard

Windows Server 2016 and Windows 10 Enterprise introduced a new security measure called Windows Defender Credential Guard. Windows Defender Credential Guard is a virtualization-based security to help isolate critical files so that only system software that is privileged can access those critical files.

Once it's enabled, a Windows 10 machine that is part of Active Directory or Azure Active Directory will have the system's credentials protected by Windows Defender Credential Guard.

After an administrator enables Windows Defender Credential Guard, the Local Security Authority (LSA) process in the operating system works with a new component named the isolated LSA. The isolated process stores and protects the system's critical data.

Once data is stored by the isolated LSA process, the system then uses the virtualization-based security to protect the data and that data is no longer accessible to the rest of the operating system.

To enable Windows Defender Credential Guard, the following requirements should be met:

- Machine must support virtualization-based security (required)
- Secure boot (required)
- TPM 1.2 or 2.0, either discrete or firmware (preferred, provides binding to hardware)
- UEFI lock (preferred, prevents attacker from disabling with a simple registry key change)

The virtualization-based security requires the following:

- 64-bit CPU
- CPU virtualization extensions plus extended page tables
- Windows hypervisor (does not require Hyper-V Windows Feature to be installed)

If an administrator wants to use Windows Defender Credential Guard in a Hyper-V virtual machine, the following requirements need to be met:

- The Windows 10 (version 1607 or higher) or Windows Server 2016/2019 system must have Hyper-V with Input Output Memory Management Unit (IOMMU).
- The Hyper-V virtual machine must be set as Generation 2 and virtual TPM needs to be enabled.

Once administrators have met the minimum requirements for setting up Windows Defender Credential Guard, they can enable it by either using the Windows Defender Device Guard hardware readiness tool or Group Policy Objects or directly in the Registry.

In Exercise 5.6, I will show you how to enable Windows Defender Credential Guard using a Group Policy Object.

EXERCISE 5.6

Windows Defender Credential Guard

1. Open the Group Policy Management editor on Windows Server 2016.

2. Create a new GPO and click the GPO and choose Edit.

3. Go to Computer Configuration ➤ Administrative Templates ➤ System ➤ Device Guard.

4. Double click the option Turn On Virtualization Based Security and then choose the Enabled option (see Figure 5.17).

5. In the Turn On Virtualization Based Security option, select Platform Security Level box, choose either Secure Boot or Secure Boot and DMA Protection.

FIGURE 5.17   Turn On Virtualization Based Security setting

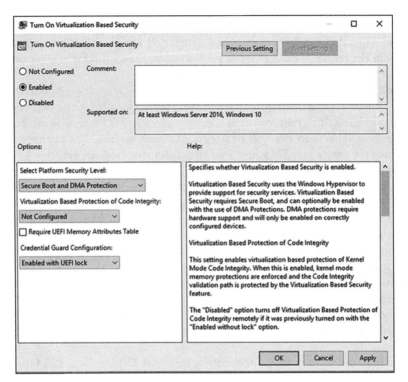

6. In the Credential Guard Configuration box, click Enabled with UEFI lock, and then click the OK button.

7. Close the Group Policy Management Console.

Implementing and Managing Windows Defender Exploit Guard

Another way that Microsoft has started protecting systems is by using Windows Defender Exploit Guard. Windows Defender Exploit Guard helps protect your Windows 10 system against malware, ransomware, and other types of attacks. It does this by reducing the attack surface of a device.

So does it mean when someone says that they are reducing the attack surface of a system? The way I always explain it is in this way. I am a huge hockey fan. When I lived in NJ, I used to go to dozens of hockey games.

Now think of a hockey net (or soccer net) as the Windows system. During one of the hockey intermissions (when the players get a break), they would bring out a piece of plexiglass and on the bottom of the plexiglass, there was an opening just a bit bigger than a hockey puck. Then they would give someone a stick and a puck and allow them to shoot at the net from the center of the ice. If the puck went in, they would win a car or money or whatever the prize was that night.

Now think of the open net as Windows 10. You can have a great goaltender (your firewall) but if someone is good enough, they can still get the puck by the goaltender. Now think of the plexiglass. The only way that someone can score is by getting the puck in that tiny little opening. This is an example of a reduced attack surface. The goaltender doesn't need to protect the entire net. They just need to protect that tiny opening.

Windows Defender Exploit Guard is your plexiglass on the Windows 10 operating system. By protecting common ways that hackers exploit the system, the hackers now have to get into the system by using that tiny little opening.

Windows Defender Exploit Guard helps protect your system from common malware hacks that use executable files and scripts that attack applications like Microsoft Office (for example, Outlook). Windows Defender Exploit Guard also looks for suspicious scripts or behavior that is not normal on the Windows 10 system.

One of the common hacks today is ransomware. This is when a hacker takes over your system and requests a ransom to release your files. During this time, the hackers hold your documents hostage until you pay. Once Windows Defender Exploit Guard is enabled, folders and files are assessed to determine if the files are safe or harmful from ransomware threats.

There are multiple ways to turn on Windows Defender Exploit Guard. Administrators can enable the Windows Defender Credential Guard by using the Windows Defender Security Center, a Group Policy Object, System Center Configuration Manager (SCCM), or Mobile Device Management (MDM) using Microsoft Intune with EMS.

In Exercise 5.7, I will show you how to enable Windows Defender Exploit Guard using the Windows Defender Security Center.

EXERCISE 5.7

Windows Defender Exploit Guard

1. Open the Settings center by clicking on the Start button and clicking on the Settings (the spoke) icon.

2. Choose Update and Security.

3. Click on Windows Security and choose Virus and threat protection.

4. Choose Ransomware Protection and make sure the setting is turned on (see Figure 5.18).

FIGURE 5.18   Turn On Ransomware setting

5.   Click on Protected folders (see Figure 5.19) to see what folders are currently protected. You can click on the + Add a protected folder to add additional folders.

FIGURE 5.19   Protected Folders screen

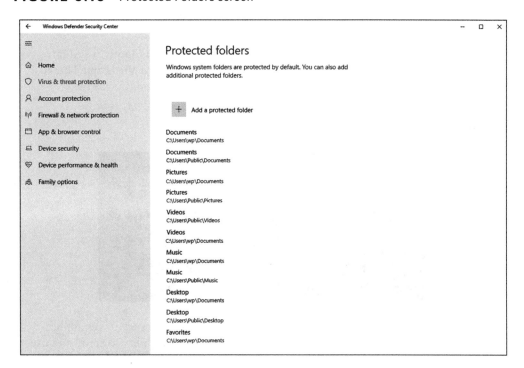

6. If you would like an application to have access, you can click on the link Allow an app through Controlled folder access. Once you click the link, you can add an application that will be allowed access (see Figure 5.20).

FIGURE 5.20   Allow an app through Controlled folder access screen

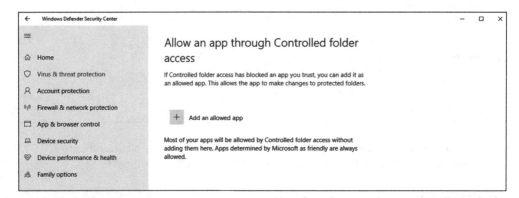

7. Close the Security Center (reboot if you made any changes).

Once Windows Defender Exploit Guard is enabled, when the Windows 10 system suspects that a file is a danger, the Windows 10 system will display a Virus and Threat Warning screen (see Figure 5.21). This protection is completed in real time as the Windows 10 system is operating.

FIGURE 5.21   Virus and Threat Warning screen

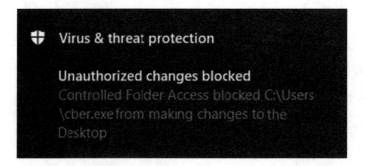

Another part of controlling application exploitation is when users try to get applications from the web and Microsoft Store. Administrators have the ability to setup and use Microsoft Windows Defender SmartScreen (see Figure 5.22).

FIGURE 5.22   Windows Defender Smart Screen

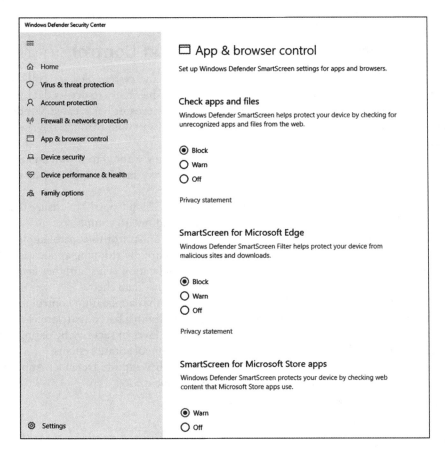

Windows Defender SmartScreen helps administrators protect their employees when they try to visit websites that have previously been reported as phishing or malware websites. Windows Defender SmartScreen also helps Windows 10 if an employee tries to download potentially malicious files.

SmartScreen allows Windows 10 to determine if a downloaded application or an application installer that may be potentially malicious. It does this by:

- Looking at downloaded files and seeing if those files are on a list of known malicious software sites or if programs that are being downloaded are known to be unsafe. If any file or program is on these lists, SmartScreen will prompt the user with a warning to let that user know that the data or site might be malicious.

- When a user downloads a file or program that isn't on the list, SmartScreen will show the user a warning prompt, to just advise caution.

Another way that your organization can help protect their users against downloading applications that are possibly harmful is using Windows Defender Application Control.

Using Windows Defender Application Control

So now that we have discussed how to protect the system and system files, let's talk about protecting applications. When an application runs, it has the ability to access data with the same access to data that a user has. Because of this, Microsoft has created Windows Defender Application Control (WDAC) to help stop attacks of data through the use of applications.

For many years, if a user had local admin rights and they wanted to install an application onto a corporate machine, they just did it. Users just assume that applications that they buy or download is just trustworthy.

Administrators can now use Windows Defender Application Control to ensure that only applications that you explicitly allow can run on the Windows 10 computers.

Windows Defender Application Control allows an administrator to control applications and this is a big advantage over just using antivirus software. By stopping applications from running unless an administrator explicitly allows the application is just another layer of protection that organizations can utilize in their war against data theft.

For many years, top level security analysts have stated that application control is one of the best ways for addressing the many threats that executable based malware is used against companies. Now, administrators can add another layer of security by listing what applications can specifically run on their own Windows 10 corporate systems.

If an administrator wants to create policies for use with Windows Defender Application Control, they need to meet the following system requirements:

- Windows 10 Enterprise
- Windows Server 2016
- Windows Server 2019

Administrators can configure Windows Defender Application Control through the use of a Group Policy Object or by using Mobile Device Management (MDM) and Microsoft Intune with EMS. After Windows Defender Application Control is set up, administrators can create and configure policies by using GPOs or Intune.

Summary

In this chapter, I discussed using Windows Defender Firewall with Advanced Security. Windows Defender Firewall helps prevent unauthorized users from connecting to the Windows 10 operating system. Windows Defender Firewall is an extra line of defense, but it should not replace a perimeter firewall for your network.

I also talked about protecting devices using Windows Defender Security. I talked about how your Organization's IT department can have even better threat protection when they combine Azure Windows Defender Advanced Threat Protection (Windows Defender ATP) with Azure Advanced Threat Protection (Azure ATP).

I then talked about using Windows Defender Application Guard. Application Guard was specifically designed for Windows 10 and Microsoft Internet browsers (Edge & Internet Explorer). Application Guard works with Windows Edge to isolate untrusted websites, thus protecting your organization's network and data while users are working on the Internet.

I spoke about using Windows Defender Exploit Guard and how it helps protect your Windows 10 system against malware, ransomware, and other types of attacks. It does this by reducing the attack surface of a device.

I then talked about using Windows Defender Credential Guard. Windows Defender Credential Guard is a virtualization based security to help isolate critical files so that only system software that is privileged can access those critical files.

Finally, I explained how Windows Defender Application Control allows an administrator to control applications and how administrators can stop applications from running unless an administrator explicitly allows the application.

Exam Essentials

Know how to configure Windows Defender Firewall.   Know how to set up and maintain Windows Defender Firewall with Advanced Security. Know that you can set up inbound and outbound rules by using Windows Defender Firewall. Know how to allow or deny applications by using Windows Defender Firewall.

Understand Windows Defender Application Guard.   Understand how Application Guard works with Windows Edge and Internet Explorer to isolate untrusted websites.

Know Windows Defender Credential Guard.   Know how Windows Defender Credential Guard uses virtualization-based security to help isolate critical files so that only system software with privileges can access those critical files.

Understand Windows Defender Exploit Guard.   Understand how Windows Defender Exploit Guard helps protect your Windows 10 system against malware, ransomware, and other types of attacks.

Know Windows Defender ATP.   Know and understand how to combine Azure Windows Defender Advanced Threat Protection (Windows Defender ATP) with Azure Advanced Threat Protection (Azure ATP).

Understand Windows Defender Application Control.   Understand how Windows Defender Application Control allows an administrator to control which applications are allowed on a Windows 10 system.

Review Questions

1. You are the administrator for an organization with 275 computers that all run Windows 10. These computers are all joined to Microsoft Azure Active and all computers are enrolled in Microsoft Intune with EMS. You need to make sure that only approved applications are allowed to run on all of these computers. What should you implement to ensure this?

   A. Windows Defender Credential Guard

   B. Windows Defender Exploit Guard

   C. Windows Defender Application Control

   D. Windows Defender Antivirus

2. You are the administrator of a large training company. All of your machines run Windows 10. You have a Windows 10 machine that has a virus that was caused by a malicious font. You need to stop this type of threat from affecting your corporate computers in the future. What should you use?

   A. Windows Defender Exploit Guard

   B. Windows Defender Application Guard

   C. Windows Defender Credential Guard

   D. Windows Defender System Guard

3. You are the administrator for an organization where all computers run Windows 10. You need to make sure that critical files are isolated so that only system software with privileges can access those critical files. What should you implement to ensure this?

   A. Windows Defender Credential Guard

   B. Windows Defender Exploit Guard

   C. Windows Defender Application Control

   D. Windows Defender Antivirus

4. You are the IT Director for a large school system. You need to set up inbound and outbound rules on the Windows 10 machines. What do you need to do to accomplish this?

   A. Windows Defender Credential Guard

   B. Windows Defender Exploit Guard

   C. Windows Defender Application Control

   D. Windows Defender Firewall with Advanced Security

5. You are the administrator for StormWind Studios. You are trying to set up your Windows Defender Firewall to allow DNS inbound and outbound rules. Which port number would you set up?

   A. Port 20

   B. Port 25

   C. Port 53

   D. Port 80

6. You are the IT Manager for WillPanek.com. The company has an Active Directory domain and a cloud-based Azure Active Directory. You need to protect your systems from common malware hacks that use executable files and scripts that attack applications like Microsoft Office (for example, Outlook). What do you need to do to accomplish this?

   A. Windows Defender Credential Guard

   B. Windows Defender Exploit Guard

   C. Windows Defender Application Control

   D. Windows Defender Firewall with Advanced Security

7. You are the administrator for StormWind Studios. You are trying to set up your Windows Defender Firewall to allow SMTP inbound and outbound rules. Which port number would you setup?

   A. Port 20

   B. Port 25

   C. Port 53

   D. Port 80

8. You are the administrator for a large organization and all computers run Windows 10. These computers are all joined to Microsoft Azure Active and all computers are enrolled in Microsoft Intune with EMS. You need to ensure that all applications installed on the Windows 10 systems are only applications that are approved by the IT department. What should you implement to ensure this?

   A. Windows Defender Application Control

   B. Windows Defender Credential Guard

   C. Windows Defender Exploit Guard

   D. Windows Defender Antivirus

9. You are the administrator of a large publishing company. All of your corporate machines run Windows 10. You need to ensure that no software will affect the Windows 10 machines from common malware hacks that use executable files and scripts to attack applications. What should you use?

   A. Windows Defender Application Guard

   B. Windows Defender Credential Guard

   C. Windows Defender System Guard

   D. Windows Defender Exploit Guard

10. You are the administrator for StormWind Studios. You are trying to set up your Windows Defender Firewall to allow FTP traffic. Which two port numbers would you setup?

   A. Port 20 and 21

   B. Port 25 and 53

   C. Port 53 and 80

   D. Port 80 and 443

Chapter

6

Configuring Auditing

MICROSOFT EXAM OBJECTIVES COVERED IN THIS CHAPTER:

✓ **Monitor devices**

- Monitor device health (e.g., log analytics, Windows Analytics, or other cloud-based tools); monitor device security

One of the tasks that administrators will need to do on a daily basis is fixing Windows 10 systems that are having issues.

There are many ways to determine what issues a Windows 10 system may be having, and there are many tools to help you solve the issues.

The best way to protect any Windows 10 system is to make sure the users' files are stored on a network server and backed up daily. But there may be times when you need to back up the Windows 10 system.

Windows 10 includes a full backup and restore application (Backup and Restore [Windows 7]) that allows a user or an administrator to maintain a backup copy of any of the Windows 10 component files and data files that are considered critical to the operation of their day-to-day business. In this chapter we will discuss using the Microsoft Azure Backup utility and how easy it is for your users and IT administrators to quickly and easily back up their documents to the cloud.

Finally, there will be times when an administrator needs to monitor the Windows 10 system. Sometimes, performance optimization can feel like a luxury, but it can be very important, especially if you can't get your Windows 10 system to run applications the way they are intended to run. The Windows 10 operating system has been specifically designed to keep your mission-critical applications and data accessible even in times of failures.

The most common cause of such problems is a hardware configuration issue. Poorly written device drivers and unsupported hardware can cause problems with system stability. Failed hardware components (such as system memory) may do so as well. Memory chips can be faulty, electrostatic discharge can ruin them, and other hardware issues can occur. No matter what, a problem with your memory chip spells disaster for your Windows 10 system.

Usually, third-party hardware vendors provide utility programs with their computers that can be used for performing hardware diagnostics on machines to help you find problems. These utilities are a good first step to resolving intermittent problems, but Windows 10 comes with many utilities that can help you diagnose and fix your issues.

In this chapter, I'll cover the tools and methods used for measuring performance and troubleshooting failures in Windows 10. Before you dive into the technical details, however, you should thoroughly understand what you're trying to accomplish and how you'll meet this goal.

Monitoring Windows

Because performance monitoring and optimization are vital functions in network environments of any size, Windows 10 includes several monitoring and performance tools.

Introducing Performance Monitor

The first and most useful tool is the Windows 10 *Performance Monitor*, which was designed to allow users and system administrators to monitor performance statistics for various operating system parameters. Specifically, you can collect, store, and analyze information about CPU, memory, disk, and network resources using this tool, and these are only a handful of the things you can monitor. By collecting and analyzing performance values, system administrators can identify many potential problems.

You can use Performance Monitor in the following ways:

Performance Monitor ActiveX Control   Windows 10 Performance Monitor is an ActiveX control that you can place within other applications. Examples of applications that can host the Performance Monitor control include web browsers and client programs such as Microsoft Word and Microsoft Excel. This functionality can make it easy for application developers and system administrators to incorporate Performance Monitor into their own tools and applications.

Performance Monitor MMC   For more common performance monitoring functions, you'll want to use the built-in Microsoft Management Console (MMC) version of Performance Monitor.

Data Collector Sets   Windows 10 Performance Monitor includes Data Collector Sets. This tool works with performance logs, telling Performance Monitor where the logs are stored and when a log needs to run. The Data Collector Sets also define the credentials used to run the set.

To access the Performance Monitor MMC, you open Administrative Tools and then choose Performance Monitor. This launches the Performance MMC and loads and initializes Performance Monitor with a handful of default counters.

You can choose from many different methods of monitoring performance when you are using Performance Monitor. A couple of examples are listed here:

- You can look at a snapshot of current activity for a few of the most important counters. This allows you to find areas of potential bottlenecks and monitor the load on your servers at a certain point in time.

- You can save information to a log file for historical reporting and later analysis. This type of information is useful, for example, if you want to compare the load on your servers from three months ago to the current load.

You'll get to take a closer look at this method and many others as you examine Performance Monitor in more detail.

In the following sections, you'll learn about the basics of working with the Windows 10 Performance Monitor and other performance tools. Then you'll apply these tools and techniques when you monitor the performance of your network.

> Your Performance Monitor grows as your system grows, and whenever you add services to Windows 10, you also add to what you can monitor. You should make sure that, as you install services, you take a look at what it is you can monitor.

Deciding What to Monitor

The first step in monitoring performance is to decide *what* you want to monitor. In Windows 10, the operating system and related services include hundreds of performance statistics that you can track easily. For example, you may want to monitor the processor. This is just one of many items that can be monitored. All performance statistics fall into three main categories that you can choose to measure:

Performance Objects   A *performance object* within Performance Monitor is a collection of various performance statistics that you can monitor. Performance objects are based on various areas of system resources. For example, there are performance objects for the processor and memory as well as for specific services.

Counters   *Counters* are the actual parameters measured by Performance Monitor. They are specific items that are grouped within performance objects. For example, within the Processor performance object, there is a counter for % Processor Time. This counter displays one type of detailed information about the Processor performance object (specifically, the amount of total CPU time all of the processes on the system are using). Another set of counters you can use will allow you to monitor print servers.

Instances   Some counters will have *instances*. An instance further identifies which performance parameter the counter is measuring. A simple example is a server with two CPUs. If you decide you want to monitor processor usage (using the Processor performance object)—specifically, utilization (the % Total Utilization counter)—you must still specify *which* CPU(s) you want to measure. In this example, you would have the choice of monitoring either of the two CPUs or a total value for both (using the Total instance).

To specify which performance objects, counters, and instances you want to monitor, you add them to Performance Monitor using the Add Counters dialog box. Figure 6.1 shows the various options that are available when you add new counters to monitor using Performance Monitor.

FIGURE 6.1 Adding a new Performance Monitor counter

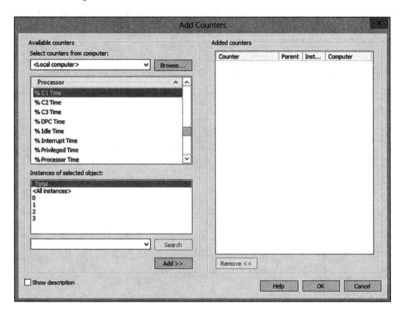

The items that you will be able to monitor will be based on your hardware and software configuration. For example, if you have not installed and configured Hyper-V, the options available within the Hyper-V Server performance object will not be available. Or, if you have multiple network adapters or CPUs on the Windows 10 system, you will have the option of viewing each instance separately or as part of the total value.

Viewing Performance Information

The Windows 10 Performance Monitor was designed to show information in a clear and easy-to-understand format. Performance objects, counters, and instances may be displayed in each of three views. This flexibility allows system administrators to quickly and easily define the information they want to see once and then choose how it will be displayed based on specific needs. Most likely, you will use only one view, but it's helpful to know what other views are available depending on what it is you are trying to assess.

You can use the following main views to review statistics and information on performance:

Graph View The *Graph view* (sometimes referred to as the Line view) is the default display that is presented when you first access the Windows 10 Performance Monitor. The chart displays values using the vertical axis and time using the horizontal axis. This view is useful if you want to display values over a period of time or see the changes in these values over that time period. Each point that is plotted on the graph is based on an average value calculated during the sample interval for the measurement being made. For example, you may notice overall CPU utilization starting at a low value at the beginning of the chart and then becoming much higher during later measurements. This indicates that the server has become busier (specifically, with CPU-intensive processes). Figure 6.2 provides an example of the Graph view.

FIGURE 6.2   Viewing information in Performance Monitor Graph view

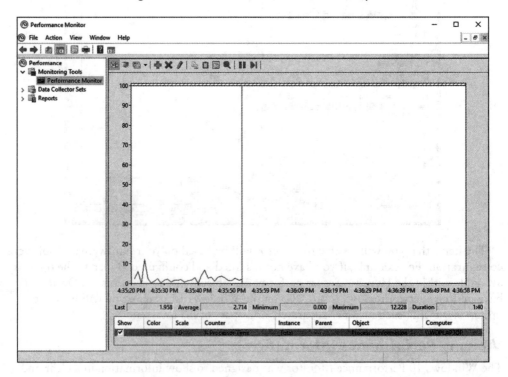

Histogram View   The *Histogram view* shows performance statistics and information using a set of relative bar charts. This view is useful if you want to see a snapshot of the latest value for a given counter. For example, if you were interested in viewing a snapshot of current system performance statistics during each refresh interval, the length of each of the bars in the display would give you a visual representation of each value. It would also allow you to compare measurements visually relative to each other. You can set the histogram to display an average measurement as well as minimum and maximum thresholds. Figure 6.3 shows a typical Histogram view.

Report View   Like the Histogram view, the *Report view* shows performance statistics based on the latest measurement. You can see an average measurement as well as minimum and maximum thresholds. This view is most useful for determining exact values because it provides information in numeric terms, whereas the Graph and Histogram views provide information graphically. Figure 6.4 provides an example of the type of information you'll see in the Report view.

FIGURE 6.3   Viewing information in Performance Monitor Histogram view

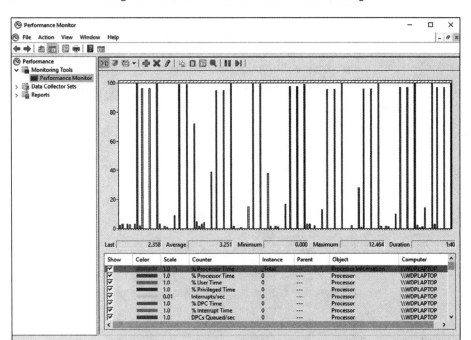

FIGURE 6.4   Viewing information in Performance Monitor Report view

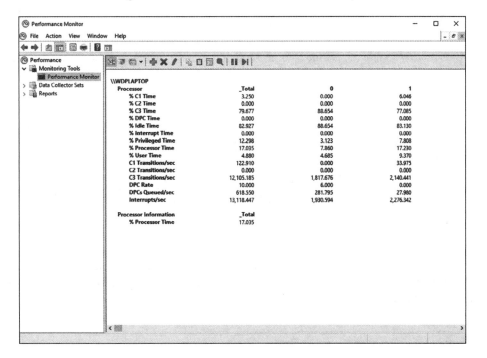

Managing Performance Monitor Properties

You can specify additional settings for viewing performance information within the properties of Performance Monitor. You can access these options by clicking the Properties button in the Taskbar or by right-clicking the Performance Monitor display and selecting Properties. You can change these additional settings by using the following tabs:

General Tab On the General tab (shown in Figure 6.5), you can specify several options that relate to Performance Monitor views:

FIGURE 6.5   General tab of the Performance Monitor Properties dialog box

- You can enable or disable legends (which display information about the various counters), the value bar, and the toolbar.

- For the Report and Histogram views, you can choose which type of information is displayed. The options are Default, Current, Minimum, Maximum, and Average. What you see with each of these options depends on the type of data being collected. These options are not available for the Graph view because the Graph view displays an average value over a period of time (the sample interval).

- You can also choose the graph elements. By default, the display will be set to update every second. If you want to update less often, you should increase the number of seconds between updates.

Source Tab On the Source tab (shown in Figure 6.6), you can specify the source for the performance information you want to view. Options include current activity (the default setting) or data from a log file. If you choose to analyze information from a log file, you can also specify the time range for which you want to view statistics. I'll cover these selections in the next section.

FIGURE 6.6 Source tab of the Performance Monitor Properties dialog box

Data Tab The Data tab (shown in Figure 6.7) lists the counters that have been added to the Performance Monitor display. These counters apply to the Chart, Histogram, and Report views. Using this interface, you can also add or remove any of the counters and change the properties, such as the width, style, and color of the line and the scale used for display.

FIGURE 6.7 The Data tab of the Performance Monitor Properties dialog box

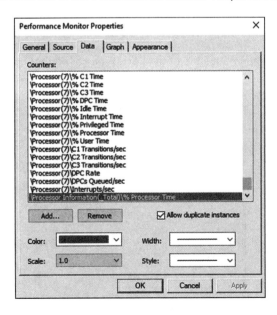

Graph Tab   On the Graph tab (shown in Figure 6.8), you can specify certain options that will allow you to customize the display of Performance Monitor views. First you can specify what type of view you want to see (Line, Histogram, or Report). Then you can add a title for the graph, specify a label for the vertical axis, choose to display grids, and specify the vertical scale range.

FIGURE 6.8   The Graph tab of the Performance Monitor Properties dialog box

Appearance Tab   Using the Appearance tab (see Figure 6.9), you can specify the colors for the areas of the display, such as the background and foreground. You can also specify the fonts that are used to display counter values in Performance Monitor views. You can change settings to find a suitable balance between readability and the amount of information shown on one screen. Finally, you can set up the properties for a border.

FIGURE 6.9   The Appearance tab of the Performance Monitor Properties dialog box

Now that you have an idea of the types of information Performance Monitor tracks and how this data is displayed, we'll take a look at another feature—saving and analyzing performance data.

Saving and Analyzing Data with Performance Logs and Alerts

One of the most important aspects of monitoring performance is that it should be done over a given period of time (referred to as a *baseline*). So far, I have shown you how you can use Performance Monitor to view statistics in real time. I have, however, also alluded to using Performance Monitor to save data for later analysis. Now let's take a look at how you can do this.

When viewing information in Performance Monitor, you have two main options with respect to the data on display:

View Current Activity   When you first open the Performance icon from the Administrative Tools folder, the default option is to view data obtained from current system information. This method of viewing measures and displays various real-time statistics on the system's performance.

View Log File Data   This option allows you to view information that was previously saved to a log file. Although the performance objects, counters, and instances may appear to be the same as those viewed using the View Current Activity option, the information itself was actually captured at a previous point in time and stored into a log file.

Log files for the View Log File Data option are created in the Performance Logs And Alerts section of the Windows 10 Performance tool.

Three items allow you to customize how the data is collected in the log files:

Counter Logs   *Counter logs* record performance statistics based on the various performance objects, counters, and instances available in Performance Monitor. The values are updated based on a time interval setting and are saved to a file for later analysis.

Circular Logging   In *circular logging*, the data that is stored within a file is overwritten as new data is entered into the log. This is a useful method of logging if you want to record information only for a certain time frame (for example, the past four hours). Circular logging also conserves disk space by ensuring that the performance log file will not continue to grow over certain limits.

Linear Logging   In *linear logging*, data is never deleted from the log files, and new information is added to the end of the log file. The result is a log file that continually grows. The benefit is that all historical information is retained.

Now that you have an idea of the types of functions that are supported by the Windows 10 Performance tools, you can learn how you can apply this information to the task at hand—monitoring and troubleshooting your Windows network.

🌐 **Real World Scenario**

Real-World Performance Monitoring

In our daily jobs as system engineers and administrators, we come across systems that are in need of our help. . .and may even ask for it. You, of course, check your Event Viewer and Performance Monitor and perform other tasks that help you troubleshoot. But what is really the most common problem that occurs? From my experience, I'd say that you suffer performance problems many times if your Windows 10 operating system is installed on a subpar system. Either the system's hardware minimum requirements weren't addressed or the operating system is not configured properly.

Using Other Performance-Monitoring Tools

Performance Monitor allows you to monitor different parameters of the Windows 10 operating system and associated services and applications. However, you can also use three other tools to monitor performance in Windows 10. They are Reliability Monitor, Task Manager, and Event Viewer. All three of these tools are useful for monitoring different areas of overall system performance and for examining details related to specific system events. In the following sections, you'll take a quick look at these tools and how you can best use them.

Reliability Monitor

Windows 10 Reliability Monitor is part of the Windows Reliability and Performance Monitor snap-in for Microsoft Management Console (MMC). The easiest way to access the Reliability Monitor is to type **perfmon /rel** in the Start Search box and press Enter.

The Reliability Monitor provides a system stability overview and allows an administrator to get details about events that may be impacting the Windows 10 reliability. Reliability Monitor calculates a stability index based on a certain period of time and it then shows that stability index in the System Stability Chart.

The Reliability Monitor shows information, all on their own separate lines, about application failures, Windows failures, miscellaneous failures, warnings, and information.

The Reliability Monitor shows an administrator a period of time on the Windows 10 system and the administrator can click on any of the events during that specific period of time and see what Information, Warnings, or Errors that may have happened during that time period.

Administrators can then use the information gathered by the Reliability Monitor to help diagnose the issues that the Windows 10 system may be having.

Task Manager

Performance Monitor is designed to allow you to keep track of specific aspects of system performance over time. But what do you do if you want to get a quick snapshot of what the local system is doing? Creating a System Monitor chart, adding counters, and choosing a view is overkill. Fortunately, the Windows 10 Task Manager has been designed to provide a quick overview of important system performance statistics without requiring any configuration. Better yet, it's always readily available.

You can easily access Task Manager in several ways:

- Right-click the Windows Taskbar, and then click Task Manager.

- Press Ctrl+Alt+Del, and then select Task Manager.

- Press Ctrl+Shift+Esc.

- Type **Taskman** in the Windows Search box.

Each of these methods allows you to access a snapshot of the current system performance quickly.

Once you access Task Manager, you will see the following seven tabs:

These tabs can be different on Windows client machines. For example, Windows 10 Home can vary from Windows 10 Enterprise.

Processes Tab   The Processes tab shows you all the processes that are currently running on the local computer. By default, you'll be able to view how much CPU time and memory a particular process is using. By clicking any of the columns, you can quickly sort by the data values in that particular column. This is useful, for example, if you want to find out which processes are using the most memory on your server.

By accessing the performance objects in the View menu, you can add columns to the Processes tab. Figure 6.10 shows a list of the current processes running on a Windows 10 computer.

FIGURE 6.10   Viewing process statistics and information using Task Manager

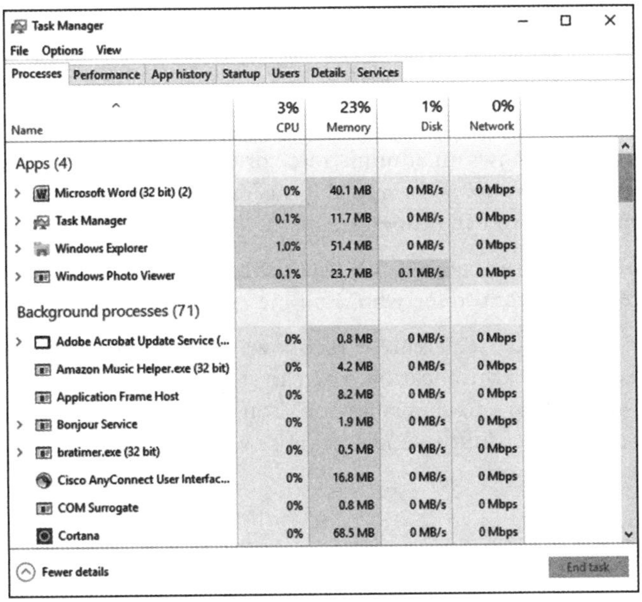

Name	3% CPU	23% Memory	1% Disk	0% Network
Apps (4)				
› ◻ Microsoft Word (32 bit) (2)	0%	40.1 MB	0 MB/s	0 Mbps
› ◻ Task Manager	0.1%	11.7 MB	0 MB/s	0 Mbps
› ◻ Windows Explorer	1.0%	51.4 MB	0 MB/s	0 Mbps
› ◻ Windows Photo Viewer	0.1%	23.7 MB	0.1 MB/s	0 Mbps
Background processes (71)				
› ◻ Adobe Acrobat Update Service (...	0%	0.8 MB	0 MB/s	0 Mbps
◻ Amazon Music Helper.exe (32 bit)	0%	4.2 MB	0 MB/s	0 Mbps
◻ Application Frame Host	0%	8.2 MB	0 MB/s	0 Mbps
› ◻ Bonjour Service	0%	1.9 MB	0 MB/s	0 Mbps
› ◻ bratimer.exe (32 bit)	0%	0.5 MB	0 MB/s	0 Mbps
◻ Cisco AnyConnect User Interfac...	0%	16.8 MB	0 MB/s	0 Mbps
◻ COM Surrogate	0%	0.8 MB	0 MB/s	0 Mbps
◻ Cortana	0%	68.5 MB	0 MB/s	0 Mbps

Task Manager
File   Options   View
Processes   Performance   App history   Startup   Users   Details   Services

⌄ Fewer details   End task

Performance Tab   One of the problems with using Performance Monitor to get a quick snapshot of system performance is that you have to add counters to a chart. Most system administrators are too busy to take the time to do this when all they need is basic CPU and memory information. That's where the Performance tab of Task Manager comes in. Using the Performance tab, you can view details about how memory is allocated on the computer and how much of the CPU is utilized (see Figure 6.11).

FIGURE 6.11   Viewing CPU and memory performance information using Task Manager

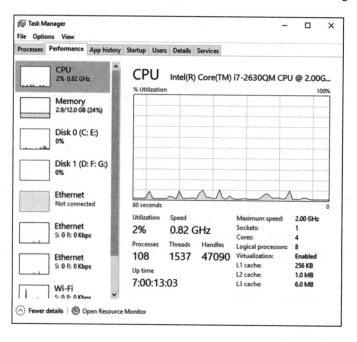

App History   This tab shows you all of the recent applications that have been running on the Windows 10 system. Users have the ability to Delete Usage History from this tab.

Startup   The Startup tab shows an administrator or user which applications get started when the machine first starts up. Some applications require that services start at system startup for the applications to run properly.

Users Tab   The Users tab (see Figure 6.12) lists the currently active user accounts. This is particularly helpful if you want to see who is online and quickly log off or disconnect users.

Details Tab   The Details tab (see Figure 6.13) shows you what applications are currently running on the system. From this location, you can stop an application from running by right-clicking the application and choosing Stop. You also have the ability to set your affinity level here. By setting the affinity, you can choose which applications will use which physical processors on your system.

FIGURE 6.12   Viewing user information using Task Manager

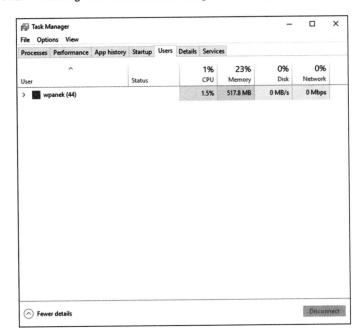

FIGURE 6.13   Viewing currently running applications using Task Manager

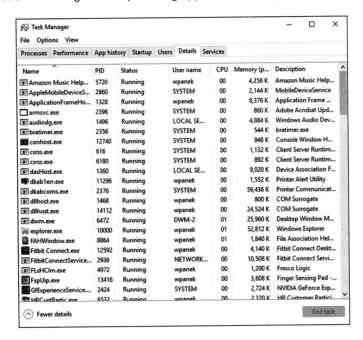

Services Tab   The Services tab (see Figure 6.14) shows you what services are currently running on the system. From this location, you can stop a service from running by right-clicking the service and choosing Stop. The Open Services link launches the Services MMC.

FIGURE 6.14   Viewing services information using Task Manager

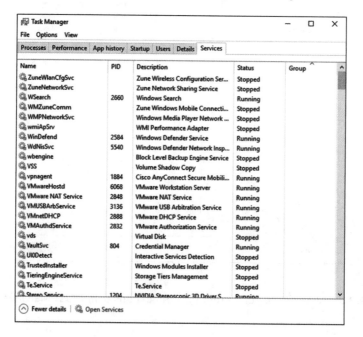

As you can see, Task Manager is useful for providing important information about the system quickly. Once you get used to using Task Manager, you won't be able to get by without it!

> Make sure that you use Task Manager and familiarize yourself with all that it can do; you can end processes that have become intermittent, kill applications that may hang the system, view NIC performance, and so on. In addition, you can access this tool quickly to get an idea of what could be causing you problems. Event Viewer and Performance Monitor are both great tools for getting granular information on potential problems.

Event Viewer

Event Viewer is also useful for monitoring network information. Specifically, you can use the logs to view any information, warnings, or alerts related to the proper functioning of the network (see Figure 6.15). You can access Event Viewer by clicking the Start button, then selecting Windows Administrative Tools ➤ Event Viewer or by right-clicking the Start button and choosing Event Viewer. Clicking any of the items in the left pane displays the various events that have been logged for each item.

FIGURE 6.15   Event Viewer

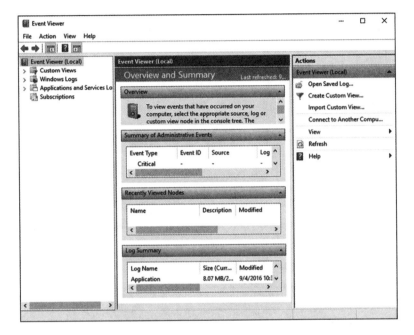

Each event that is preceded by a blue "i" icon designates that these events are informational and do not indicate problems with the network. Rather, they record benign events such as Microsoft Office startup or a service starting.

Problematic or potentially problematic events are indicated by a yellow warning icon or a red error icon (see Figure 6.16). Warnings usually indicate a problem that wouldn't prevent a service from running but might cause undesired effects with the service in question.

Error events almost always indicate a failed service, application, or function. For instance, if the dynamic registration of a DNS client fails, Event Viewer will generate an error. As you can see, errors are more severe than warnings because, in the case of DNS, the DNS client cannot participate in DNS at all.

Double-clicking any event opens its Event Properties dialog box, shown in Figure 6.17, which displays a detailed description of the event.

FIGURE 6.16 Information, errors, and warnings in Event Viewer

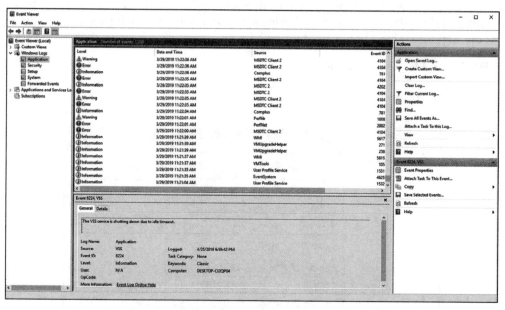

FIGURE 6.17 An Event Properties dialog box

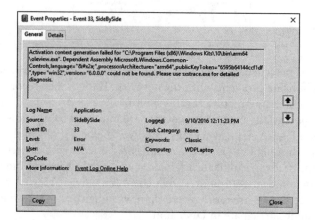

Event Viewer can display thousands of different events, so it would be impossible to list them all here. The important points of which you should be aware are the following:

- Information events are always benign.
- Warnings indicate noncritical problems.
- Errors indicate show-stopping events.

Let's discuss some of the logs and the ways that you can view data:

Applications and Services   The *applications and services logs* are part of Event Viewer where applications (for example, Hardware events) and services log their events. Internet Explorer events would be logged in this part of Event Viewer. An important log in this section is the Key Management Service log (see Figure 6.18). This is where all of your Key Management Service events get stored.

FIGURE 6.18   The applications and services logs

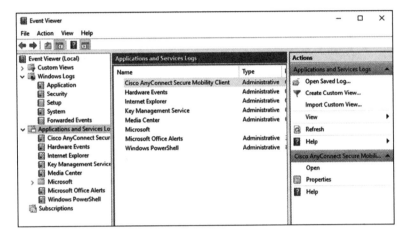

Custom Views   *Custom views* allow you to filter events (see Figure 6.19) to create your own customized look. You can filter events by event level (critical, error, warning, and so on), by logs, and by source. You also have the ability to view events occurring within a specific time frame. This allows you to look only at the events that are important to you.

FIGURE 6.19   Create Custom View dialog box

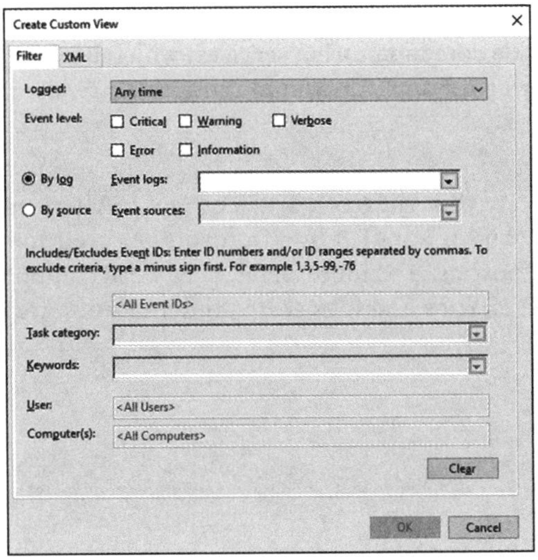

Subscriptions *Subscriptions* allow a user to receive alerts about events that you predefine. In the Subscription Properties dialog box (see Figure 6.20), you can define what type of events you want notifications about and the notification method. The Subscriptions section is an advanced alerting service to help you watch for events.

FIGURE 6.20   Subscription Properties dialog box

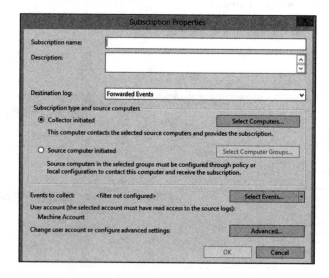

Monitor Cloud-Based Tools

Microsoft offers a couple different cloud-based tools for monitoring services. These include:

- Azure Monitor, which is designed for the cloud but can also be used to monitor on-premises systems.
- System Center Operations Manager (SCOM), which is designed for on-premises and for the cloud.

These two tools provide core monitoring services, which include alerts, service uptime tracking, health monitoring for application and infrastructure, diagnostics, and analytics.

Azure Monitor

Azure Monitor is software that runs as a service (SaaS). All of the supporting infrastructure runs in Azure and is handled by Microsoft. Azure Monitor was created to perform analytics, diagnostics, and monitoring. The core components of the infrastructure, such as collectors, metrics and logs store, and analytics are run by Microsoft (see Figure 6.21).

Many of the following figures were taken directly from Microsoft's website. Since many of the figures point out specific issues, most of the following figures were taken from Microsoft's website to demonstrate those points.

FIGURE 6.21   Azure Monitor Dashboard

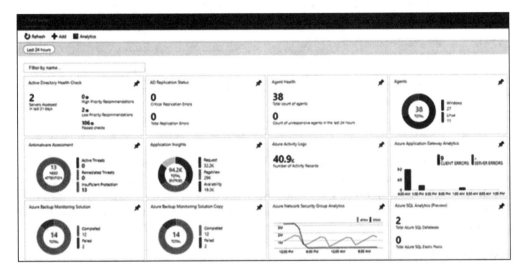

Here are a few things that you can do with Azure Monitor:

- With Application Insights you can detect and diagnose issues across applications and dependencies.

- For VMs and Azure Monitor for Containers you can compare infrastructure issues.

- Using Log Analytics for troubleshooting and deep diagnostics you can monitor data.

- Using smart alerts and automated actions you can support operations at scale.

- Using Azure dashboards and workbooks you can create visualizations

The following figure provides a view on how Azure Monitor works, shown in Figure 6.22. In the middle are the two fundamental types of data used by Azure Monitor, these are the data stores for metrics and logs. On the left side are the sources that populate the data stores. On the right side are the various functions that Azure Monitor can perform with this collected data.

As I mentioned earlier, all the data that is collected by Azure Monitor fits into one of two fundamental types, metrics and logs.

- Metrics are numerical values that express a piece of the system at a specific point in time. They are capable of supporting real-time scenarios.

- Logs contain other kinds of data, which is arranged into records with different sets of properties for each type.

FIGURE 6.22 How Azure Monitor Works

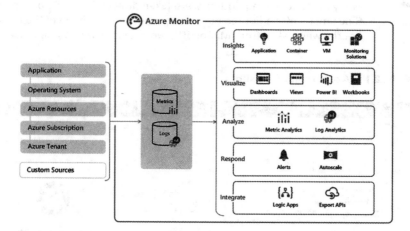

Data collected by Azure Monitor will appear on the right-hand side on the Overview page in the Azure portal. You may notice several charts that display the performance metrics. If you click on any of the graphs, it will open the data in Metrics Explorer, shown in Figure 6.23, so you can chart the values of various metrics over a given period of time. You can also view the charts or pin them to a dashboard to view them with other visualizations.

FIGURE 6.23 Metrics Explorer

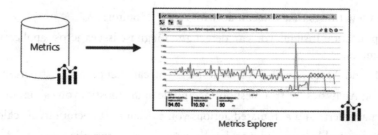

Metrics Explorer

Log data that is accumulated with Azure Monitor can be analyzed by using queries. You can create and test queries by using Log Analytics in the Azure portal (see Figure 6.24).

FIGURE 6.24 Log Analytics

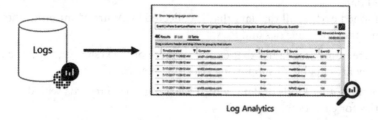

Log Analytics

Azure Monitor collects data from a wide variety of sources, including data collected from the following tiers:

- Application monitoring data is about the performance and functionality of the code written, regardless of its platform.

- Guest OS monitoring data is about the operating system on which the application is running.

- Azure resource monitoring data is about the operation of an Azure resource.

- Azure subscription monitoring data is about the operation and management of an Azure subscription, including the data on the health and operation of Azure itself.

- Azure tenant monitoring data is about the operation of tenant-level Azure services, such as Azure Active Directory.

Azure Monitor starts collecting data as soon as you create an Azure subscription and start adding resources. The Activity log records when resources were created or modified and the Metrics will show how the resources are performing.

Using the Data Collector API, Azure Monitor can collect log data from any REST client which will allow you to create custom monitoring scenarios.

Azure Monitor includes several features and tools that can provide helpful insights into your applications and other resources. These features include; Application Insights, Azure Monitor for containers, and Azure Monitor for VMs.

Application Insights

Application Insights monitors the availability, performance, and usage of web applications that are either hosted in the cloud or on-premises. It uses Azure Monitor to provide insight into an application's operations and to diagnose problems without waiting for a user to report it. Application Insights includes connection points to several different development tools and can integrate with Visual Studio to support DevOps processes (see Figure 6.25).

FIGURE 6.25   Application Insights

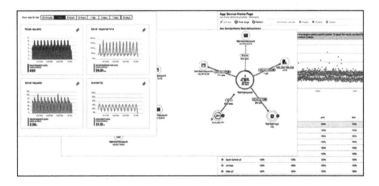

Azure Monitor for Containers

Azure Monitor for Containers is a feature intended to monitor the performance of container workloads. It shows performance visibility by collecting memory and processor metrics from controllers, nodes, and containers. Container logs are also collected (see Figure 6.26).

FIGURE 6.26   Azure Monitor for Containers

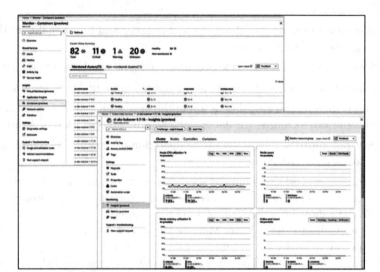

Azure Monitor for Containers monitors the performance and health of Azure Kubernetes Services or Azure Container Instances. It also collects container logs and inventory data about containers and their images.

Azure Monitor for VMs

Azure Monitor for VMs monitors the Azure virtual machines (VMs) by analyzing the performance and health of the Windows and Linux VMs. This includes support for monitoring performance and application dependencies for VMs hosted on-premises or on another cloud provider (see Figure 6.27).

FIGURE 6.27   Azure Monitor for VMs

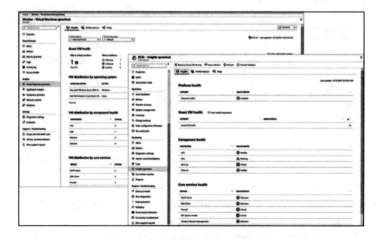

Azure Monitor for VMs delivers health monitoring for the guest Azure VMs when you're monitoring Windows and Linux virtual machines. It evaluates the health of major operating system components to determine the current health state. When it determines the guest VM is experiencing an issue, it will generate an alert.

In addition to monitoring data, Azure Monitor allows you to perform other functions to meet your needs. You can perform the following:

- Alerts inform you of critical conditions and can attempt to take corrective action. Alert rules (see Figure 6.28) provide near real-time alerting based on metric numeric values, while rules based on logs allow for complex logic across data from numerous sources. Alert rules use action groups, which contain unique sets of recipients and actions that can be shared across multiple rules.

FIGURE 6.28   Alerts

Subscription	Resource group	Time Range
Contoso IT - demo	mms-eus	Past Hour

Contoso IT - demo › mms-eus

Total Alerts	Smart Groups	Total Alert Rules		Learn More
29	**1**	**15**		About Alerts
Since 8/1/2018, 4:38:39 PM	96.55% Reduction	Enabled 13		

SEVERITY	TOTAL ALERTS	NEW	ACKNOWLEDGED	CLOSED
Sev 0	26	26	0	0
Sev 1	0	0	0	0
Sev 2	3	3	0	0
Sev 3	0	0	0	0
Sev 4	0	0	0	0

- Autoscale allows just the amount of resources needed in order to handle application workload. Azure Monitor allows you to create rules that use metrics collected to determine when resources will be added automatically to handle increases in workload and can save money by removing idle resources. You can specify a minimum and maximum number of instances and the logic for when to increase or decrease resources (see Figure 6.29).

FIGURE 6.29   Autoscale

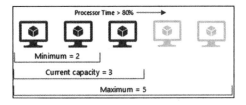

- Azure dashboards allow you to join different kinds of data, including metrics and logs, into a single pane in the Azure portal (see Figure 6.30).

FIGURE 6.30   Azure Monitor Dashboard

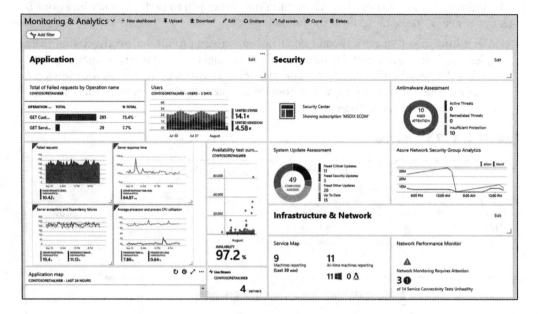

- Views show log data in Azure Monitor. Each view includes a single tile that can be depicted as bar and line charts and lists summarizing critical data (see Figure 6.31).

FIGURE 6.31   Views

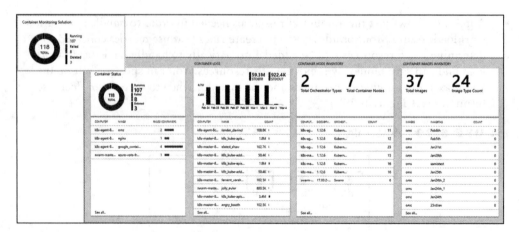

- Power BI is a business analytics service that provides interactive visualizations across a wide variety of data sources and makes data available to others either within or outside the organization. You can configure Power BI to import log data automatically from Azure Monitor (see Figure 6.32).

FIGURE 6.32 Power BI

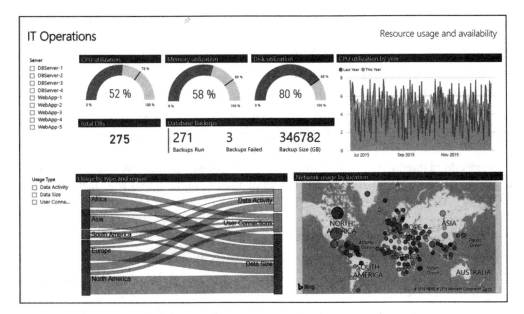

- Azure Event Hubs are a streaming platform and event breakdown service that transforms and stores data using any real-time analytics provider. Use Event Hubs to stream Azure Monitor data to partner SIEM and monitoring tools.

- Logic Apps is a service that allows the automation of tasks and processes using workflows that combine different systems and services. Activities are available that read and write metrics and logs in Azure Monitor, which allows you to build workflows integrating with a variety of other systems.

- Multiple APIs are available to read and write metrics and logs to and from Azure Monitor, as well as accessing generated alerts. You can also use them to configure and retrieve alerts.

System Center Operations Manager

From 2015 until April 2018, Operations Management Suite (OMS) was a bundle of the following Azure management services:

- Azure Automation
- Azure Backup

- Application Insights

- Operational Insights (later called Log Analytics)

- Site Recovery

The functionality of the services that were part of OMS did not change when discontinued; they were realigned under Azure Monitor.

In March 2019, Microsoft released System Center 2019.

System Center 2019 enables deployment and management of Windows Server 2019 at a larger scale to meet data center needs.

System Center 2019 provides the following:

- Tools to monitor and manage data centers.

- Support and management capabilities in the most current versions of Windows Server.

- Enables hybrid management and monitoring capabilities with Azure.

System Center 2019 is a Long Term Servicing Channel (LTSC) release and provides five years of standard support and five years of extended support.

Service Map integration with System Center Operations Manager (SCOM) allows you to automatically create distributed application diagrams in Operations Manager (OM) that are based on the dynamic dependency maps in Service Map.

Azure Management Pack allows you to perform the following tasks:

- View performance and alert metrics in SCOM

- Integrate with web application monitoring in Application Insights

- Monitor additional platform as a service (PaaS) services, such as Azure Blob Storage, Azure Data Factory, etc.

Virtual Machine Manager (VMM) 2019 (see Figure 6.33) enables simplified patching of VMs by integrating with Azure Update Management.

FIGURE 6.33   Virtual Machine Manager (VMM) 2019

Monitor Azure Device Security

Azure IoT Central Applications is an Internet of Things (IoT) application platform that lessens the load and cost of developing, managing, and maintaining enterprise-grade IoT solutions. Azure IoT Central Applications provides you with the ability to focus energy, money, and time working with a business with IoT data rather than simply maintaining and updating an intricate and continually changing IoT infrastructure. Use Microsoft Azure IoT Central Applications to monitor devices and change settings.

Azure IoT Central Applications are hosted by Microsoft, which reduces the administration overhead of managing applications.

The web user intake allows you to monitor device conditions, create rules, and manage devices and their data through their life cycle. It also enables you to act on device insights by extending IoT intelligence into line-of-business applications.

Azure IoT Central allows for the following:

- Reducing management burden

- Reducing operational costs and overheads

- Easily customizing applications while working with the following:

  - Industry-leading technologies such as Azure IoT Hub and Azure Time Series Insights

  - Enterprise-grade security features such as end-to-end encryption

Azure IoT Central Applications has four personas who interact with an Azure IoT Central Application. They are the builder, operator, administrator, and device developer. Each is described below:

- A builder is responsible for defining the types of devices that connect to the application and customizing the application for the operator.

- An operator manages the devices connected to the application.

- An administrator is responsible for administrative tasks such as managing users and roles within the application.

- A device developer creates the code that runs on a device connected to your application.

After the builder defines the types of devices that can connect to the application, a device developer creates the code to run on the devices. The device developer utilizes Microsoft's open-source Azure IoT SDKs to create the device code. These SDKs have broad language, platform, and protocol support to meet your needs to connect the devices to the Azure IoT Central Application. The SDKs can help you implement the following device capabilities:

- Create a secure connection.

- Send telemetry.

- Report status.

- Receive configuration updates.

An operator uses Azure IoT Central Applications to manage the devices. Operators perform tasks such as:

- Monitoring the devices connected to the application.
- Troubleshooting and remediating issues with devices.
- Provisioning new devices.

As a builder, you create custom rules and actions that operate over data streaming from connected devices. An operator can enable or disable these rules at the device level.

An operator can:

- Use the Device Explorer page to view, add, and delete devices connected to the Azure IoT Central Applications.
- Maintain an up-to-date inventory of devices.
- Keep device metadata up-to-date by changing the values stored in the device properties.
- Control the behavior of devices by updating a setting on a specific device from the Settings page.

To View an Individual Device

1. On the left navigation menu, choose Device Explorer.
2. Choose a device template from the Templates list.
3. In the right-hand pane of the Device Explorer page, you will see a list of devices created from that device template. Choose an individual device to see the device details page for that device (see Figure 6.34):

FIGURE 6.34   Templates

Another way an administrator can view the events collected from a specific computer in Azure is to run a query in Logs Analytics. Administrators can run the following query:

`Event | where Computer = = "ComputerName"`

To Add a Device to an Azure IoT Central Application

1. On the left navigation menu, choose Device Explorer.

2. Choose the device template to create a device.

3. Choose + New.

4. Choose Real or Simulated. A real device is for a physical device that you connect to your Azure IoT Central Application. A simulated device has sample data generated for you by an Azure IoT Central Application.

To connect a large number of devices to an application, you can bulk import devices using a CSV file. The CSV file should have the following columns and headers:

- IOTC_DeviceID (The device ID name should be all lowercase.)

- IOTC_DeviceName (This column is optional.)

To Bulk Register Devices in an Application

1. On the left navigation menu, choose Device Explorer.

2. On the left panel, choose the device template to bulk create the devices.

3. Select Import (see Figure 6.35).

FIGURE 6.35   Select Import

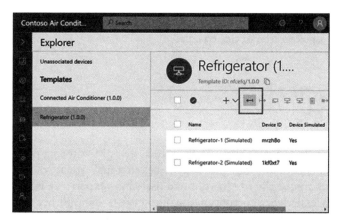

4. Select the CSV file that has the list of device IDs to be imported.

5. Device import starts once the file has been uploaded. You can track the import status at the top of the device grid.

6. Once the import completes, a success message is shown on the device grid (see Figure 6.36).

FIGURE 6.36   Import Complete Success Message

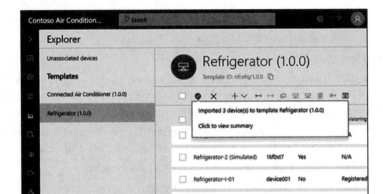

To Delete a Device (Either Real or Simulated) from an Azure IoT Central Application

1. On the navigation menu, choose Device Explorer.

2. Choose the device template of the device to delete.

3. Check the box next to the device to delete.

4. Choose Delete.

Summary

The chapter covered monitoring the Windows 10 system. Monitoring performance on Windows 10 is imperative to rooting out any issues that may affect your network. If your systems are not running at their best, your end users may experience issues such as latency, or worse, you may experience corruption in your network data. Either way, it's important to know how to monitor the performance of your systems.

We also examined how to use the various performance-related tools that are included with Windows 10. Tools such as Performance Monitor, Task Manager, and Event Viewer can help you diagnose and troubleshoot system performance issues. These tools will help you find typical problems related to memory, disk space, and any other hardware-related issues you may experience.

Knowing how to use tools to troubleshoot and test your systems is imperative, not only to passing the exam, but also to performing your duties at work. To have a smoothly running network environment, it is vital that you understand the issues related to the reliability and performance of your Windows 10 systems.

I next discussed using Monitor Cloud-Based Tools. Microsoft offers a couple different cloud-based tools for monitoring services and these include Azure Monitor and System Center Operations Manager (SCOM). These two tools provide core monitoring services, which include alerts, service uptime tracking, health monitoring for application and infrastructure, diagnostics, and analytics.

Finally, I talked about Monitor Azure Device Security. Azure IoT Central is an Internet of Things (IoT) application platform that lessens the load and cost of developing, managing, and maintaining enterprise-grade IoT solutions. Azure IoT Central provides you the ability to focus energy, money, and time working with a business with IoT data, rather than simply maintaining and updating an intricate and continually changing IoT infrastructure.

Use Microsoft Azure IoT Central Applications to monitor devices and change settings. Azure IoT Central Applications are hosted by Microsoft, which reduces the administration overhead of managing applications.

Exam Essentials

Know the importance of common performance counters.   Several important performance-related counters deal with general system performance. Know the importance of monitoring memory, print server, CPU, and network usage on a busy server.

Understand the role of other troubleshooting tools.   Windows Task Manager and Event Viewer can both be used to diagnose and troubleshoot configuration- and performance-related issues.

Understand how to troubleshoot common sources of server reliability problems.   Windows 10 has been designed to be a stable, robust, and reliable operating system. Should you experience intermittent failures, you should know how to troubleshoot device drivers and buggy system-level software.

Know Monitor Cloud-Based Tools   Microsoft offers a couple different cloud-based tools for monitoring services and these include Azure Monitor and System Center Operations Manager (SCOM).

Understand Monitor Azure Device Security   Azure IoT Central is an Internet of Things (IoT) application platform that lessens the load and cost of developing, managing, and maintaining enterprise-grade IoT solutions.

Review Questions

1. You are the administrator for an organization that uses a hybrid onsite and Azure network. You use Microsoft Azure Log Analytics workplace to collect all of the event logs from the computers at your organization. You have a computer named Laptop1. Laptop1 has Windows 10 loaded on the system. You need to view the events collected from Laptop1. Which query would an administrator run in Log Analytics?

    A. Eventview | where SourceSystem = = "laptop1"

    B. Eventview | where Computer = = "laptop1"

    C. Event | where SourceSystem = = "laptop1"

    D. Event | where Computer = = "laptop1"

2. You need to stop an application from running in Task Manager. Which tab would you use to stop an application from running?

    A. Performance

    B. Users

    C. Options

    D. Details

3. You are the network administrator for Stellacon Corporation. Users in the sales department have been complaining that the Sales application is slow to load. Using Performance Monitor, you create a baseline report for one of the computers, monitoring memory, the processor, the disk subsystem, and the network subsystem. You notice that the disk subsystem has a high load of activity. What other subsystem should you monitor before you can know for sure whether you have a disk subsystem bottleneck?

    A. Memory

    B. Processor

    C. Network

    D. Application

4. You are the network administrator for an organization that has decided to migrate to Windows 10. Part of your job requires that you are able to complete the following:

    ▪ Collect data from the local or remote Windows 10 computers on the network. You can collect data from a single computer or multiple computers concurrently.

    ▪ View data as it is being collected in real time, or historically from collected data.

    Which Window 10 application can you use to achieve your task?

    A. Event Viewer

    B. Computer Monitor

    C. Windows 7 Monitor

    D. Performance Monitor

5. You are the network administrator for a large organization. You are running Windows 10 machines throughout your network along with Windows Server 2019. You need to use Event Viewer to review event logs for Critical and Error events only. You need to see ALL of these events from the logs. What do you do to achieve this?

A. Use the Administrative Events view.

B. Create a custom view and choose Administrative Events.

C. Do a search on the system log for all of these events.

D. Create a custom view and select Critical, Error, and Verbose for all logs.

6. You are the network administrator for an organization that runs Windows Server 2019 and Windows 10. On a Windows 10 machine, you are asked by your IT manager to collect performance data for a period of three weeks. The IT manager wants CPU utilization, disk utilization, and memory utilization all included in the data collected. How should you accomplish this?

A. Create a User Defined Data Collector set.

B. Create a custom performance set.

C. Create a Trace event.

D. Create a session Data Collector set.

7. While using Performance Monitor, you use the following output mode. Which output mode are you using?

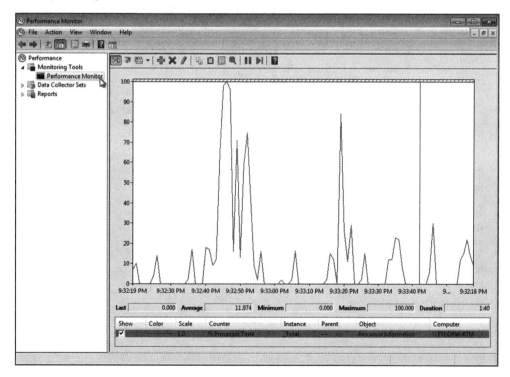

    A. Histogram Bar view

    B. Graph view

    C. Report view

    D. Line view

8. While using Performance Monitor, you use the following output mode. Which output mode are you using?

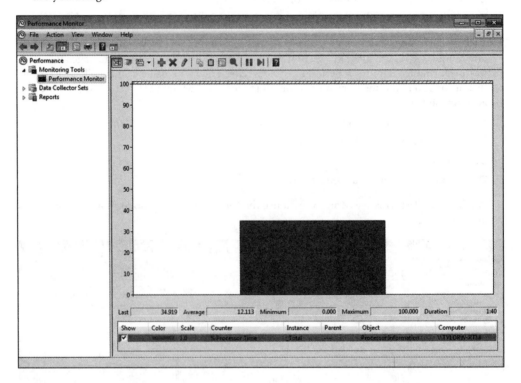

    A. Histogram Bar view

    B. Graph view

    C. Report view

    D. Line view

9. You are the administrator for a large organization that has started using Azure. You need to use a Microsoft Azure monitoring tool to monitor devices and change settings. Which of the following tools can you use?

    A. Performance Monitor

    B. Microsoft Azure IoT Central Applications

    C. Azure Performance Center

    D. Intune Performance Center

10. You are the administrator for a large training organization that uses an Azure network. You have decided to use Microsoft Azure Log Analytics workplace to collect event logs from all of the different Azure connected machines. You have a computer named AzureSystem1 and AzureSystem1 uses Windows 10. An administrator wants you to view the events collected from AzureSystem1. Which query would an administrator run in Log Analytics?

A. Eventview | where SourceSystem = = "AzureSystem1"

B. Event | where Computer = = "AzureSystem1"

C. Eventview | where Computer = = "AzureSystem1"

D. Event | where SourceSystem = = "AzureSystem1"

Appendix

Answers to Review Questions

Chapter 1: Installing and Updating Windows 10

1. **A, E.** If you are going to implement the Secure Boot feature of Windows 10, then make sure the system firmware is set up as Unified Extensible Firmware Interface (UEFI) and not BIOS. You also need to make sure the disks are converted from Master Boot Record (MBR) disks to a GUID Partition Table (GPT) disk.

2. **B.** Windows Autopilot profiles allow an administrator to choose how the Windows 10 system will be set up and configured on Azure AD and Intune.

3. **B.** When installing or upgrading Windows 10, the version of Windows 10 that is installed must match the CPU version. For example, if your system is a 32-bit system, you must use a 32-bit version of Windows 10. If your system is a 64-bit system, you can install either the 32-bit or 64-bit version of Windows 10.

4. **D.** You would use the Sysprep utility. The /generalize option prevents system-specific information from being included in the image.

5. **A.** The DISM utility with the /get-drivers switch allows you to find out which drivers are installed on the WIM.

6. **D.** Windows Autopilot profiles allow an administrator to choose how the Windows 10 system will be setup and configured on Azure AD and Intune.

7. **B.** wdsutil is a command-line utility that can be used to configure the WDS server. Several other configuration options need to be specified on the WDS server, and you can set them using wdsutil.

8. **C.** Windows System Image Manager (SIM) is used to create unattended answer files in Windows 10. It uses a GUI-based interface to set up and configure the most common options that are used within an answer file.

9. **C.** You enable WDS servers to respond to client requests through the Windows Deployment Services (WDS) Microsoft Management Console (MMC) snap-in. In the PXE Properties dialog box, enable the option Respond To Client Computers.

10. **B.** The /generalize option prevents system-specific information from being included in the image. The sysprep.exe command can be used with a variety of options. You can see a complete list by typing sysprep/? at a command-line prompt.

Chapter 2: Managing Authentication

1. **B.** Azure AD Identity Protection allows an Azure administrator to use the same type of protection that Microsoft uses to protect and secure users' identities.

2. **D.** Administrators can use the New-AzureADPolicy command to create a new Azure AD policy.

3. A. The `Get-AzureADPolicy` command allows an Azure admin to view an Azure AD policy.

4. C. The Password Reset section of Azure AD allows an administrator to determine if they want to enable Self-service password resets (SSPR). If an organization decides to enable this feature, users will be able to reset their own passwords or unlock their accounts.

5. B. Azure AD Connect is a Microsoft utility that allows you to set up a hybrid design between Azure AD and your on-site AD. Azure AD Connect allows both versions of AD to connect to each other.

6. B. Administrators can use the `Add-AzureADApplicationPolicy` command to add an application policy.

7. D. Administrators can use the `Set-AzureADPolicy` command to update an Azure AD policy.

8. D. Administrators can't change or delete the initial domain name that is created but Azure administrators do have the ability to add their organization's new or existing domain names to the list of supported names.

9. A. Administrators can use the Custom Domain Names section of Azure AD to create your organization's new or existing domain names to the list of supported names.

10. B. Administrators can use the `Get-AzureADDirectorySetting` command to view their directory settings.

Chapter 3: Managing Devices

1. D. You can upgrade your devices by using a device configuration profile. The option that you want to configure is Edition Upgrade. Edition Upgrade allows you to upgrade Windows 10 (and later) devices to a newer version of Windows.

2. B. One of the options you have in device configuration profiles is the ability to set up custom profiles. Custom profile settings allow an Intune administrator to configure options that are not automatically included with Intune. For example, as an administrator, you can set a custom profile that allows you to create ADMX-backed policy or even enable self-service password resets.

3. A. Kiosk settings allow an administrator to configure a Windows 10 (and later) device to run a single application or run many applications. Kiosk systems are normally designed in a location where many people can use the same device and that device will only run limited applications.

4. A. One of the options that you can set in device configuration profiles is the ability to setup custom profiles. Custom profile settings allow an Intune Administrator to configure options that are not automatically included with Intune. For example, an administrator can set a custom profile that allows you to create ADMX-backed policy or even enable self-service password resets.

5. D. Both Windows 10 and Windows XP Professional support FAT32 and NTFS, so both file systems will be viewable on both operating systems.

6. D. Dynamic disks are supported by all Windows operating systems above Windows Server 2000. Windows 10 supports mirrored volumes.

7. A. The Disk Defragmenter utility is used to rearrange files so that they are stored contiguously on the disk. This optimizes access to those files. You can also defragment disks through the command-line utility Defrag.

8. B. Endpoint protection allows you to set Windows 10 (and above) options for BitLocker and Windows Defender settings. For example, you can set Windows Defender for a threat score setting. If a user with a high threat score rating attempts to access cloud-based resources, you can stop this device from accessing your resources.

9. D. One of the options that you can set in device configuration profiles is the ability to setup custom profiles. Custom profile settings allow an Intune Administrator to configure options that are not automatically included with Intune. For example, an administrator can set a custom profile that allows you to create ADMX-backed policy or even enable self-service password resets.

10. C. One of the advantages to using Azure is the ability to protect corporate data by ensuring that users and devices meet certain requirements. When using Intune, this is referred to as compliance policies. Compliance policies are rules and settings that your users and their devices must follow in order to connect and access Intune.

Chapter 4: Planning and Managing Microsoft Intune

1. A. Administrators have the ability to limit and monitor network usage by configuring the network as a metered network. Network metering allows network downloading to be watched or metered and then administrators can charge users or departments for the network usage.

2. D. To review a policy report on the deployment status for the Windows 10 update ring, sign in to the Microsoft Endpoint Manager Admin Center. Then, select Devices ➤ Overview ➤ Software Update Status. To review software updates, select Monitor, and then below Software Updates, select Per Update Ring Deployment State and choose the deployment ring to review.

3. C, D. As long as the salesperson's personally owned Windows 10 laptop is being managed by the management infrastructure agent, administrators can use the remote wipe feature. When you do a remote wipe, all of the company's data gets wiped from the device.

4. D. An Apple Push Notification service (APNs) certificate must be imported from Apple so that the school can manage iOS devices. This certificate allows Intune administrators to manage iOS.

5. A. You will want to go to device configuration. To do this sign in to the Azure portal and click on Intune. Create a new device configuration profile by going to Device Configuration ➤ Profiles ➤ Create Profile. Configure any needed settings. Click OK and then click Create.

6. **C, D.** If using Configuration Manager, Administrators must configure Configuration Manager to manage mobile devices. To do this, it requires administrators to create a Windows Intune subscription and use a connector to synchronize user accounts.

7. **A.** Before you can setup any Intune policies regarding applications, you must first add that application to Intune.

8. **C.** By default, licensed users can add up to 15 devices to their accounts. Device Administrators have the ability to add devices to Intune but users do have the ability to enroll 15 devices on their own. The limit was changed from 5 to 15 for a user. So, a single Intune user can now enroll up to 15 devices using a single Intune license.

9. **D.** Sideloading an application means that you are loading an application that you already own or one that your company created into a delivery system (i.e. Intune, Microsoft Store, or images).

10. **B, C.** Intune Administrators have the ability to setup different notifications to different emails based on alert type. So you can send all alerts, critical alerts, warnings, and informational alerts to different IT members.

Chapter 5: Managing Security

1. **C.** Administrators can use Windows Defender Application Control to ensure that only applications that you explicitly allow can run on Windows 10 computers.

2. **A.** Windows Defender Exploit Guard helps protect your system from common malware hacks that use executable files and scripts to attack applications like Microsoft Office (for example, Outlook). Windows Defender Exploit Guard also looks for suspicious scripts or behavior that is not normal on the Windows 10 system.

3. **A.** Administrators can use Windows Defender Credential Guard to help isolate critical files so that only system software with proper privileges can access those critical files.

4. **D.** Windows Defender Firewall with Advanced Security allows you to set up inbound and outbound rules by using Windows Firewall.

5. **C.** To configure your Windows Firewall to allow DNS inbound and outbound traffic, you would set up port 53. Port 20 is for FTP data, port 25 is for SMTP (mail), and port 80 is HTTP.

6. **B.** Windows Defender Exploit Guard helps protect your system from common malware hacks that use executable files and scripts that attack applications like Microsoft Office (for example, Outlook). Windows Defender Exploit Guard also looks for suspicious scripts or behavior that is not normal on the Windows 10 system.

7. **B.** To configure your Windows Defender Firewall to allow SMTP inbound and outbound traffic, you would set up port 25. Port 20 is for FTP data, Port 53 is for DNS, and Port 80 is HTTP.

8. A. Administrators can use Windows Defender Application Control to ensure that only applications that you explicitly allow can run on Windows 10 computers.

9. D. Windows Defender Exploit Guard helps protect your system from common malware hacks that use executable files and scripts to attack applications like Microsoft Office (for example, Outlook). Windows Defender Exploit Guard also looks for suspicious scripts or behavior that is not normal on the Windows 10 system.

10. A. To configure your Windows Defender Firewall to allow FTP traffic, you would set up ports 20 and 21. Port 25 is for mail and Port 53 is for DNS. Port 80 is HTTP, and Port 443 is for HTTPS.

Chapter 6: Configuring Auditing

1. D. Administrator can view the events collected from a specific computer in Azure is to run a query in the Logs Analytics.

2. D. All of the applications that are running on the Windows 10 machine will show up under the Details tab. Right-click the application and end the process.

3. A. You should check the memory counters. If your computer does not have enough memory, it can cause excessive paging, which may be perceived as a disk subsystem bottleneck.

4. D. Performance Monitor allows you to collect data from your local computer or remote Windows 10 machine from a single computer or multiple computers concurrently, view data as it is being collected in real time, or historically from collected data, have full control over the selection of what data will be collected, by selecting which specific objects and counters will be collected, choose the sampling parameters that will be used, meaning the time interval that you want to use for collecting data points and the time period that will be used for data collection.

5. D. You would have to create a custom view to achieve this task. You could not use the Administrative Events view (default custom view) because it also includes all warnings.

6. A. Data collector sets are used to collect data into a log so that the data can be reviewed. You can view the log files with Performance Monitor.

7. D. The graphic is an example of a Line view output. The three options are Line view, Histogram Bar view, and Report view.

8. A. The graphic is an example of a Histogram Bar view output. The three options are Line view, Histogram Bar view, and Report view.

9. B. Use Microsoft Azure IoT Central Applications to monitor devices and change settings. Azure IoT Central Applications are hosted by Microsoft, which reduces the administration overhead of managing applications.

10. B. Administrator can view the events collected from a specific computer in Azure is to run a query in the Logs Analytics.

Index

K

L

M

X–Y–Z

Online Test Bank

Register to gain one year of FREE access after activation to the online test bank to help you study for your MCA Modern Desktop Administrator certification exam—included with your purchase of this book! All of the chapter review questions and the practice tests in this book are included in the online test bank so you can practice in a timed and graded setting.

Register and Access the Online Test Bank

To register your book and get access to the online test bank, follow these steps:

1. Go to bit.ly/SybexTest (this address is case sensitive)!
2. Select your book from the list.
3. Complete the required registration information, including answering the security verification to prove book ownership. You will be emailed a pin code.
4. Follow the directions in the email or go to www.wiley.com/go/sybextestprep.
5. Find your book on that page and click the "Register or Login" link with it. Then enter the pin code you received and click the "Activate PIN" button.
6. On the Create an Account or Login page, enter your username and password, and click Login or, if you don't have an account already, create a new account.
7. At this point, you should be in the test bank site with your new test bank listed at the top of the page. If you do not see it there, please refresh the page or log out and log back in.